D1797845

INSECURITY!

INSECURITY!

The spread of weapons in the
Indian and Pacific oceans

Editor Robert O'Neill

Australian National University Press
Canberra, A.C.T., Norwalk, Conn. 1978

First published in Australia 1978

Printed in Australia for the Australian National University Press, Canberra

Wholly set up and printed by Academy Press Pty Ltd, Brisbane

National Library of Australia
Cataloguing-in-Publication entry

Insecurity!

    ISBN 0 7081 0546 7.
    1. Weapons systems—Addresses, essays, lectures.
    2. International relations—Addresses, essays,
    lectures. 3. Pacific Ocean—Addresses, essays,
    lectures. I. O'Neill, Robert John, 1936– , ed.

355.8209164

North America: Books Australia, Norwalk, Conn., USA
Southeast Asia: Angus & Robertson (S.E. Asia) Pty Ltd, Singapore
Japan: United Publishers Services Ltd, Tokyo

Editor's Foreword

The Conference on which this volume is based was organised as part of the program of arms control and international security studies conducted within the Research School of Pacific Studies of the Australian National University by the Department of International Relations and the Strategic and Defence Studies Centre. This program aims to place emphasis on those wider regional issues which relate to the Pacific and Indian Ocean area and in which members of the Department and the Centre have special interests and experience. The program's activities include scholars from many nations but principally from those of East, South-east and South Asia and the South Pacific. It is broadly international in its approach, recognising that the security of any individual state within this region relates to that of the region as a whole and that events within the region are influenced by a wide range of factors —economic, social, political, diplomatic, technological and military —which operate at global, regional and national levels.

We are fortunate to have been given support for this program by the Ford Foundation for the period 1975–78. One of its essential elements, we considered, should be a major international conference to bring together leading scholars from near and far so that, first, our activities could benefit from their direct contributions and, second, the program might make a direct offering to the international debate through a volume such as this one. Hence we are particularly grateful to the Ford Foundation for without its generous support, a conference of these dimensions would not have been possible.

While I am beholden to all of the contributors for their efforts, I would like to make special mention of those who journeyed from afar to a very wintry Canberra in July 1977 and of Dr Steven Rosen who prepared his excellent paper on extremely short notice, at a time when he had other pressing commitments to attend to.

My further thanks are due to Professors J.D.B. Miller and Hedley Bull for their assistance in planning the Conference, to Colonel J.O. Langtry for administering it, to Dr Desmond Ball and Mrs Jolika Tie for help in many ways, to Mrs Billie Dalrymple for assisting both Colonel Langtry and myself, to Mrs Shirley Steer, Miss Dianne Mahalm and Miss May McKenzie for assisting with typing, to Mr Brian Clouston, Director of the A.N.U. Press for excellent co-operation in the rapid publication of this volume, and to Professor Wang Gungwu for his support and advice throughout.

Robert O'Neill
Canberra, August 1977.

Introduction
Wang Gungwu

In the past three years the Strategic and Defence Studies Centre of our Research School of Pacific Studies has conducted several conferences on a wide range of issues; from the strategic nuclear balance between the superpowers, through the relationship between Australia, Indonesia and Papua New Guinea, to questions of Australian defence policy. Hence it is timely that we should now be considering an issue which is germane to each of these segments of recent activities. The proliferation of weaponry in the Indian and Pacific Ocean area is of direct concern to the superpowers, to the stability of its major sub-regions and to the security of all nations, both great and small, which are situated in the area.

The growing destructive power, accuracy and range of modern weaponry, both nuclear and conventional, means that there are very few people in the world who do not have real concerns for their own security. At the same time international interaction is growing steadily, thereby raising many issues in which the interests of individual states or groups of states come into collision. Thus there are ample reasons both for the major powers to seek to supply weaponry to the smaller ones and for these latter states to seek such external sources of assistance, and this in turn creates new relationships of dependence. In order to minimise this dependence, many of the middle and smaller powers have developed their own weapons industries and thus the sources of proliferation are both numerous and heterogeneous.

Against this background of increasing difficulties there is at least the ray of hope that the great powers are aware of the damage that each can do to the others and so a powerful deterrent mechanism is operating to inhibit direct conflict at that level. However despite over thirty years of cold war, limited war and détente, it must be acknowledged that the stability of the great power balance rests largely on the constantly shifting foundation of technology. Any new scientific breakthrough by one side or the other which deprives its adversary of an assured second strike capacity, or significantly limits the effectiveness of a second strike, could invalidate what has been called the relationship of Mutual Assured Destruction. Agreements such as SALT I and Vladivostok may provide some reassurance by restricting numerical proliferation but they do little to halt the more serious competition in terms of the quality of opposing weapons sytems which goes on within their framework.

Another cause for serious concern regarding the possibility of major conflict amongst the great powers is the propensity for their lesser allies and clients to engage in hostilities which then induce a state of acute tension between their patrons. In this type of situation the risky policy of self-limitation by the great powers concerned is the only safeguard against escalation. Delicate and politically controversial decisions have to be made by their leaders to balance the credibility of an alliance relationship against the direct costs and dangers of entering into a proxy conflict with another great power. The wars in Korea, the Middle East and Indo-China which have occupied most of the period since 1945 have shown us many examples of these problems. Currently all three of these conflicts are in a quiescent phase but no experienced observer would dismiss their potential for re-eruption, particularly the first two. We must also bear in mind the existing rivalries in Africa in both the Horn and the Southern region. Clearly there are no grounds for complacency about the stability of great power relationships in any of these situations. We may hope that the great powers will show adroitness and skill in their diplomacy in handling these regional problems but we would be foolish to take the exercising of these qualities for granted.

Even if stability is preserved amongst the great powers, there is still a large proportion of the world's population which has good cause to be concerned about its security from local attack. Principally these people inhabit the developing countries of Asia, Africa and Latin America but even the most developed societies have had recent experience of problems such as those caused by terrorism. War has been a major factor in international relations for too long for it to be easily eradicable and it would be naive to expect therefore that nations which feel threatened will not seek security through building strong defences. All that one can hope for in the immediate future is that individual governments will recognise that one state's security can easily be the cause of another state's insecurity and so where a choice of weaponry is possible, we might hope that they opt for a more defensive, rather than a more offensive, posture.

Apart from the direct dangers posed by regional conflicts to the life, limbs and property of the people involved, one cannot help but be concerned at the high economic costs actually incurred in maintaining national defences. These costs include not only the direct outlays made on manpower and weaponry but also the opportunity costs incurred by the diversion of scarce resources and technological knowledge away from the production of goods and services. Hence the objectives of this Conference relate not only to the potential costs of warfare but also to the actual and constantly recurring costs of building and maintaining credible military forces.

In the light of the above considerations it was appropriate that the Conference on which this volume is based should have been organised in two tiers: the first covering global trends; and the second covering regional issues which are of prime concern in Australia's wider neighbourhood. In the first tier our authors examine the proliferation of nuclear weapons throughout the world, the development of the conventional arms trade and the spread of the major forms of conventional weaponry, both sea-based and land-based. In the second they discuss the dynamics of the security problems of four significant regions within or adjoining the Indian-Pacific Ocean area, the ways in which the proliferation of weaponry affects the security perspectives of the member states of those regions and the possibilities for achieving some degree of arms control within them.

Every one of these regions is quite different in terms of its security problems and so we have invited a leading specialist from each to analyse its problems. North-east Asia must pay particular attention to the Korean problem. Recent frictions between Japan and the Soviet Union regarding their fishing rights, the extent of their exclusive economic zones and the four northern islands off the Hokkaido coast point to new forms of tension. South-east Asia remains divided between Communist and non-Communist states. Direct military conflicts between the two groups have been limited but the current situation on the borders of Thailand remains a cause for concern. Minority or communal problems continue to exist within several of the major states of South-east Asia, thereby complicating the already difficult problems of achieving national development at a satisfactory rate for all. The Indian Ocean adjoins several groups of antagonistic littoral states, from Africa through the Middle East to South Asia and is also the scene for naval rivalry between the two superpowers. The South-west Pacific area is not currently troubled by serious internal disputes but, as an area of rapid political and economic change, which is also of interest to the superpowers, it remains prone to the possibility of local arms races in which outside powers play a leading part and which could threaten the existing peace of the area.

I hope that out of this volume will come a wider discussion of these issues and of their implications for the region as a whole. Should this prove to be the case, then the contributors may be well satisfied by their efforts.

Contents

1
Global Trends in Nuclear Proliferation
Michael Nacht

The problem of nuclear weapons proliferation is now a fundamental concern of a large number of national governments and is a matter intimately related to the basic energy needs of both the developed and developing nations. It is fast becoming an issue of high politics on a global scale.

This is a new development. While fear of the spread of nuclear weapons has been with us since the United States first developed these instruments of mass destruction more than three decades ago, it is only events of the last four years that have produced this sense of urgency. The 1973 oil embargo by the Organization of Petroleum Exporting Countries (OPEC) clarified as never before the significance of being dependent on external sources for energy supplies and stimulated an enormous quest for energy independence by nations throughout the world. Because of the widespread belief that nuclear energy is the only technologically-feasible alternative to fossil fuels for the balance of this century, the demand for nationally-owned facilities capable of using nuclear energy for electric power generation has markedly increased. The furore resulting from the 1975 agreement of cooperation between the Federal Republic of Germany and Brazil—the so-called German-Brazilian nuclear deal—underscored, however, that a strong linkage is present between nuclear energy and nuclear weapons. Sensitive nuclear facilities, particularly those used for uranium enrichment and for reprocessing of spent fuel, can provide a nation with sufficient amounts of weapons-grade material to produce a credible nuclear weapons option as a by-product of a domestic nuclear energy program. The prospect of thirty or forty nations obtaining this option by the year 2000 is viewed by many as a fundamental challenge to world order. The recognition of the nuclear energy—nuclear weapons connection, is, of course, not new. The Baruch Plan offered at the United Nations after World War II, the 'Atoms for

Peace' Program launched in 1953, and the Nuclear Non-Proliferation Treaty (NPT) signed in 1968 all address this connection. It is the fact that this connection is more easily made today that is the source of concern.

The Indian peaceful nuclear explosion of May 1974 illustrated two further points: that sufficient weapons-grade material could be obtained to fabricate a nuclear weapon even from a research reactor, and that the concept of a 'peaceful' nuclear explosion could be used by nations as a rationale for developing devices which are indistinguishable in their effects from nuclear weapons.

As a consequence of these developments a vigorous debate arose, first in the United States and then in a number of the advanced industrial societies, concerning the most efficacious means of dealing with or managing or coping with or preventing or minimising the spread of nuclear weapons. Out of this debate a number of general points have emerged:

1. A consensus developed in American governmental and academic circles that a combination of security- related and energy-related strategies needed to be implemented by the United States and other developed nations in order to combat nuclear proliferation.[1] Individuals and groups associated in one form or another with the United States nuclear industry, however, opposed those strategies that threatened or were perceived to threaten the growth and profitability of the industry.

2. A number of the developed nations, particularly France and the Federal Republic of Germany, were suspicious that American energy-related strategies were motivated not by a concern over the spread of nuclear weapons but by a desire to perpetuate American dominance of the nuclear export market. This suspicion has resulted in a reluctance by both the French and German governments to accept the American position.

3. By and large the American position has been rejected in the developing world. It is argued that the United States, in the name of nuclear non-proliferation, seeks to implement policies that are highly discriminatory vis-à-vis non-nuclear states and that are designed to maintain American political, military and economic power at the expense of the poorer nations.

4. Few students of the nuclear proliferation problem expect it to be solved. Rather attention has shifted from stopping the spread to discouraging it and to learning to live with it.

5. The view that nuclear proliferation will be a stabilising force in world politics, while widely rejected in the United States, commands many adherents, especially among individuals whose

nations are caught in the grip of intense regional conflict situations. The argument is made that the system of mutual deterrence that nuclear weapons has brought to the Soviet-American relationship is not peculiar to this relationship and can in fact be replicated in the Middle East, South Asia and elsewhere.

Hence there is by no means a global consensus on either the threat posed by nuclear proliferation or the steps that should be taken to deal with it. Indeed there is even disagreement on the definition of a new nuclear state. Despite its known inadequacies, the only commonly accepted definition is a state that explodes a nuclear device. This definition not only masks the status of states such as Israel that have a 'bomb in the basement', but it fails to distinguish between those states that might have a small stockpile of nuclear weapons and those that have an arsenal of sophisticated delivery vehicles capable of posing a serious military threat. Therefore it is not surprising that the issue has inflamed domestic debate in many nations, has strained alliance relationships, has sharpened the confrontation between the North and the South, and has served to complicate concepts of national and international security.

This paper will examine global trends in nuclear proliferation by first reviewing the American policy initiatives of recent vintage and the reactions to these initiatives, will then proceed to review some of the significant developments in the threshold countries, and will conclude by highlighting some of the underlying difficulties in maintaining a non-proliferation regime.

American Policy Initiatives
On 7 April 1977 President Carter announced a seven-point program as the foundation for his administration's policy on nuclear power. The program was given the highest priority by the President and reflected previous initiatives taken by the Ford administration near the end of its term and the position on nuclear power espoused by Mr Carter during the 1976 Presidential campaign. The main elements of the program are these:

— an indefinite deferral of the commerical reprocessing and recycling of the plutonium produced in U.S. nuclear programs, and the decision not to use federal funds or federal government influence to complete the plant at Barnwell, South Carolina as a reprocessing facility.
— a restructuring of the U.S. breeder reactor program to give greater priority to alternative breeder designs, and deferral of

the date when breeder reactors will be put into commercial use.

— a redirection of funding of U.S. nuclear research and development programs to accelerate research into alternative nuclear fuel cycles which do not involve direct access to materials usable in nuclear weapons.

— an increase in U.S. production capacity for enriched uranium to provide adequate and timely supply of nuclear fuels for domestic and foreign needs.

— a decision to propose the necessary legislative steps to permit the United States to offer nuclear fuel supply contracts and to guarantee the delivery of nuclear fuel to other countries.

— continuation of the decision to embargo the export of equipment or technology that would permit uranium enrichment and chemical reprocessing.

— endorsement of continuing discussions with supplying and recipient countries on a variety of international approaches and frameworks that will permit nations to achieve their energy objectives while reducing the spread of nuclear explosive capability. These will include exploring the establishment of an international fuel cycle evaluation program aimed at developing alternative fuel cycles as well as a variety of international and U.S. measures to assure access to nuclear fuel supplies and spent fuel storage for nations sharing common non-proliferation objectives.

It is the Carter administration's position that the nuclear proliferation problem is a matter of both intentions and capabilities and that the United States should adopt policies that will steer the intentions of non-nuclear states away from nuclear weapons acquisition while at the same time minimising their capabilities to acquire such weapons. Intentions are to be influenced by providing incentives (e.g., the United States expects to provide economic incentives to non-nuclear states so that they will not seek to develop the full fuel cycle in their own domestic energy programs). Capabilities are to be influenced by implementing both controls (e.g., safeguards for nuclear power facilities) and denials (e.g., no reprocessing or enrichment facilities). Particular emphasis is to be placed on providing assured supply of non-sensitive nuclear fuels on a timely, adequate, reliable, and economic basis, and to ensure sufficient spent fuel and nuclear waste storage capacity.

The Carter policy is quite similar in some respects to the initiatives announced by President Ford in his 28 October 1976 statement. The Carter policy reaffirms the importance of light water reactors as the bedrock of nuclear power programs for at least the next ten years; it reaffirms the significance of the International Atomic Energy Agency (IAEA) as the organisation responsible for both providing technical assistance to non-nuclear weapon states that are party to the Nuclear Non-proliferation Treaty (NPT) and for implementing a system of safeguards to verify that the parties to the NPT are in compliance with it; and it reaffirms a moratorium on reprocessing in the United States.

There are a number of significant differences, however. The Carter policy provides for an indefinite deferral on re-processing in the United States rather than for a three-year period. Moreover, with respect to breeder reactors there has been a noticeable decline in enthusiasm from Ford to Carter. While the Carter policy does not call for either the cessation of research on breeders or for other nations to foresake their breeder programs, it clearly places the development of breeder reactors within the context of minimising the spread of nuclear weapons rather than letting their design be governed strictly by energy and economic considerations.

The international nuclear fuel cycle evaluation program is a new initiative by President Carter. It would be designed to provide information to prospective recipients of nuclear energy facilities on alternative fuel cycles, fuel availability, improved methods for the operation of light water reactors, and other datum that would be useful in the recipient's decision-making process. It is intended to be an addition to the London Suppliers Group with the advantage that it would be established in such a manner as to avoid being seen as a 'rich man's club,' the principal deficiency of the Suppliers Group.

The Carter administration has also restructured American nuclear export policy. It is the aim of Mr Carter that nuclear export agreements be carried out through negotiations that emphasise a number of criteria: a comprehensive safeguards program for all nuclear facilities; the penalty of a cutoff in fuel supply and in technical assistance by the United States should the non-nuclear state detonate a peaceful nuclear explosion; the right of the United States to rule on the permissibility of the transfer of nuclear technologies from the recipient state to third parties; and the right of the United States to rule on the permissibility of the recipient state acquiring or developing an indigenous reprocessing capability. A procedural change has been instituted whereby the President can override an export decision made by the Nuclear Regulatory Commission (NRC) justified on the basis of whether the NRC's decision is consistent with U.S. non-proliferation policy. This change eliminates the ad hoc nature that had previously characterised U.S. nuclear export decision-making. And, by emphasising international fuel assurances and considering as an interim solution the establishment of an international spent fuel depository, the Carter administration seeks to increase the sensitivity of American policy to the concerns of the recipient nations.

There appears to be, in addition, a considerable change in emphasis from Ford to Carter in how the United States will deal with its allies on nuclear matters. Despite the adoption of a visible stance in opposition to nuclear proliferation by Mr Ford, it was nonetheless characteristic of his administration that the United States, to paraphrase one high-level official, would not sacrifice alliance relationships on the altar of nuclear non-proliferation. In other words the Ford administration felt particularly concerned about applying too much pressure on France, the Federal Republic of Germany and Japan with respect to their nuclear energy programs and export policies for fear of creating great tension in America's relations with these states. The Carter administration has, on the other hand, been willing to incur such risks. As President Carter stated in his address on foreign policy at Notre Dame University on 22 May 1977 'we are attempting, even at the risk of some friction with our friends, to reduce the danger of nuclear proliferation.' Although initial negativism toward Mr Carter, particularly by the West Germans, was temporarily overcome at the London summit meeting in May, it is readily apparent that strains in alliance relationships are likely to be a significant by-product of American initiatives to stem the spread of nuclear weapons.[2]

Reactions
Although it is not possible to assess with any definitiveness the reaction to the Carter initiatives, given that the policy is but a few months old, sufficient responses have been registered to be able to formulate some preliminary generalisations.

Within the United States, first of all, there is a general sense that the policy is a fragile one and that its likelihood of success, however success is to be measured, is highly problematical. It is increasingly clear, for example, that security guarantees as tools of nuclear non-proliferation policy have limited applicability. The United States is having sufficient difficulty in retaining its existing relationships in Western Europe and Japan; the prospect of acquiring new security partners appears to be exceedingly remote. Indeed, existing treaty arrangements with both South Korea and Taiwan are now under serious review—the first because of the Carter commitment to withdraw American ground troops from the

Korean peninsula within five years, and the second because of the growing desire by the Carter administration to normalise relations with the People's Republic of China. The South-east Asia Treaty Organization (SEATO) has within the last month literally had a 'going out of business sale' and is now defunct. Strains have developed in American relations with Israel following the electoral victory of the Likud Party, and with Brazil as a consequence of 1) American attempts to roll back the German–Brazilian deal and 2) American criticism of the Brazilian government's infringement on the human rights of its own citizens. Attempts by the Carter administration, and particularly by United Nations Ambassador Andrew Young, to endorse vociferously the movement for majority rule in southern Africa has, whatever its positive effects in Black Africa, seriously strained relations between Washington and Pretoria. While these developments may in fact be highly transient, the initial pattern that is emerging supports the contention that the foreign policy priorities of the Carter administration outside of the nuclear non-proliferation area are by-and-large tending to undermine the very considerable effort on the part of the administration to slow the spread of nuclear weapons.

The Carter policy toward conventional arms control illustrates this point particularly well. Mr Carter and his associates have been consistent in their desire to reverse the trend established during the Nixon-Ford years, largely at the initiative of Henry Kissinger, of transferring large numbers of highly sophisticated conventional weapons including high-performance aircraft, anti-tank weapons and surface-to-air missiles to a number of developing nations—with concentration in the Middle East and the Persian Gulf—in order to retain or enhance American political influence. In late May Mr Carter announced a major shift in American conventional arms transfer policy.

> The United States will henceforth view arms transfers as an exceptional foreign policy implement, to be used only in instances where it can be clearly demonstrated that the transfer contributes to our national security interests . . . We will continue to utilize arms transfers to promote our security and the security of our close friends. But, in the future, the burden of persuasion will be on those who favour a particular arms sale, rather than those who oppose it.

In his statement Mr Carter made it clear that the NATO countries, Japan, Australia, New Zealand and Israel were to be exempt from these restrictions. But it is the basic aim of the policy to reduce the sales volume of conventional arms, to prohibit the development of advanced weapon systems in the United States that are specifically designed for export, to eliminate the American role as the 'first supplier' of advanced weapons to countries seeking 'new or significantly higher combat capability' and to cease production agreements with other countries for 'significant weapons.'

While this initiative is most admirable from an arms control perspective, there is little doubt that it will tend to exacerbate the nuclear proliferation problem. As unpalatable as it may seem, there very definitely appears to be a tradeoff between conventional arms control and nuclear non-proliferation. Denying Pakistan high-performance A–7 aircraft, for example, is likely to increase rather than decrease the need felt by Pakistani officials for nuclear weapons as a means of guaranteeing Pakistan's national security. Whether the Carter administration will in the long run be able to retain both its vigorous resistance to nuclear proliferation and its tough stand on conventional arms transfers is, therefore, highly uncertain. This problem is often referred to as the 'dove's dilemma'. It is complicated by the fact that threshold states can seek to take advantage of this tradeoff to obtain sophisticated conventional weapons, while still leaving their nuclear options open.

There are a number of additional concerns about the Carter non-proliferation policy that are keenly felt in the United States. There is a real question as to the Congressional reaction to the Carter policy and, in particular, to the attitude of key Congressmen on the question of American incentives to dissuade non-nuclear states from seeking to acquire a full nuclear fuel cycle. There is some disquietness about the overzealous approach of the administration's export policy, the 'overloading' of important bilateral relationships, and the fear of nationalist reactions that could produce exactly the opposite effect from what was intended. There is concern that the policy is not well understood and has been poorly explained. But there remains a feeling, particularly in government circles, that as long as the NPT remains intact, as long as the nuclear suppliers group does not unravel, and as long as some positive reactions can continue to be identified—the halt in further funding of the German breeder program and the decisions by Germany and France not to export reprocessing facilities beyond existing commitments to Brazil and Pakistan respectively are all cases in point—the policy will be retained and its validity will have been demonstrated.

Initial reactions outside the United States to the Carter program have been generally quite unsympathetic. Only a few days after Mr Carter's 7 April statement a major conference on the transfer of nuclear technology was convened in Persepolis sponsored by the

Iranian government in cooperation with the American Nuclear Society, the European Nuclear Society and the Japan Atomic Energy Society. The conference attracted nearly 500 participants from forty–one countries, including more than half from the developing nations. The tone of the conference was established in an opening address by Mr Akbar Etemad, Director of the Iranian Atomic Energy Organization, who described the prevailing nuclear policies and practices of the technologically advanced nations as 'formulated in a piecemeal and isolated manner at the risk of being conservative, unidimensional and distortive.' Mr Etemad claimed that natural resources and technology are 'the essential property of man.' Yet the advanced nations seek to maintain a near-absolute sovereignty over technology while demanding free and unconditional access to natural resources. Moreover, Mr Etemad noted that the NPT has not been universally accepted and that its spirit and letter have been clearly violated by the 'unilateral and secretive decision-making' of the London Suppliers Group.

With specific reference to the Carter policy, a number of points were raised that evidently claimed wide acceptance among the conference participants:

— reprocessing of fuel and recycling of fissile isotopes are essential to the operation of any breeder reactor, and the Carter suggestions that both reprocessing and recycling are unacceptable is viewed with alarm because it strikes at the heart of future nuclear power programs.

— unlike the United States, many other nations cannot afford to defer use of the breeder.

— the near-monopoly by the United States of uranium enrichment services is viewed by the developing nations with alarm rather than with equanimity.

— the Carter policy is considered to be particularly threatening because it indicates that the United States plans to interfere directly in the implementation of enrichment, reprocessing and recycling technologies in the importing nations. The importing nations desire to determine their own courses of implementation dependent only upon the rate of growth of the energy needs of the various countries, the world supply of uranium, and the policies of the uranium exporting nations.

— the Carter statement is regarded by some as an abrogation of Article IV of the NPT which stipulates that 'parties to the Treaty in a position to do so shall cooperate . . . to the further development of the applications of nuclear energy for peaceful purposes, especially in the territories of non-nuclear-weapon states party to the Treaty, with due consideration for the needs of the developing areas of the world.'

— restrictions on reprocessing of spent fuel are further criticised on the grounds that they will not be an effective deterrent to nuclear weapons proliferation—the price is too high for a marginally effective safeguard—and, further, that many nations are legally committed to reprocessing as the only feasible route to the safe and ultimate disposal of radioactive wastes.

— the portion of the Carter statement citing the exploration of alternative breeder designs and fuel cycles is viewed with scepticism. 'There are no fuel cycles which are consistent with breeding and which provide an effective technological barrier to proliferation.'

— the Carter statement will strengthen the political position of anti-nuclear power groups in the United States and other supplier nations, thereby increasing the uncertainty that commitments made by supplier nations to recipient nations can indeed be met.

The Carter policy is therefore judged essentially to be an ineffective attempt to provide a technical fix to a largely political problem. It has created fears in the developing world that the United States, as a leading industrial nation with great influence on the actions taken in many other countries, will undermine the ability of nations to adopt the only sound alternative for their energy supplies. The policies are considered to be highly discriminatory vis-à-vis the developing world and in contravention to international agreements. To the extent that it signals a general strategy of withholding by the supplier nations, the Carter initiative will stimulate rather than retard proliferation.

Beyond the reactions expressed at Persepolis, the most noteworthy public responses have come from the Federal Republic of Germany in the form of statements to the press by both government officials and representatives of Kraftwerk Union, the German nuclear facility manufacturer. It is the German position that reprocessing of spent fuel assemblies, recycling of regained residual uranium and plutonium, and the intensive pursuit of the development of the fast breeder reactor are integral parts of the nuclear energy program of the Federal Republic. Reprocessing and recycling are considered essential in order to decrease the potential risk associated with nuclear waste disposal and thereby increase the German public's willingness to accept nuclear energy. Foregoing reprocessing would also drastically increase the Federal Republic's needs for importing natural uranium, intensifying Germany's dependence on external sources of supply. The fast breeder reactor, moreover, is viewed as the only option within a reasonable time which would decrease German dependence on foreign suppliers for primary energy. Motivated by questions of job security and the reliable access to raw materials unavilable in the country, the Federal Republic is also highly dependent on the export of nuclear systems and technologies. Although Chancellor Helmut Schmidt, in a joint press conference with French President Valéry Giscard d'Estaing in mid-June, announced that West Germany would not export nuclear reprocessing technology beyond existing contracts, he noted that this decision was valid 'for the time being' and it remains rather unclear whether, in the long run, the Federal Republic will adhere to the export guidelines set forth by Mr Carter.

On balance, therefore, German policy is not likely to be terribly responsive to the Carter initiative. Instead the Federal Republic expects to proceed with the orderly development of its nuclear energy program, including the establishment of a major waste management facility and the expansion of its ultra-centrifuge enrichment capacity, while relying on the NPT regime and IAEA safeguards as the principal means for controlling the spread of nuclear weapons.[3]

There is still one additional problem confronting the Carter policy that is likely to promote adverse reaction. That is the linkage between 'vertical' proliferation—the enhancement of the nuclear arsenals of the United States and the Soviet Union—and 'horizontal' proliferation—the spread of nuclear weapons to non-nuclear states. The case has long been made, particularly in the developing world, that vertical proliferation is a principal cause of horizontal proliferation, and that the superpowers are hypocritical in adopting non-proliferation policies since they have failed to achieve nuclear arms control themselves. Undoubtedly, for some states this is a legitimate expression of their national position and national mood: a feeling of being discriminated against by the superpowers. For other states it is more likely an excuse to proceed with a nuclear weapons program. Indeed within an individual threshold state, both attitudes are surely present.

Unfortunately, however, the prospects for substantial Soviet-American nuclear arms control are not at all bright. The deterioration in Soviet-American relations since the signing of the Strategic Arms Limitation Talks (SALT) agreements of May 1972—a result of the continuing superpower political and ideological competition, the aggressive stance of Soviet foreign policy, and the pronounced Soviet military buildup—and the technological evolution of advanced weaponry make it exceedingly unlikely that substantive arms control agreements will be reached that will satisfy the threshold states. Consequently it can be expected that the lack of superpower arms control will be raised consistently as a point of criticism of American non-proliferation policy.

Regional Trends
While the Carter initiatives and reactions to them have been perhaps the most dramatic recent developments concerning nuclear proliferation, events in various parts of the world over the last few years indicate a continuing movement toward the spread of nuclear weapons. These events can be summarised by region.

Western Europe
Among the least interesting regions of the world from the perspective of nuclear proliferation, Western Europe remains very much in a holding pattern. A number of the states in the region —West Germany, Sweden, Switzerland, the Netherlands, Italy and Belgium—clearly have the requisite technological, economic and manpower resources to acquire nuclear weapons. They merely lack the political will. Because of its past history, however, West Germany's intentions receive particularly close attention. The prevailing view at this writing is that an independent German nuclear capability will not materialise unless the NATO alliance loses much of its credibility, thereby exposing Germany to serious threats from the Soviet Union and its Warsaw Pact allies, or unless a large number of new nuclear states emerge in a short period of time producing a momentum which impacts on German political will. Indeed the prospect that the Federal Republic may acquire long-range cruise missiles armed with conventional warheads during the next decade should be reassuring to those concerned about German nuclear weapons. Although there are some who are concerned about the surreptitious transfer of weapons-grade material from Brazilian facilities to Germany in ten or fifteen years, it seems clear that nothing less than a fundamental shift in Germany's perception of its own national security would prompt the Federal Republic to acquire nuclear weapons.

Spain is one additional West European country that is receiving attention from nuclear proliferation watchers. The Spanish government has made a commitment toward nuclear power and expects to have more than a dozen nuclear power plants in operation by 1982. But the democratisation of the Spanish political system in the last few years and the desire within Spain to join the European Community and NATO all tend to mitigate against a Spanish nuclear weapons program.

Canada and Australia, although not in the region (except in the minds of fuzzy-headed Americans), are in similar positions to the states of Western Europe. Political will is the only barrier to nuclear weapons acquisition in these states. For Canada—a member of NATO, closely linked to the United States, and without any serious threats posed to its national security—a nuclear weapons program makes little sense. Indeed the most radical speculation about Canada is that in the event the Quebec separatist movement succeeds, the other Canadian provinces will become affiliated in some manner with the United States. While this is a highly unlikely development it would nonetheless work against Canadian nuclear proliferation. Australia, on the other hand, could conceivably convince itself that it needed nuclear weapons if 1) the People's Republic of China developed a substantial intercontinental ballistic missile force that appeared threatening to Australians or 2) the Soviet navy became a significant force in areas that impinged on Australian national interests or 3) Japan or Indonesia or both became significant military powers in the South-western Pacific and 4) there was an appreciable deterioration in Australian-American relations. The likelihood of these developments coming to pass in the next ten-to-fifteen years is sufficiently remote, however, that Australia cannot be considered a likely entrant into the nuclear weapons club during this time period. The principal Australian concern in the nuclear field is, instead, whether to develop its very considerable uranium deposits for export. But the Australian debate on this subject is dominated by environmental considerations and does not address the nuclear weapons option.

Eastern Europe

The grip that the Soviet Union exercises on the decision-making authority of the governments of the Eastern European countries is so great that the prospect of nuclear weapons proliferation in this region must be judged to be exceedingly dim. The one exception is Yugoslavia. As the Yugoslav succession crisis grows nearer, hints that the Yugoslav government might seriously consider a nuclear weapons option have grown stronger. In 1976 a Yugoslav communist party publication maintained that nuclear weapons might be necessary to repel a nuclear-armed aggressor, presumably the Soviet Union. More recently a Yugoslav military official claimed that Yugoslavia's security concerns are tied to the activities of the London Suppliers Group. He warned that the Yugoslav government would continue to resist efforts by the nuclear states to establish a nuclear monopoly. Yugoslavia expects to begin commerical operation of its first nuclear facility for electrical power generation at the end of calendar year 1978. But it has had in operation a research reactor for several years and it is not at all clear whether the Yugoslavs would have to rely on a power reactor in order to obtain sufficient amounts of weapons-grade material to fabricate one or more nuclear weapons. The deliberate uncertainty with which Yugoslavia is approaching the nuclear weapons decision is somewhat similar to the stance adopted by Israel. It is assumed in this discussion that the Soviet Union will continue to retain its non-proliferation stance and will in no way attempt to assist other nations down the nuclear weapons path in Eastern Europe or elsewhere. There is no reason to assume otherwise.

Middle East and Persian Gulf

In the Middle East it is widely held that Israel already possesses nuclear weapons capable of being delivered at short notice against its opponents in the region. Israel is not a member of the NPT and steadfastly refuses to permit outside inspection if its Dimona reactor. The Israeli stance of fostered ambiguity in which nuclear weapon possession is neither admitted nor denied—'we will neither be the first nation to introduce nuclear weapons into the Middle East nor will we be the second'—may have in fact exercised a certain amount of deterrent effect vis-à-vis the Arab states in both the 1967 and 1973 wars, although this remains a highly contentious matter. In April 1977 doubts concerning Israeli possession of sufficient amounts of natural uranium to produce highly enriched uranium for bombs were punctured in a paper delivered at the Salzburg Conference for a Non-Nuclear Future by Paul Leventhal, former legislative assistant to U.S. Senator Abraham Ribicoff. Leventhal claimed that:

> In 1966 or 1967 a ship carrying about 200 tonnes (440,000 pounds) of natural uranium from Belgium to Italy disappeared. A few weeks later the ship reappeared with a new name, a new registry, a new crew, but no uranium. The intelligence services of several nations investigated, but eventually closed their files on the case without positively locating the hijacked uranium. It is generally assumed, however, that the material was unloaded in Israel. The shipment was under EURATOM safeguards, but the diversion was never publicly reported.

Although there has been a spirited debate in recent years on the question of whether Israel would be better off declaring that it had nuclear weapons or even detonating a device, its ambiguous policy seems to have broad support within Israel and, short of another war, no alteration is to be expected.

As long as Israel refrains from openly conceding its possession of nuclear weapons and as long as the nuclear weapon states—the United States, the Soviet Union, China, Great Britain, France and now India—continue to refrain from transferring weapons-grade material to other states, it may be many years before Middle Eastern nations besides Israel acquire nuclear weapons. The American nuclear reactor deal with both Egypt and Israel remains stalled and may not become untracked for a very long time. Libya has failed in its attempts to purchase nuclear weapons. And no other Middle Eastern state has yet completed the commercial arrangements to obtain nuclear power facilities.

In the Persian Gulf, however, Iran continues to seek the acquisition of nuclear power plants. Two 1200 megawatt pressurised water reactors have been ordered from West Germany and two 900 megawatt pressurised water reactors have been ordered from France. Given the widespread belief that Iran seeks regional hegemony in the Persian Gulf region, that it is acquiring a considerable military capability, and that it continues to seek to obtain both reprocessing and enrichment facilities, it must be ranked as a prime candidate for nuclear weapons possession in the next twenty years. And whether such possession will trigger similar responses in Iraq and Saudi Arabia cannot be lightly dismissed.

Sub-Saharan Africa

The only threshold country south of the Sahara in Africa appears to be South Africa. A principal source for natural uranium,[4] South Africa has ordered two pressurised water reactors from France that are scheduled to begin commerical operation by 1982–83. But it is highly doubtful that the South African government is relying on power reactors to obtain weapons-grade material. Instead South Africa has established a uranium enrichment plant which ironically is known as 'Valindaba', a contraction of the Zulu expression meaning 'the talking is over'. South Africa has not signed the NPT, has sent more than 120 scientists for training at nuclear establishments in the West, and has been rumoured to be cooperating with Israel in nuclear weapons development. As South Africa's political situation becomes less tenable, the government may move to a nuclear option, if it has not already done so. While the argument has been made that nuclear weapons would do little for the white Afrikaners in a guerrilla war against the blacks, it is possible that Prime Minister Vorster's government hopes to relinquish some territory, expel the blacks, establish an all-white South

African garrison state, and use nuclear weapons as a deterrent against a black invasion. South Africa must be considered a prime candidate for nuclear weapon possession within the next decade.

South Asia

In South Asia the surprising development of the last three years is that India has failed to explode a second nuclear device. The predictable development is that Pakistan seems to be striving to develop its own nuclear capability. India has a long-established nuclear research community that dates back to World War II. It has been able to obtain fuel for its Tarapur reactors even in the wake of its peaceful nuclear explosion. It expects to have eight nuclear power plants in operation by 1982. And it clearly has the wherewithal to field a credible nuclear force placing tens of nuclear weapons on a variety of delivery vehicles—if it chooses to do so. The Indian position remains, however, that it seeks to use nuclear energy solely for peaceful purposes and that it will strive for a nuclear weapons program of substantial magnitude only if the superpowers fail to curb their own nuclear arms competition. While it is premature at this stage to assess the differences on nuclear policy between the newly-elected Desai government and the administration of Mrs Gandhi, it may well be that India will exercise nuclear restraint unless Pakistan develops a nuclear arsenal of its own or Sino-Indian relations again deteriorate to the point of conflict.

Pakistan has had a small 125 megawatt reactor in operation since December 1972 and it now seeks to purchase a reprocessing plant and associated nuclear technology from France. At this writing the French position is that it will proceed with the sale once the political turmoil in Pakistan has ceased. Whether the deal is made or not, there is little doubt that Pakistan feels severely threatened by India and seeks nuclear weapons as the great equaliser on the Indian subcontinent. Pakistan is one nation whose nuclear weapons capability might well be determined by the ability of the supplier states to control effectively the spread of sensitive nuclear energy technologies.

East Asia

In East Asia four states are potential possessors of nuclear weapons: South and North Korea, Japan and Taiwan. As the United States paves the way for withdrawal of its ground troops from South Korea, it is doing what it can to minimise the destabilising effects of the withdrawal by considering retention of a U.S. Air Force presence on the peninsula, by stressing the proximity of the U.S.

Pacific Fleet to the region, and by engaging in close diplomatic consultation with both Seoul and Tokyo. It is highly questionable whether these steps will satisfy South Korean concerns. The United States will no doubt find its political leverage over South Korean policy reduced significantly once the ground troops have been removed, and it is precisely this leverage that was used to force cancellation of the previously completed Franco–South Korean arrangement that would have brought a French reprocessing plant to South Korea. Efforts by the Park regime to acquire an independent nuclear capability must be expected in the years ahead. Should this capability be acquired the North Koreans will be in a strong position to pressure both the Soviet Union and China for assistance in obtaining nuclear weapons of their own.

The Japanese situation is an extremely complex one and cannot be easily summarised. A double-edged problem faces Japan: on the one hand, it suffered as much as any other nation as a result of the 1973 OPEC oil embargo and it has striven to remove itself from a dependent energy position by moving vigorously toward nuclear power, with some 27 nuclear power plants expected to be in operation by 1982; on the other hand, it has an enormous psychological, political and legal aversion to the acquisition of nuclear weapons. Perhaps nowhere is the nuclear energy-nuclear weapons connection more intertwined than in Japan, which seeks reprocessing facilities to guarantee supplies of nuclear fuels for its Tokai facilities, which is extremely nervous about the American pullout from Korea in the wake of American defeat in South-east Asia, which is uncomfortable in its relations with both the Soviet Union and China, and which, at least for the moment, still sees no threat to its national security that would necessitate taking the nuclear weapons option. It may well be that a Japanese nuclear weapons program may only come about if other states in the region precede them.

In Taiwan there seem to be most of the necessary ingredients for a nuclear weapons program. Taiwan was one of the first nations in Asia to operate a research reactor, it has a cadre of well-trained nuclear engineers, scientists and technicians, it expects to have eight nuclear power plants in operation by 1984, it is becoming increasingly isolated in the international community and, based on recent reports, it may shortly lose its security agreement with the United States. Taiwan would most likely seek to acquire nuclear weapons to deter an attack from China, but acquisition would also complicate nuclear decision-making for South Korea and Japan. Taiwan seeks at all costs to prevent from being blackmailed by China. If a Taiwanese nuclear weapons program is the only means available to prevent this condition from occurring, Taiwan can be expected to take whatever steps are necessary to acquire this capability.

Latin America

In order to improve attitudes toward nuclear arms control in Latin America the Carter administration signed Protocol 1 of the Treaty of Tlatelolco, the so-called Latin American Nuclear Free Zone Treaty which establishes Latin America and the Caribbean as a region free of nuclear weapons. By adhering to the Protocol, the United States is precluded from retaining nuclear weapons on its military bases in Puerto Rico, Cuba and the Panama Canal Zone. Whether this effort will now result in Argentina, Brazil and Chile becoming parties to the Treaty remains to be seen.

There is little doubt that Brazil seeks to become a power of the first rank, that its nuclear energy program will not only promote economic development within the country but will provide it with a realisable nuclear weapons option, and that this prospect is viewed with alarm particularly by Brazil's chief political rival, Argentina. The German-Brazilian deal, if seen to completion, will provide Brazil in fifteen years with an autonomous nuclear industry including reprocessing facilities and an enrichment plant utilising the Becker nozzle process developed in West Germany. The fundamental conclusion to be reached from this development is that Brazil will, well before the end of the century, be able to become a significant nuclear weapons power if it chooses to do so. Argentina, which has a long-established nuclear energy research community, would then have to face the choice of being subject to possible intimidation by its rival or acquiring nuclear weapons of its own.

Maintaining A Non-Proliferation Regime

As this brief regional sketch suggests, pressures to acquire nuclear weapons are mounting in various parts of the world and are probably beyond the ability of any nation or group of nations to control. The Carter initiatives which represent the most vigorous effort by any government to control the spread of nuclear weapons are already meeting substantial resistance and are not likely to be fully successful. Other factors which are not even addressed in this paper—laser enrichment of uranium and the use of nuclear weapons by terrorist groups—are real prospects that will greatly exacerbate the nuclear proliferation problem. The inability of the United States and the Soviet Union to curb their nuclear weapons appetites, as demonstrated in the long-deadlocked Strategic Arms Limitation

Talks (SALT), sets a poor example for non-nuclear states and provides a rationale for those nations that seek an independent nuclear weapons capability. Indeed it is fast becoming possible for non-nuclear states to cooperate solely with each other in order to acquire nuclear weapons, by-passing the supplier states altogether. In sum it is difficult to be optimistic that the spread of nuclear weapons can be controlled.

In order to minimise the spread, however, and to maintain as much of a non-proliferation regime as possible, it will be necessary for the supplier states to coordinate their nuclear policies more effectively in the future than they have in the past, it will be necessary to begin an effective dialogue between the suppliers and the recipients, and it will be necessary for the community of nations to impose severe sanctions on any state that explodes a nuclear device, whether for peaceful purposes or in anger. Failure to pursue with vigour each of these approaches will only quicken the pace of proliferation and promote international instability.

For the moment the debate in the United States over nuclear non-proliferation policy has subsided. The implementation phase of the Carter policy has begun. And with it, the world's reactions to this policy are beginning to be formed. The acceptability of the policy and of associated measures stemming from it may well determine the extent to which there will be any hope of controlling nuclear proliferation in the future.

Footnotes

1. These strategies are reviewed in Michael Nacht, 'The United States in a World of Nuclear Powers' *The Annals of the American Academy of Political and Social Sciences*, March 1977, pp. 162–174.

2. At this writing particularly sensitive negotiations are in progress between Japan and the United States concerning the future status of Japanese reprocessing facilities, with the parties reportedly being far from agreement. More generally, it should be noted that some American observers believe the Soviet Union sees the nuclear proliferation issue as a major development likely to undermine Western alliance cohesion. These observers argue for a 'go slow' approach.

3. The German position highlights two more general points worth noting. First, the argument that economic necessity compels the Federal Republic and other nations to make early commitments to reprocessing and breeder reactors has not gone unchallenged. In a recent American study, for example, the conclusion is reached that uranium needs in this century appear capable of being met from resources producible at less than $20 per pound of uranium oxide, that prices under $10 per pound in the first quarter of the twenty-first century are a reasonable possibility, and that at such prices processed plutonium fuels make no economic sense. See Vince Taylor, *The Myth of Uranium Scarcity*, Pan Heuristics Inc., Los Angeles, May 1977. Second, the German response tends to de-emphasise the significance of the London Suppliers Group. The original seven-nation group (Canada, West Germany, France, Japan, the Soviet Union, Great Britain and the United States) was expanded to fifteen in 1976 with the addition of Belgium, Czechoslovakia, East Germany, Italy, the Netherlands, Poland, Sweden and Switzerland. The group meets in closed sessions and has so far failed to reach substantive agreements beyond a set of 1975 guidelines endorsing IAEA safeguards.

4. A study by the Organization for Economic Cooperation and Development projects that by 1985 production of natural uranium will be distributed as follows: United States—46%; South Africa—16%; Canada—13%; Niger—7%; Australia—6%; France—4%; and all others—8%. See *Nuclear Power: Issues and Choices.* A report of the Nuclear Energy Policy Study Group, Ballinger Publishing Co., Cambridge, Mass. 1977. p.82.

2

The Development of the Conventional Arms Trade
Ron Huisken

Introduction[1]

The international transfer of armaments is by no means a new phenomenon.[2] There are, however, good reasons for discussing the trade since 1945 separately. Since World War II the major powers have used arms supplies as one of the principal instruments for the achievement of foreign policy objectives. A second and closely related reason is that the volume of the trade rapidly achieved dimensions unprecedented in history.

It is the trade with the Third World which is of primary interest to this study since only three countries in the Indian-Pacific region are normally considered developed—Australia, Japan and New Zealand. Data compiled by the U.S. Arms Control and Disarmament Agency (ACDA) suggest that for at least a decade, perhaps longer, the value of the arms trade with the Third World has exceeded that with or rather among the developed countries.[3]

A far more significant indicator of the importance of the arms trade with the Third World is that the weapons supplied have been systematically used in conflict. Nearly all the wars since 1945—some 119 of them through 1975 on one definition[4]—have occurred in the Third World and virtually without exception the weapons used were supplied by the developed countries.

Despite this the arms trade has attracted comparatively little attention from those concerned with arms control and disarmament. Nuclear weapons have monopolised the arena. It is really only since 1973, in the aftermath of the latest Arab–Israeli conflict and the associated oil crisis, that serious and comparatively widespread concern over the traffic in conventional armaments has emerged. As we shall show, this long delay has immeasurably complicated the question of controlling and moderating this trade.

The chapter is divided into three main sections. The first is an empirically-oriented description of the development of the arms trade with the Third World since 1945. The second section attempts to identify the main forces that have shaped this development. The final section discusses the principal effects of the arms trade on recipients and the implications for the future if present trends go unchecked. This section concludes with some suggestions for controlling or moderating the traffic in arms.

Section I: The Development of the Arms Trade with the Third World[5]
Since World War II the trade in arms with the Third World has escalated almost continuously. This is true almost regardless of the index chosen: the volume of resources involved, the sophistication and modernity of the weapons and equipment transferred or the number of countries involved as either suppliers or recipients. In this section we shall try to document this escalation on all three counts.

The Arms Trade in Terms of Resources
The value of the resources absorbed is perhaps the most logical aggregate measure of trends in the arms trade. In practice it is a very difficult measure to construct. Apart from the United States none of the arms suppliers provide comprehensive and disaggregated data on their arms exports. Even the U.S. data is deficient in that, for example, exports of surplus weapons and equipment are usually recorded at one-third of the acquisition cost although some items are brand new. Similarly, recipient nations do not report the value of arms imports in any readily identified way.

If the objective is to measure the actual financial flows associated with arms transactions, further complications arise because of the dearth of information on the terms of individual transactions. These range from outright grants to cash on delivery, with a variety of discount, barter and credit arrangements in between.

In this situation the only recourse is to value independently all identified transactions or deliveries. This involves the compilation of an arms trade register and the construction of a list of comparable prices of all the items traded. While a number of institutions compile arms trade registers only two attempt to value these transactions—the Stockholm International Peace Research Institute (SIPRI) and ACDA. SIPRI valuations cover only major weapons—aircraft, ships, missiles and armoured vehicles—while ACDA purports to cover in addition, non-armoured military vehicles, spare parts, support equipment, communications and electronic equipment, artillery, infantry weapons, small arms, ammunition and equipment for defence industries. This difference in coverage makes direct comparisons and joint use impossible and we have elected to use the SIPRI data.[6]

Development of the Conventional Arms Trade. 23

The SIPRI data on the value of the arms trade attempts to do
no more than reflect the trend in volume of resources transferred
in the form of weapons. For this reason they are shown in Chart
1 in index form. The ACDA figures are also presented since the
necessary assumption—that the total trade bears a reasonably close
and stable relation to the trade in major weapons—seems a
reasonable one.

Despite considerable year-to-year fluctuations the underlying
trend is clearly strongly upward. The SIPRI data show that the
value of major weapons delivered increased almost twenty-fold over
the period 1950–76, implying an average annual rate of increase
of about 12 per cent. Since 1970 the rate of increase has been

CHART 1
**INDICES OF THE VALUE OF ARMS IMPORTS BY THIRD WORLD
COUNTRIES,
1950–76**

Based on constant price data, 1970 = 100

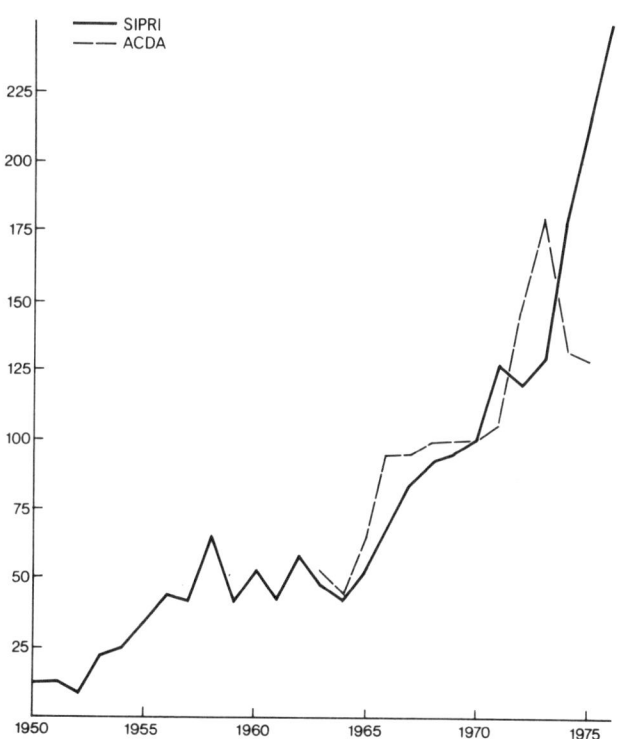

considerably faster; more than 17 per cent annually on the average. Indeed the total value of deliveries during the 1970s already exceeds that for the preceding 20 years by about 20 per cent.

As is well known the Middle East has absorbed a large and increasing fraction of total arms deliveries to the Third World: one-quarter of the cumulative deliveries during the 1950s, one third during the 1960s and one half for the period 1970–76. According to SIPRI the region has absorbed over 4,000 jet combat aircraft and some 13,500 tanks over the 25 years 1950–75.[7] A coalition of factors has contributed to this massive inflow of weaponry, most notably the region's strategic importance, the bitter and enduring Arab–Israeli dispute and the more recent oil-funded arms build-up around the Persian Gulf. The latter development has been sufficiently extravagant to permit all the major arms suppliers to increase their sales significantly. The U.S.A., however, with $21.6 billion in Foreign Military Sales (FMS) orders from Gulf States in the 10 years 1967–76, has clearly taken the lion's share of the market.[8]

Although the scale and rate of increase in arms deliveries to the Middle East are uniquely large it is by no means the only region in the Third World that has experienced an escalation in the value of arms imported. This is apparent from Chart 2. Five year moving averages have been plotted because the annual totals fluctuate markedly in some cases.

A few comments can be made. The major increase in the rate of delivery to the Far East after 1963 is due almost entirely to the conflict in Vietnam. The impact of the U.S. 'Vietnamisation' program and the accelerated deliveries to both sides prior to the January 1973 ceasefire agreement can be seen. If Vietnam is factored out, average deliveries to the remaining countries in the Far East remained at about the 1963 level, but with a major increase taking place in 1975 and continuing in 1976. In Africa the two phases of rapid increase—in the early 1960s and the early 1970s—reflect widespread increases throughout that continent, i.e., deliveries escalated to North African and Sub-Saharan states and to South Africa.

Trends in the Sophistication of the Armaments traded.
One of the most conspicuous features of the post-war military scene has been the fast pace of technological change. With few exceptions the complexity and sophistication of successive generations of weapons systems have escalated remarkably as advances in all the relevant fields of technology are incorporated. This qualitative improvement in weaponry, as distinct from quantitative growth in

CHART 2
VALUE OF IMPORTS OF MAJOR WEAPONS, BY REGION,
1952–74

US $ mn, constant (1975) prices, five-year moving averages

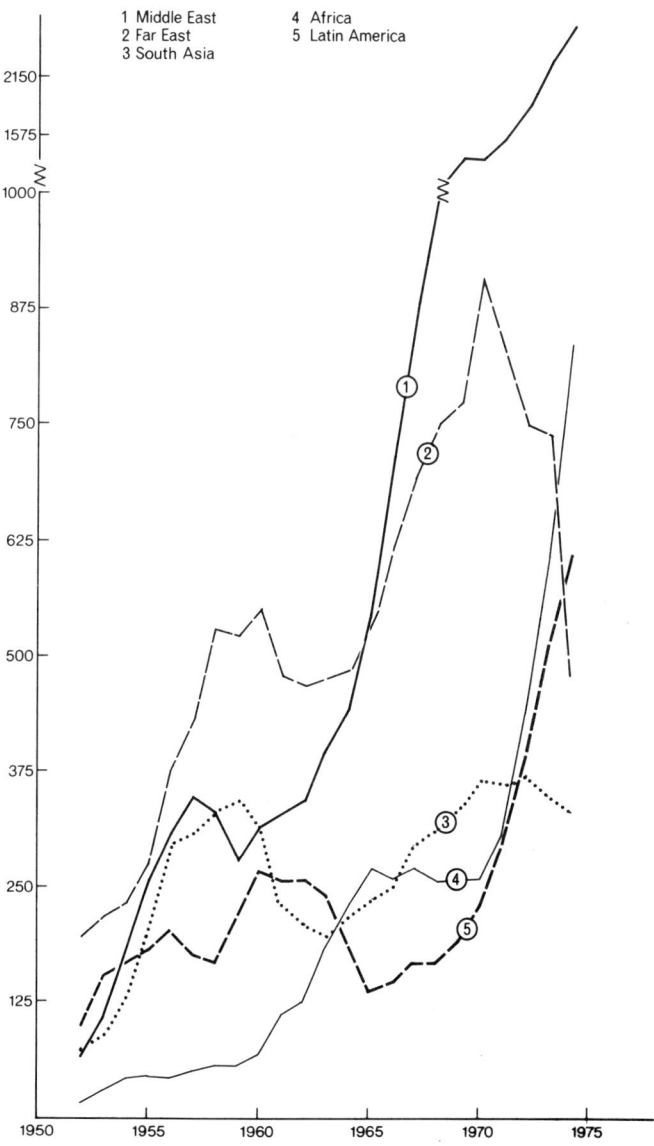

1 Middle East   4 Africa
2 Far East   5 Latin America
3 South Asia

military arsenals, is the central feature of the main East–West military competition.

The arms trade has been the primary mechanism in the global proliferation of the desire to seek continuous qualitative improvement in military arsenals. Moreover, it has steadily become a more direct mechanism in the sense that the weaponry traded has increasingly become more up-to-date and so the speed of proliferation has increased.

There are a variety of trends that can be documented to substantiate this thesis. First of all one can note the rate and/or the extent of the proliferation of certain key weapon systems that can be regarded as advanced or sophisticated, e.g., supersonic aircraft, long and medium-range surface-to-air missile systems, missile-equipped major surface warships and submarines. Table 1 shows this proliferation with respect to supersonic aircraft and surface-to-air missile systems. At the end of 1976 Third World navies possessed a total of nearly 280 major surface warships of which 26, distributed over nine countries, were equipped with missile systems. Missile-equipped patrol boats were both more numerous and more widespread; 21 countries with a total of about 165 units. Submarines are also proliferating rapidly. In 1960, seven Third World countries possessed a total of 21 units: at the end of 1976 there were 15 countries with 73 units.

Table 1: The proliferation of sophisticated weapons to the Third World, 1955–1976

	Number of countries, cumulative				
	1955	*1960*	*1965*	*1970*	*1976*
1. Supersonic Aircraft	1	3	14	30	44
2. Surface-to-air missiles	—	1	8	16	26

A second indicator of the developing sophistication of the international trade in arms is the expanding range of military capabilities being made available for export. Examples here would include long- and medium-range surface-to-surface missile systems and integrated air defence systems. With respect to surface-to-surface missiles the ice was broken in 1973 when the Soviet Union provided Egypt with some 280 kilometre range SS–IC Scud missiles, possibly to deter the use by Israel of its indigenous Jericho system although there is still no evidence that the development of the Jericho has been completed.[9] In any event, Israel subsequently requested the 140 kilometre range MGM–52 Lance missile from the U.S.A. and deliveries commenced in 1975. Syria and Iraq have also received Scud units from the Soviet Union in 1974 and 1975 respectively.

A phenomenon related to the spread of new capabilities is the adoption by Third World countries of recently-developed military tactics and the systems appropriate to these tactics. The most conspicuous example is the use of helicopters as airborne gunships and anti-tank platforms pioneered by the U.S.A. in Vietnam. Iran is currently receiving 202 AH–IJ Sea Cobra helicopter gunships and Saudi Arabia is reported to be another customer for this system: Egypt has 42 French Gazelle helicopters on order that will be equipped with the Franco-German HOT anti-tank missile. Another instance could be the use of helicopters as launching platforms for anti-ship missiles. It appears that Pakistan may be the first customer for the French AM.39 air-launched version of the Exocet missile.

A third dimension of the trend under review in this section is the modernity of the equipment transferred. In this respect the arms trade with the Third World can be said to have gone through three broad phases. In the initial post-war period the bulk of the deliveries consisted of obsolete World War II weapons. This phase was followed by the transfer of equipment rendered obsolescent by the technological arms race. The final phase, only recently begun, is the transfer of the latest equipment straight from the production lines.

There have always been, of course, important exceptions to this broad scheme. Indeed the exceptions during the first two phases played an instrumental role in accelerating the emergence of stage three. There have been two main types of exceptions. First, the major powers have always regarded some countries as privileged recipients of armaments. For the United States privileged recipients in the Third World were the so-called 'forward-defence' countries on the Asian mainland and Israel. For the Soviet Union, Egypt, Syria and Iraq and to a lesser extent North Korea and, for shorter periods, Indonesia and Cuba, have been high priority recipients. At the present time Libya is probably at or near the top of the Soviet list. These countries tended to receive more modern equipment and/or in larger quantities than the two major suppliers were inclined to make available to other recipients. Early in 1977, for example, Libya took delivery of the first of 12 TU–22 Blinder A aircraft from the Soviet Union. This is the first time that a developing country has acquired a supersonic bomber.

The other type of exception involves the second-order arms suppliers, particularly France. For reasons that will be considered in the next section, these countries regard arms exports as vital to the preservation of their defence industries. As a result there have been numerous instances in which France has sold equipment markedly superior to that extant in a given country or region. An indirect indication of this propensity is provided by the fact that many of the major weapon systems developed in France since World War II have been exported to Third World countries within a year or two of reaching operational status in France.[10]

Both types of exceptions had the same effect, namely to generate pressures in a growing number of countries for more sophisticated armaments.

The third phase, the supply of current generation weapons on an increasingly general scale, has much to do with the fact that most arms transactions now take place on commercial terms which gives recipients a much greater role in determining the nature of weapons transferred. Little or no effort has been made in the arms producing countries to develop low and intermediate technology weaponry suited to the circumstances prevailing in most Third World countries. The weaponry that has proliferated via the arms trade has, in general, been the weaponry that was or had been in use in the producing country. Now that recipients are paying for their armaments the demand is, perforce, for the latest high technology hardware.

The size of the Third World market for armaments (some $6–8 billion annually at the present time), the confident expectations that it will remain a strong market for many years to come and the intense competition among suppliers has led, particularly in recent years, to a marked easing of restrictions on the type of weaponry available for export. Some manifestations of this trend have already been mentioned. The tendency to make newly-developed weapon systems available for export, noted with respect to France, has become a general phenomenon. Perhaps the best known example was the U.S. decision to sell the F–14A with the remarkable Phoenix missile system to Iran in 1974, the same year in which the aircraft became operational in the U.S. Navy. The Soviet Union MiG–23 Flogger, which entered service in 1971, appeared in the Middle East and North Africa 2–3 years later.

In many cases the situation has developed a stage further with export orders being taken prior to the completion of the development program for a weapon. A case in point is the U.S. Harpoon anti-ship cruise missile. This weapon will enter service in the U.S. Navy in 1977 but by the end of June 1976 firm export orders for 507 missiles had been taken, some from developing countries and several more applications are being received.

An even higher stage of development has been reached in which a developing country commissions one of the arms producing nations to develop a particular weapons system or sub-system. There are several examples of this phenomenon. The repeat Iranian order for 1200 Chieftain main battle tanks included the funding of a development program to up-grade significantly the capability of this weapon.[11] Iran is also funding the development in the U.K. of the tracked, fully self-contained Rapier surface-to-air missile system. France is developing a similar system, called Chahinn for Saudi Arabia, employing the Crotale missile.[12] Finally Saudi Arabia is reported to have funded the development in the U.S.A. of a single-rail launcher for the Maverick air-to-surface missile because the standard triple launcher could not be fitted onto the F–5E Tiger II aircraft which that country is receiving.

The Third World market for armaments is now apparently sufficiently large to justify the risk of developing even major weapons exclusively for the export market. Taking the requirements of potential export customers into account to the maximum extent possible in national weapon development programs is not new. This has long been a feature of British and French weapons programs. What is new is, for example, the announced intention of Dassault in France to develop privately for export a twin-engined multi-role version of the Mirage 2000 interceptor. Another example is the Northrop-McDonnell Douglas F–18L, a privately developed land-based version of the aircraft which these two companies are developing for the U.S. Navy. As a final example we can take the West German Type 209 submarine. Some 20 Type 209s, which are larger and more advanced than any submarine in the German Navy, have been produced or are on order, all for export.

There is one last aspect of the developing sophistication of the international trade in arms that is in itself noteworthy and closely related to the subject matter of the next section. Some of the major arms deals negotiated in recent years have been elaborate and comprehensive package deals going far beyond the delivery of a squadron of aircraft or a number of missile batteries. To some extent this trend may simply reflect the availability of lavish cash resources (the outstanding examples involve the Persian Gulf States) but it presumably also reflects a growing appreciation of the full significance of the complexity of modern warfare and the implications of the 'weapons system' concept. There have been several instances—Indonesia in the past, Libya at the present time—in which developing countries have acquired lavish quantities of major weapons but the military effectiveness of these arsenals has generally been very small. The effective operation of an arsenal of advanced weapons requires a pool of diversely skilled people to operate, maintain, supply and manage the systems; it requires workshops, training schools, headquarters, communication centres and so on. These are the capabilities that some of the wealthier states are seeking to acquire in addition to the weapons themselves.

Saudi Arabia provides perhaps the clearest illustration of this. By Middle Eastern standards the Saudi armed forces are small and modestly equipped. Following a U.S. survey in 1974 of its military requirements an expansion and modernisation program has been started. The orders for weapons are, in general, not outstandingly large,[13] again by Middle Eastern standards. What is outstanding is the totality of the military capability the Saudis are seeking to import. For example the Saudis have on order from the U.S.A. what amounts to a complete naval establishment: the construction of two naval bases, repair facilities, a training centre, housing, a headquarters complex, a communications centre and, of course, naval vessels, some of which are being specifically designed to suit Saudi Arabian requirements. Saudi Arabia is admittedly the extreme example but the tendency for recipients to seek a more comprehensive transfer of military capabilities is observable on a far wider scale than ever before.

The Arms Trade: Number of Participants
A third index that can be used to assess the development of the post-war trade in arms with the Third World is the number of countries participating in this trade, either as recipients, suppliers, or both. As far as the number of recipients is concerned the growth was very rapid indeed, particularly during the 1950s and early 1960s. The U.S. Military Assistance program, for example, covered four countries in 1948, 14 in 1950 and reached a peak of 69 countries in 1963, by which time nearly all the recipients were Third World countries. In 1973 72 developing countries in Africa, the Middle East, South Asia, the Far East and Latin America were eligible under the Foreign Military Sales Act to purchase defence articles from the United States.[14] The list includes several countries that acquire significant quantities of arms from the Soviet Union and other Eastern European suppliers or from China. There is a far greater overlap, of course, with other Western suppliers. In short there is no country in the world that does not have access to modern weapons from one or more of the major arms suppliers.

An important factor accounting for the geographic spread of the arms trade is the large number of states that have achieved independence since World War II. A military establishment is an essentially indispensable symbol of nationhood. A second important consideration, of course, is that in many areas throughout the Third

World there is acute mutual suspicion and enmity between states. But other factors have also been at work, above all the powerful demonstration effect that armaments have. It requires only one country in a particular region to upgrade its arsenal either quantitatively or qualitatively to create ultimately irrepressible pressures in surrounding countries for off-setting acquisitions. It is not even necessary that surrounding countries perceive a military threat, although more often than not this is the case. Considerations of prestige and respectability seem in themselves to be sufficient motives.

In every major region of the world there have been countries that either have the resources and the ambition to seek a relative preponderance of military strength or are regarded by one or other of the two major powers as strategically important and thus have acquired disproportionately large military arsenals. This process of induced exposure to modern armaments is by now essentially complete. The tendency to seek continuous qualitative improvement of military arsenals, to acquire successively more advanced, more complex and more lethal weaponry, is to all intents and purposes a global phenomenon.

In parallel with the increasing number of recipients there has been an increase in the number of suppliers. In relative numerical terms the increase in the number of suppliers has been extremely modest but this trend nonetheless has major long-term implications not least for the prospects for arms control and disarmament.

There are several dimensions to this problem. One dimension concerns the transfer of weaponry from the original recipient to a third party. There are a growing number of countries whose military arsenals are sufficiently large or who are transitioning relatively quickly to more advanced weaponry to make them potential arms suppliers even in the absence of a local defence industry. With occasional exceptions the scale of these re-transfers is not large but they are often controversial. An early example was a sale in the mid-1960s of 90 ex-Luftwaffe F–86 Sabres to Iran. But the aircraft overshot their destination and ended up in Pakistan.

At the present time Iran is transitioning from the F–5A light fighter to the more advanced F–5E model and the former aircraft are being re-transferred, with U.S. approval, to Turkey, Jordan, Pakistan and Kenya. A more controversial example was the sale of Jordanian Hawker Hunter aircraft, Tigercat surface-to-air missile batteries and Centurion tanks to South Africa.[15] The controversy arose over speculation that the weapons were really intended for Rhodesia. Reportedly, Egypt intervened to prevent the sale of the aircraft but the other weaponry was already in South Africa by May 1974, two months before the first reports on the deal appeared in the press.[16]

A final illustration might be the transfer of Libyan Mirage IIIs to Egypt during the October 1973 war with Israel. French acknowledgement that this transaction had taken place was almost certainly a factor contributing to the decision, in August 1974, to lift the embargo on arms sales to the belligerent Arab States. The Libyan re-transfer demonstrated that, to make the embargo effective, France would have to forego arms sales to all Arab States and this was evidently too large to give up. Among the immediate fallout of this decision was the sale of 38 Mirage IIIs, ordered and paid for by Saudi Arabia, but delivered to Egypt, and an Egyptian order for 42 SA-341 Gazelle helicopters armed with HOT anti-tank missiles. Libya has continued to make major arms purchases from the Soviet Union as well as France and has also intimated that it will, when necessary, serve as an arsenal for friendly states.

A second dimension concerns the increasing number of countries offering indigenously developed and manufactured weapons or major sub-systems of weapons on the international market. What is of interest here is not so much countries like the U.K. or France with well-established and reasonably comprehensive defence in-dustries or countries like Italy and Czechoslovakia with smaller, less comprehensive but still significant defence industries. Rather the interest is in those countries that have a very narrowly-based indigenous capability in the defence field and no discernible ambition to develop comprehensive defence industries but who are nonetheless important suppliers of selected weapons or major electronic sub-systems. The dramatic growth in the monetary value of the international arms market in recent years and the increasing willingness of recipients to 'shop around' has given these peripheral or specialist suppliers an increasingly important role, particularly in intensifying the competition for orders.

The countries concerned, together with their main area of specialisation, include: the Netherlands, naval fire control systems; Switzerland, land-based air defence systems; Belgium, small arms; and Finland, mortars. This situation has produced some unusually complex arms transactions in recent years. For example, the British Type 42 frigates under construction for Brazil have French anti-ship missiles, Australian anti-submarine missiles, British and Dutch warning radars, an Italian weapon control and tracking radar and U.S. sonars. Most submarines produced in West Germany for export have fire control equipment developed and produced by

Hollandse Signall, a Dutch firm.

This trend obviously reflects a growing sophistication on the part of Third World recipients and a natural inclination to exploit the existence of several potential suppliers in virtually every field of weaponry and equipment. It also reflects the new, liberal atmosphere that surrounds the development, production and export of armaments. Egyptian MiG–21s are being test-flown with a British weapon-aiming system and consideration has been given to re-equipping Egyptian tanks with Yugoslav fire-control systems that incorporate a laser designator developed and produced in Sweden. The Orao advanced jet trainer and ground attack aircraft jointly developed by Yugoslavia and Rumania (a member of the Warsaw Pact) is powered by Rolls Royce engines.

A final observation that can be made in this context is that the industrialised countries that currently pursue very restricted arms export policies but have considerable potential as exporters— notably West Germany, Sweden and Japan—are experiencing increasingly severe internal pressures to liberalise these policies. The general argument is that lucrative export opportunities are being foregone to no practical purpose. In the case of West Germany these pressures are amplified via the link with France on collaborative weapons programs—the Alfajet and the Roland, HOT and MILAN missile systems. Indeed, it could be argued that a less restrictive arms export policy was inherent in the West German decision to enter into collaborative programs with France.

A third dimension is the evident popularity in Third World countries of *establishing* defence industries. In 1975 13 developing countries were producing major weapons under licence and three more were preparing to undertake their first ventures in this field. In 1960 the number was two or three. The scope of this activity is summarised in Appendix 1.

This trend appears to be the result of a mixture of political, military and economic motives. The few Third World countries that have made a large and sustained effort to establish and extend their indigenous capacity to manufacture modern armaments—notably India, Israel and South Africa—have all been subject to arms embargoes by their traditional suppliers. To achieve a measure of self-sufficiency in arms production and thereby greater potential independence is a costly and long-term undertaking. The standard pattern is to proceed from the maintenance and repair of imported weapons through assembly under licence and increasing local production of components to indigenous design and development.

Whether the local production of arms increases the degree of independence is arguable. Self-sufficiency in small arms and ammunition plus a local capacity to maintain and repair major systems obviously increases the length of time for which combat operations can be sustained without external assistance. However the production under licence of sophisticated major weapons by a developing country probably increases its degree of dependence on the licenser state in that the recipient must make a major commitment in plant and machinery and in the training of personnel. This investment will be heavily dependent for an extended period of time on external technical expertise and imports of critical components such as powerplants. That is to say, the more extensive the transfer of technology and industrial know-how the more dependent the recipient becomes, at least for an extended period. The risks can be partially offset by securing licences from several countries. It is also the case that it is in practice easier to secure the uninterrupted delivery of components than of complete weapon systems.

Apart from the desire for greater political independence several other considerations play important roles in motivating countries to undertake the local manufacture of armaments. One such consideration, the tendency to regard defence industries as status symbols, is immune to analytical scrutiny but there can be little doubt that this perception plays an influential role. A second is the widely-held belief that the military sector breeds a high rate of technological advance and that this will induce a similar trend in other sectors of the economy. A closely related phenomenon is the expectation that the local production of armaments will stimulate the development of ancillary industries useful to the civilian economy, for example, metallurgy, chemicals and electronics. A third consideration often cited is that while production under licence or co-production almost inevitably involves an absolute cost penalty over direct import[17] it does offer the prospect of reducing the expenditure of foreign reserves, a particularly scarce and valuable resource in most developing countries.

This is not the place to assess the validity of these various arguments, although some comments will be made on them in the third section of this paper. However, two comments, one broad, one specific, can be made in passing. Firstly, one can have intuitive doubts about the value of transferring to underdeveloped, poverty-stricken countries the mostly highly refined and specialised technology available in the industrialised world. Secondly, the ambition to save foreign exchange is difficult to realise in practice. Indian production of the MiG–21 is a case in point. The average unit manufacturing cost of these planes has been calculated at 14.4 million rupees of which 8.3 million rupees were in foreign exchange to cover Soviet-supplied materials and components. The cost of a fully-imported aircraft was 6–7.5 million rupees.[18]

The sale of military technology in addition to or instead of military end items is a conspicuous recent development in the arms trade with the Third World. Although nations and firms tend to regard technology as a critical resource, the dissemination of which must be tightly controlled, there has been an unmistakable relaxation of inhibitions to export technology. Iran has combined nearly every major purchase of weapons in recent years with arrangements for ultimate licence-production (Rapier missiles and Chieftain tanks are examples) or the establishment of a local support facility for the weapons concerned (TOW anti-tank and Maverick air-to-surface missiles are examples).[19] Argentina, Brazil, Peru and Venezuela have all recently placed orders for sophisticated major surface warships. In every case some units will be built in the purchasing country with the suppliers, in this case the U.K. and Italy providing all the necessary materials and technical support. These are just examples. The extent of these arrangements in the regions of interest to this conference has been summarised in Appendix 1.

The primary explanation for this development undoubtedly lies in the large size of the international market for arms and the unprecedented role played by commercial forces in determining who gets the orders. It is essentially a buyer's market and for the reasons listed above buyers are insisting on a more comprehensive transfer of technology in conjunction with purchases of arms. This does not mean that suppliers are being totally coerced in this direction. Technical assistance contracts—such as Lockheed's $250 million contract with Greece to establish an aircraft industry—can be very lucrative. There is also some evidence that co-production and assembly arrangements are more profitable than direct sales.[20] In addition there is the well-established practice of setting up subsidiaries in developing countries to take advantage of low labour costs and to be better placed to meet the requirements of the local market. An example which seems relevant here is Avimo Singapore (Pty) Ltd, a subsidiary of United Scientific Holdings (U.K.). The company, which specialises in military optics, commenced operation in October 1974 and was reportedly commercially viable in its first year.[21] Finally, the suppliers are presumably confident that they can stay ahead of the game in the sense that there is little prospect that developing countries, even the most ambitious of them, will be able to assimilate and master all the technologies involved in a given weapons system as fast as new developments are spawned in the industrialised countries.

Despite the negligible prospects for complete independence of developing states from the major suppliers of weapons, the proliferation of the capacity to manufacture modern armaments has major implications. Perhaps the most significant implication is the enhanced capacity to sustain combat operations independently of the actions of the principal arms suppliers. The dependence of Third World nations on arms supplies from the major powers has been singularly unsuccessful as an instrument for preventing the outbreak of conflict but it has on several occasions been used successfully to bring about an early termination of hostilities.

A second implication is an increase in the number of countries capable of being the immediate suppliers of a weapon. This permits indirect transactions that do not attract as much attention as direct sales and occasionally violate the spirit and even the letter of the arms export policy in force in the country that ultimately owns the weapons. A good example was the delivery to Turkey of 40 F–104S Starfighters by the Italian licensee Aeritalia at the time of the U.S. embargo on arms sales to the country. Italian licensees have also delivered U.S.-designed CH–47C transport helicpoters and M–113 armoured personnel carriers to Libya in recent years. Had Libya approached the U.S. directly for these items it would almost certainly have been turned down. Other examples, more relevant to our discussion, include the delivery to Thailand of West German-designed fast patrol boats manufactured in Singapore and the recent Indonesian order for U.S.-designed missile-armed patrol boats from a South Korean shipyard.

A final implication is the longer-term prospect of an increase in the number of countries offering indigenously-designed and developed weapons for export. Moreover, given the disproportionately large effort that a developing nation must make to achieve this capacity, it can be anticipated that export policies will be flexible. Israel, though in many respects a special case, illustrates the ramifications of this development. Israeli arms exports have raced from $10 million in 1966 to a forecast $1000 million in 1977.[22] The export drive is broadly-based in terms of products—aircraft, missiles, warships, infantry weapons and electronic equipment—and sales have been made to countries in Europe, Africa, the Far East and Latin America. This extraordinary performance is due to a significant extent to past U.S. largesse in transferring military technology to Israel. The ramifications of this generosity have only recently begun to be appreciated in the U.S.A. Apart from unfavourable commercial implications for U.S. manufacturers, the contradiction between burgeoning Israeli arms exports heavily based on U.S. technology and continuing large-scale assistance to Israel under the Foreign Military Sales credit program, U.S. defence officials are concerned about the proliferation, in modified form of new and highly advanced U.S. technology which enhances the prospects that it will fall into the wrong hands. Furthermore some recipients of Israeli weapons, actual and prospective, are either countries to which the U.S.A. will not sell weapons (South Africa) or countries that the U.S.A. tries to discourage from acquiring sophisticated weapons (countries in Latin America). Israeli efforts to sell the Kfir fighter-bomber in Latin America are thus contrary to U.S. policy although in this particular instance the U.S.A. can prevent any sales because the aircraft is powered by a U.S. engine.[23]

Israel is unique in the speed with which it has emerged as an important arms exporting country but the trend towards the transfer of military technology suggests that the ranks of the arms suppliers will continue to grow. Apart from Israel a number of other developing countries—Argentina, Brazil, India, South Africa and Taiwan—have significant indigenous weapon development programs under way. India formally announced its intention to enter the arms export market in April 1972, a decade after the war with China which provoked a major expansion in Indian weapon development and production activity. To date sales appear to have been confined largely to infantry weapons and equipment and artillery.

The various developments described in this section are producing increasingly complex and obscure patterns of interaction and interdependence between suppliers and recipients and this in turn is compounding the difficulty of devising effective measures to control and moderate the trade in arms.

Section II. Forces shaping the Development of the Post-War Arms Trade with the Third World

In this section we will discuss, very briefly, what appear to have been the main factors shaping the evolution of the post-war arms trade documented in Section I.

The United States and the Soviet Union

With the possible exception of the first years after World War II the United States and the Soviet Union have been the predominant exporters of armaments. Indeed, the rapid emergence after World War II of an enduring enmity between these two powers has been the primary determinant of the scale and pattern of the post-war international trade in arms.

In the late 1940s, building on the extension of economic and military assistance to Greece and Turkey after the U.K. had indicated that it could no longer afford to do so, the U.S.A. undertook to subsidise the economic reconstruction and modest rearmament of Western Europe. The outbreak of war in Korea in June 1950, apart from enormously expanding and accelerating the European rearmament program, demonstrated that the threat of conflict between the two camps was not confined to Europe. The result was that the scope of the U.S. military assistance program expanded rapidly to cover all the major regions in the Third World but with a necessary emphasis on those countries on the Asian landmass that bordered on the Soviet Union and China.

The U.S. military assistance program had the primary objective of 'containing' the expansion of Communism by military means. The supply of arms, particularly on a grant basis, symbolised a security connection with the recipient nation and implied the existence of a common enemy. Indeed, for a time in the early 1950s recipients of U.S. military assistance were required to issue public statements to the effect that Communism was the common enemy.

For a period of nearly five years the U.S.A. had virtually a free hand in endeavouring to secure friendship and support in the Third World through the provision of economic and military assistance. Then in October 1955 the Soviet Union, via Czechoslovakia, concluded a military assistance agreement with Egypt. This step drastically changed the parameters of the arms trade. The Soviet Union did not insist on any public declarations of support and its availability as an alternative supplier provided recipient nations with a degree of leverage which they previously lacked. For the U.S.A. it meant that the criteria for the supply of arms had to be significantly relaxed. It was no longer practicable to supply arms only if it maintained or expanded the Western sphere of influence; it was enough to prevent the Soviet sphere from growing.

As a late starter in the competition for influence in the Third World the Soviet Union found its principal openings in areas where regional disputes and rivalries were predominant and where the policies of the Western powers eventually resulted in one of the parties feeling alienated. And as a late starter the Soviet Union was not inclined, at least in the initial period, to be cautious in exploiting such opportunities as did arise. The scale of deliveries to Egypt, Syria, Iraq, Indonesia and Cuba in the late 1950s and early 1960s demonstrates this point.

As arms suppliers to opposing parties in regional disputes, the broader competition between the United States and the Soviet

Union provided a built-in escalatory mechanism for levels of armament in such regions. The broad result, particularly of the U.S. military assistance program, but with the Soviet Union and other Western arms suppliers also playing a significant role, was the exposure of many countries in every major region of the Third World to modern major weapons (see Table 2). In my view this

Table 2: Selected indicators of the quality of military arsenals in the Third World in 1960.

	Jet combat aircraft	Tanks	Surface ships >1500 tons	Submarines
Far East	Burma Indonesia North Korea South Korea Philippines Taiwan* Thailand	North Korea South Korea Taiwan North Vietnam South Vietnam	Indonesia Taiwan	Indonesia
South Asia	Afghanistan India* Pakistan	Afghanistan India Pakistan	India Pakistan	
Middle East	Egypt Iran Iraq Israel* Jordan Lebanon Saudi Arabia Syria	Egypt Iran Iraq Israel Jordan Kuwait Lebanon Saudi Arabia Syria Yemen	Egypt Israel	Egypt Israel
Africa	Ethiopia Rhodesia South Africa	Ethiopia Guinea Libya Morocco Sudan Tunisia South Africa	South Africa	
Latin America	Dom. Republic Mexico Argentina Brazil Chile Colombia Ecuador Peru Uruguay Venezuela	Cuba Dom. Republic Guatemala Honduras Mexico Brazil Chile Paraguay Peru Uruguay Venezuela	Argentina Brazil Chile Colombia Peru Venezuela	Argentina Brazil Peru Venezuela

Source: SIPRI Arms Trade Registers.   * Including supersonic aircraft.

amounted to a gigantic exercise in the creation and/or strengthening of a demand for advanced major weapons which was subsequently to sustain and accelerate the trade in arms.

Other major Suppliers
A second important escalatory pressure has been the competition between the arms producing nations of the Western world. At the end of World War II only a handful of countries, essentially the U.S.A., the U.S.S.R. and the U.K., retained a capacity to develop and manufacture modern armaments. In Japan and Germany production facilities were totally destroyed and their reconstruction essentially banned. The French, Italian and, although less extensive, Dutch and Belgian industries were also substantially destroyed. Moreover, in terms of research and development capacity these countries were nearly a decade out of date, in years of exceedingly rapid technological change in weaponry.

In the immediate post-war period the re-establishment of these industries could not be entertained. The devastation of Europe was such that economic reconstruction had overwhelming priority. Regulations on the U.S. aid extended under the Marshall Plan tightly circumscribed the diversion of resources to the establishment of defence industries. Even the rearmament plans formulated in conjunction with the establishment of NATO were relatively modest so as not to conflict with economic reconstruction. Most importantly it was hoped that the various members of the alliance would develop complementary rather than competitive military, scientific and industrial capabilities.

The prospects for a gradual and considered program for the rebuilding of Europe's defence industries were shattered by the Korean War. The rearmament of Europe, including defence industries, became suddenly urgent. A variety of programs was initiated to accelerate the development of European defence industries. One was the off-shore procurement program under which the U.S.A. paid for the production of weapons and equipment in allied countries. A second was the Foreign Military Facilities Assistance program, later renamed the Weapons Production Program under which the U.S.A. contributed to the investment costs of establishing or expanding production facilities. A third was the Mutual Weapons Development Program under which the U.S.A. provided financial support for weapon development projects in allied countries. Finally the U.S.A. pursued a liberal policy in regard to the extension of licence production rights. The U.K. also played a major role in this regard, particularly for aircraft and aeroengines.

As a result of these various developments, strongly reinforced by considerations of national prestige and the desire for independence, the European capacity to develop and manufacture modern armaments re-emerged very rapidly. And, to re-iterate, no significant effort was made to coordinate this build-up so that there was a considerable degree of overlap between countries, particularly France and the United Kingdom.

Despite the general consensus on the need for expansion of European defence industries and the considerable assistance provided by the U.S.A. the European nations faced major problems. Perhaps the most important of these was the punishing rate of change in military technology imposed by the two superpowers, particularly the United States.

By 1957 expenditure on military research and development in the United States exceeded total military expenditure in both the U.K. and France. All aspects of the cost of weapons—development, manufacture, operation and maintenance—increased extremely fast. In the 1940s the development costs of tactical aircraft (for example the F–86 Sabre or F–89 Scorpion in the U.S.A. were of the order of $20–30 million in today's prices. For current fighter aircraft a development bill of $500 million is considered cheap. The F–16 low-cost light fighter is expected to cost $575 million to develop, to which must be added the $100 million spent in developing the F–16 and F–17 competitive prototypes. As regards trends in manufacturing costs Table 3 summarises the results of a study prepared by the U.S. Department of Defense. It is worth pointing out that this study factored out both inflation and the impact of declining production runs for major weapons. The costs of operating and maintaining weapons are more difficult to document in a concise manner but for most major weapons the costs

Table 3: Cost growth in selected categories of U.S. weapon systems

Type of system	Period	Average annual increase in real cost per cent
1. Main battle tanks	1940–1980	4.8
2. Attack/utility helicopters	1950–1980	4.3
3. Solid fuel ballistic missiles	1960–1974	4.8
4. Tactical aircraft: high mix	1960–1975	9.2
high/low mix	1960–1985	5.3
5. Major ships, submarines, aircraft carriers	(1945–1975)	(4.5)
6. Average all major weapon systems	(1940–1985)	(5.5)

Source: See footnote 24.

of ownership over the effective life of the weapon are considerably greater than the initial acquisition cost.

One result of these trends was that countries like the U.K. and France were forced to compromise continuously in their ambitions to have indigenous capacity to develop and manufacture the full range of modern weapons and equipment. A second result was that a high premium came to be placed on arms exports to help minimise the extent to which the indigenous effort had to be restricted.

In an absolute sense—for example, in relation to total employment or total export earnings—the production of arms for export is not of major economic significance to the principal arms producing nations. However, from the viewpoint of the defence industry in isolation, production for export generates diverse benefits. First development and other fixed costs associated with a particular weapon can be spread over a larger number of units. Second, in the manufacture and assembly of a complex piece of equipment, there is considerable scope for improving efficiency through a process known as 'learning by doing'. For example, the Swedish shipyard Karlskrona Varvet, which recently completed the production of 12 Spica II-class patrol boats, reported a 30 percent reduction in manhours for each of the first five units.[25] This process is subject to diminishing returns but if domestic orders fall in the declining portion of the cost curve and if export orders can be secured prior to the start of series production the unit cost to all customers can be reduced.

Very little information is available on the actual extent of the 'savings' produced through export sales. One exception is a study made by the U.S. Congressional Budget Office. On the basic assumption that the U.S.A. would not significantly alter the defence production base in the absence of production for export this study concluded that an $8 billion foreign sales program, composed of the current mix of weapons, services and construction would reduce U.S. defence costs by $560 million annually.[26]

In addition to these quantifiable factors there are other benefits from arms exports that are probably at least as important if not more so. In particular, production for export can help to prevent severe fluctuations in employment and work-loads in the defence industry resulting from the periodic nature of major orders from the national forces. The scientific and industrial teams working in this field are typically regarded as national assets that cannot be allowed to disintegrate without risk to the nation's ability to keep abreast of foreign developments in technology. The supply of armaments also yields some political influence over the recipient, which most exporting governments find attractive, and a trade relationship in armaments can be exploited to promote a wider range of business.

The emerging arms suppliers in Western Europe, seeking exports to alleviate the heavy cost of the technological arms race, found the European markets almost totally monopolised by the United States, initially as a result of the grant military assistance program and subsequently (after 1961)[27] of an aggressive sales campaign in which the U.S.A. used an irresistible combination of technological superiority, cost advantages and political leverage to capture the more important orders for major weapons. These countries therefore turned increasingly to the Third World for export markets.

Thus the tendency for the competition between the U.S.A. and the Soviet Union to escalate the trade in arms both quantitatively and qualitatively was exacerbated by competition from France, the U.K., Italy and a number of lesser arms producing nations where the primary motive was economic. The propensity for the arms trade to escalate as a result of this dual competitive pressure can perhaps best be illustrated by way of examples.

It was argued above that the U.S.-Soviet competition in the 1950s led to the exposure of many countries in every region to modern major weapons. Even the training programs conducted by these two countries created a latent demand for such weapons. The second-order arms suppliers were able to meet the derived demand for armaments from countries that were not major recipients of grant or concessionary supplies from either of the superpowers. They were also able to meet demands for weapons more modern and more capable than the two superpowers were prepared to make available to their less favoured clients. Thus, over time, as the capabilities of European-designed weapons improved, this stimulus became mutual. In several instances it was the European arms suppliers and not the U.S.A. or the U.S.S.R. that first introduced a major new military capability into a country and this usually precipitated a regional escalation in the capability of the weapons imported.[28]

As modern weapons proliferated the desire to establish and preserve regional military balances became an increasingly prominent consideration governing the supply of arms, particularly, it seems, in the United States. In practice this has usually resulted in escalating levels of armament. One analyst has put the matter as follows using Egypt and Israel as an example.

> To illustrate this, let's assume that Israeli intelligence sources report a delivery of 100 Soviet T–54 tanks to Egypt (give or take an error of 10 percent), and that an average of 15

percent of both Israeli and Egyptian tanks are normally out of service at any given time for repairs. Now, under worst-case planning, the Israeli defence staff will assume that the intelligence report is on the low side, that 100 percent of the Egyptian tanks will be operational on the eve of battle, and that Israel will be minus its usual 15 percent. The net result is that Israel needs 130 tanks to 'balance' the Egyptian T–54s. But since a shipment to Israel of this size would show up on Egyptian intelligence reports as falling in the 120 to 140 tank range, Egyptian planners, using the same principle, would now need 65 additional tanks to compensate for the perceived Israeli advantage.[29]

The probability that the objective of preserving a military balance will result in higher and higher levels of armament is significantly increased if three or more external suppliers are involved. If, for example, the U.S.A. and the Soviet Union are the predominant suppliers an isolated sale of major weapons by a third party can generate a wave of adjusting supplies from the two superpowers. Moreover the number of countries able to supply weapons capable of disturbing the military status quo in several areas of the world is tending to increase, Israel being the latest addition.

A multiplicity of suppliers also adds to the difficulty of stabilising the inflow of weapons to a given region because each nation's weaponry has its unique advantages and disadvantages. All the states of a region may have, say, current generation fighters, surface-to-air missiles, anti-ship missiles and tanks. But if these are a mixture of U.S., Soviet, British, French, German and Italian weapons then pressures will inevitably arise for additional acquisitions to counter the advantages of the weapons possessed by other countries and to offset the disadvantages of one's own weapons.

At various times over the post-war period one or the other of the major arms suppliers has imposed selective unilateral constraints on exports. In virtually every case this restraint was abandoned as a result of the policies pursued by the other suppliers. One instance occurred as early as 1948. Early in that year the U.K. negotiated a major arms contract with Venezuela which included 80 Meteor jet fighters. At that time the U.S.A. prohibited the sale of front-line fighters to Latin American countries which naturally led U.S. aircraft manufacturers to complain that they could not compete on equal terms with the British. In November 1948 the U.S. Department of State announced that the F–80 and F–84 fighters could be exported to Latin America. Both these aircraft were in front-line service with the U.S. Air Force at the time.

A decade and a half later the roles were reversed. U.S. acknowledgement, in 1964, that it had authorised the sale of Hawk surface-to-air missiles to Israel prompted the U.K. to announce that it would review its existing policy of not supplying sophisticated weapons to states in the Middle East.

As a final example we can cite the Congressional ban imposed in 1968 on the sale of 'sophisticated' (the term was never defined) U.S. weapons to Latin America. This unilateral restraint proved to be a bonanza for arms-producing countries in Europe with France, the U.K. the Federal Republic of Germany and Italy all securing major contracts.

It is largely a history of experiences such as these that has made the argument that 'if we don't sell the arms somebody else will' so persuasive. By refusing a request to sell arms the supplier incurs the disfavour of the potential recipient, loses whatever political leverage the transaction might have made possible and, of course, loses business. It is argued that since the demand will be met anyway there are no positive considerations to offset the various negative effects of unilateral restraint.

Throughout this section we have stressed the factors on the supply side of the arms trade equation that have promoted escalation in the trade with the Third World. It goes virtually without saying that these pressures would have come to nothing if there were no demand for armaments. There is very little evidence that Third World nations have been coerced into acquiring armaments although some countries have presumably expanded their arsenals reluctantly in response to a build-up in a neighbouring state. This is not to suggest that the arms suppliers, governments and manufacturers alike, have been passive agents. On the contrary their collective actions have significantly accelerated the development of the market for armaments in non-producing nations and they have long actively promoted their products to maintain and increase their share of this market.

In one fundamental sense the major powers are responsible for the world-wide demand for armaments. Since World War II they have maintained a highly visible and unshakeable dedication to the notion that military strength is the best means of preserving national security and promoting national interest. It can be argued that the emerging nations in the Third World were given no alternative, although some have undoubtedly shown excessive zeal in emulating the example set by the major powers. In addition, whether the demand for armaments stems from realistic calculations of the requirements of self-defence or whether considerations of prestige and respectability are predominant, the standards set since World War II have been very high indeed.

Section III: Trends and Implications for the Future

The arms trade with the Third World has clearly come a long way in the last thirty years. We have documented the trends in the scale and content of the trade and the gradual relaxation of inhibitions regarding the transfer of highly capable and/or highly sophisticated weapons systems and equipments. In parallel with these developments there has been a gradual **under**mining of the perception that the export or import of armaments has any special significance in the general relationship between states. The quality and strength of the arguments considered adequate to justify the export of weaponry have been much reduced.

The major exporting countries have increasingly based their policies on straight-forward economic considerations and on the role that exports play in sustaining the national defence industry.[30] Foreign policy considerations and the desire to sustain a general presence on the international stage certainly still play an important role but the traditional argument that the supply of arms provides a useful degree of influence over the policies pursued by the recipients is recognised as having little validity. Experience has shown that this influence is least when it is most needed, that is, in a crisis. A survey of attempts by the U.S.A. and other countries to use arms embargoes as a policy tool came to the following conclusion:

> In sum, it is probably true that the provision of military aid is usually a positive factor in the relations of two countries, and that it furnishes some incentive to the recipient to avoid provoking the supplier. However, an explicitly hinted, definitely threatened, or actually implemented suspension of military aid as a means of forcing the recipient to follow a certain course of action is at best a risky policy. While it can succeed under certain specific (and relatively unusual) conditions, it all too often can fail completely; in either case, furthermore, the high pressure tactic can have serious detrimental effects on the long-term relations between the supplying nation and the recipient.[31]

This study was prepared in 1969. Developments since then, such as more suppliers and a conspicuous tendency among recipients to diversify their sources of armaments, would reinforce its conclusions.

To put the matter in a slightly different perspective there has been a gradual change in perceptions of who is doing whom a favour in arms transactions. In the hey-day of grant and concessionary military aid the supplier assessed requirements and determined the types and quantities of the weapons transferred. In the 1950s even U.S. military sales were termed 'reimbursable aid'. Today there is a far greater willingness to accept recipient assessments of their requirements. Now that most arms are traded on commercial terms the argument, long advanced by recipients, that they are sovereign states and free to dispose of their resources as they see fit carries a lot more weight. At the same time the commercialisation of the arms trade has made it easier for the suppliers to absolve themselves of any responsibility for the impact, whether economic, political or military, that the arms supplied may have. Most analysts supported the transition from grants to sales on the grounds that it would force recipients to face the full budgetary implications of arms imports. In retrospect it seems clear that by the time sales became the predominant mode of arms transfer the militarisation of the Third World was too far advanced for this to serve as a significant deterrent.

In the light of these observations the most confident prediction that can be made on the future of the arms trade is that it will remain large and dynamic and that the pattern of the trade will become increasingly complex and obscure. The extraordinary escalation in the volume of the trade since the oil-crisis in 1973/74 will certainly taper off although the oil-rich states will continue to be the major source of demand for armaments in the Third World. One can also be confident that the developments spear-headed by the OPEC States, particularly those on the Persian Gulf, will filter through to other regions. The 'demonstration effect' is exceedingly powerful in the field of armaments and suppliers will either not be inclined or will find it extremely difficult to apply less liberal policies to non-OPEC States.

With regard to the content of the trade in the coming years the pressure to transfer weapons that have become obsolescent in the major powers will persist. In some cases, notably the F–4 Phantom fighter-bomber, the transfer of these weapons could have particularly serious implications for the balance of military forces in some regions and for the potential scale of conflict.

Apart from this two areas of rapid growth can be predicted with some confidence. The first is naval forces in general. At least two reasons for this can be identified. The first, and probably less important, is that some long-standing regional conflicts, for example in the Middle East and South Asia, have increasingly taken on a naval dimension. The second is the growing appreciation of the importance of the oceans as a continuing source of food and as a major future source of raw materials. A closely related issue is, of course, the 200–mile maritime economic zone. The impact of these developments is already apparent. One calculation suggests that the estimated capital value of the stock of fighting ships in Third World navies increased by more than one-half between 1970 and 1976.[32] On-going construction and new orders for naval units by Third World countries are substantial.

The second area of rapid growth is likely to be in the area of precision guided munitions (PGMs). The weapons described by this general heading are the product of advances in the miniaturisation of electronic components, warhead design and, above all, guidance technology. Generally speaking they are highly effective, easy to use, relatively inexpensive and require little maintenance. Each attribute makes these weapons particularly attractive to developing countries and they are already proliferating rapidly.

The Arms Trade and Conflict
The high incidence of warfare in the Third World inevitably raises the issue of whether or not this is causally linked with the arms trade. The evidence is inconclusive and will probably remain so. But two propositions can be advanced to support the thesis that the arms trade, as it has evolved since World War II, has at least not diminished the propensity for conflict. The first is that the large, complex weapon systems that dominate the military scene have led to the emergence of professional military establishments. In most Third World countries the military has considerable political influence and a significant number of countries are ruled by the military. At the very least this must mean that the military input in political decision-making is large.

The second proposition is perhaps easier to appreciate. The clearest indictment that can be brought against the arms trade, in so far as it may be causally related with the high incidence of warfare in the Third World, is the unmistakable atmosphere of military escalation that it generates. New countries are constantly joining the list of recipients of major weapons and existing recipients are constantly filling out and up-grading their arsenals. Weapons can be produced and delivered far more quickly than they can be designed and developed, particularly so when several suppliers are involved. For these reasons the military scene in virtually the whole of the Third World is one of rapid change, certainly more rapid at the visible level than in Europe or in the U.S.A. and the U.S.S.R.

Whether this change is more appearance than substance—and increasingly it is substance—is really beside the point. An atmosphere of rapid military change is destabilising and increases the probability of conflict.

Whatever its impact on the probability of conflict, the arms trade has immeasurably raised the potential scale of conflict. The larger and more intense a conflict the greater the likelihood of major power involvement and the longer its legacy will impede relations among the states involved.

Economic Implications of the Arms Trade
This is a relatively neglected but undoubtedly important aspect of the arms trade. Governments in developing countries bear a large responsibility for bringing about economic and social development. In other words the resources that the government commands must be regarded as particularly scarce and the opportunity cost of resources devoted to military uses as particularly high. Furthermore, establishing and maintaining modern armed forces places heavy demands on precisely those resources which are typically in short supply in developing countries—foreign exchange and skilled manpower of all varieties.[33]

The seemingly intractable problem of underdevelopment and the widening gaps in material well-being between rich and poor states are perhaps the most serious long-term problems the world community faces. Yet there is no evidence of any systematic attempt to study the inter-relationship between the trade in arms and the closely-related production of modern armaments in developing countries and such issues as the volume of development assistance, debt-servicing problems and improving the terms of trade for developing countries. The arms trade is obviously not a central factor in these issues but it has almost certainly ceased to be a negligible one.

A final comment on this general theme concerns the transfer of technology. One analyst claims that ' . . . roughly half the technology imported by Third World countries is military related.'[34] Even if this is exaggerated it can be accepted that armaments are an increasingly important mechanism for the transfer of technology. This being the case several comments can be made. Military technology is typically the most advanced and complex technology available in the developed countries. For developing countries to attempt to master this technology, even partially, must be extremely costly. The prospects for 'spin-offs' beneficial to the economy at large, distinctly limited even in the countries developing these technologies, are probably negligible. There are wider implications too. Modern armaments are the products of the world's highly industrialised nations whose social and economic structures are by no means necessarily appropriate as models for developing countries. Yet the import of modern armaments forces recipient countries to duplicate these structures. The rigidities are inherent in the concept of the 'weapons system'. To operate a weapons system requires a rigid organisation of personnel and their specialisation in particular tasks. To support, and even more, to manufacture a weapons system dictates a specific range of technical and industrial capacities.

What can be done?

The long neglect and the associated rapid evolution of the international arms transfers phenomenon has vastly complicated the issue of arms control among developing (non-arms producing) nations. For several reasons arms control among developing nations should be more simple and entail less risk than among the major powers: the smaller size of military arsenals, the lower level of military technology, the absence of weapons of mass destruction, the absence of a local defence industry to widen and strengthen internal pressures for a large and dynamic military establishment and the absence of an indigenous military research and development capacity to bedevil verification procedures are all factors which should simplify the control of arms races amongst Third World countries.

It is apparent that all of these simplifying factors have been significantly eroded over the past 10 or 15 years and continue to be eroded at a fast pace. Moreover, the increasing size and lethality of military arsenals has almost certainly exacerbated the mutual suspicion of all states and thus made them more reluctant to negotiate arms control agreements.

The regions and sub-regions covered by the term 'Indian-Pacific Ocean region' are heterogenous in the extreme with wide divergencies in the intensity and character of local conflicts, disputes and rivalries, the degree of interest and involvement by external powers and in the size and composition of military arsenals. There is little point, therefore, in attempting to devise measures of controlling the inflow of armaments that would have universal applicability.

Perhaps the first question to be asked is whether the initiative for controls of the arms trade should come from suppliers or recipients. Most developing countries have consistently opposed suggestions to control the arms trade on the grounds that they discriminate in favour of arms-producing nations and constitute undue interference with the sovereign right of self defence. Even the relatively innocuous suggestion for an international register of arms transfers without any controls—proposed at the United Nations by Malta in 1965 and by Denmark in 1968—was strongly opposed and not brought to a vote. The attempts at unilateral restraint by one or other of the major powers were all, sooner or later, undermined owing to the absence of common political interests among the larger producers. In any event multi-lateral restraint on arms transfers would almost certainly focus on transfers to developing countries. It is highly unlikely that restraints on intra-NATO and intra-Warsaw Pact transfers would be entertained. This, of course, would make such proposals even more unpalatable to developing countries. Furthermore, such restraints may in the longer run be counterproductive if they led more countries to establish national defence industries and accelerate their development. Mention must be made here of the new guidelines that will govern U.S. arms transfers after 1977, announced by President Carter on 19 May 1977. The new policy is directed at all countries except those with which the U.S.A. has major defence treaties. In other words NATO countries, Japan, Australia and New Zealand will be exempted. Israel will also be treated as a special case. The status of South Korea and Taiwan, both obvious candidates for special treatment, was not made clear. Outstanding obligations under the FMS program and commercial agreements through FY 1977—obligations approaching $40 billion—will not be affected.

The new policy reiterates some aspects of the old but the new or qualitatively different aspects of the Carter policy are as follows. First, the annual value of arms sales under the FMS program will be lower than that recorded for FY 1977. Second, co-production agreements for significant weapons, equipment and components will in future be banned. Given the trend of developments in the arms trade documented earlier this initiative could have important implications and will certainly be heavily criticised by potential recipients. In particular, South Korea and Taiwan, insofar as they are not accorded special status, will have to restructure signficantly or redirect their on-going efforts to develop local defence industries on the basis of U.S. technology.

Third, there will be a ban on the development or significant modification of advanced weapons solely for export. This requirement will presumably prevent, for example, Northrop from developing a land-based version of the U.S. Navy's F–18 Hornet multi-purpose fighter unless U.S. forces opt to acquire it.

It is clear that the impact of the new policy will depend very much on how key terms are interpreted. The White House statement detailing the new policy referred to the sale of weapons with a 'new or significantly higher combat capability', the co-production of 'signifcant' weapons and the 'significant modification of advanced weapons'. The general context in which proposed arms sales would be reviewed suggests that these terms may be interpreted rather rigorously. Specifically, President Carter indicated that arms transfers would henceforth be regarded as an exceptional foreign policy instrument and that '. . . the burden of persuasion will be on those who favour a particular arms sale rather than those who oppose it.'.[35]

As the world's leading arms supplier the impact of these unilateral U.S. initiatives should not be minimised. On the other hand the prospects of enlisting the co-operation of the other major supplier and the likelihood of a significant diminution in the arms trade even if this co-operation is secured are not particularly high.

An article in *Pravda* on 2 June 1977 focussed on the exceptions to the new policy and the potential loopholes referred to above. The article implied that the U.S.S.R. would adopt a wait-and-see attitude. The initial French reaction was also cool with an official pointing out that France considered it a matter of policy that every country should have the right to acquire the arms needed for self-defence.

It can be anticipated that the other suppliers will be sorely tempted to make themselves available to pick up any additional business that the U.S. initiative may yield. A study prepared by the National Security Council points out that if other countries step into fill the gaps created by U.S. refusals ' . . . it will be difficult to sustain unilateral U.S. restraint over the longer term'.[36] Even if a multi-lateral approach is achieved, each supplier, following the U.S. lead, may make exceptions for selected recipients in the Third World and so the prospects for a follow-the-leader escalatory cycle will remain high in most regions. And finally, of course, the developing countries will be less than enthusiastic about restrictive arms sales policies that do not apply to the non-arms producing developed countries.

In short one is led to the conclusion that the initiative in restraining the proliferation of weapons is best taken by regional or sub-regional groupings of recipient states. The almost predictable negative political and economic ramifications of even a co-ordinated restriction on the supply of armaments imposed without the approval of the non-producing nations make such a development unlikely. However, a commitment by the non-producing nations, or any sub-group of these nations, to restrict demand carries no similar penalties. Recipient states, after all, now bear the full cost of arms imports and stand to reap the benefits of controlling and moderating the rate of inflow of arms. Furthermore, for most nations, the predominant consideration shaping force requirements is the military capability of neighbouring states.[37]

This having been said it must be acknowledged that in most regions formidable political and psychological problems will have to be surmounted before meaningful restraint arrangements can be attained. It is not surprising, therefore, that few proposals have emerged from regional groupings of recipient states. To date, all such proposals have come from Latin America beginning with a suggestion by Costa Rica in 1958 that the members of the Organisation of American States agree to limits on their armed forces. The latest proposal, included in the Ayacucho Declaration in December 1974, involved eight states who expressed their intent to 'make possible the effective limitation of armaments and their acquisition for offensive purposes, so that all possible resources might be devoted to the economic and social development of every country in Latin America'. The fast pace of arms acquisition in this region before and since 1974 indicates that these political initiatives need to be followed up very rapidly with concrete measures for their implementation.

There are several ways in which the developed countries and institutions such as the United Nations could foster the adoption and implementation of regional measures to control the inflow of arms. First, of course, any such arrangement would benefit from the discreet support of the major arms suppliers to minimise the incentive and the opportunity for any participating state to violate the spirit of the accord.

Second, very little is known about the implications of militarisation and participation in the technological arms race for the economic and social development of Third World countries as distinct from crude economic growth. The results of systematic research in this area may provide an important incentive for adopting measures of control.

Third, there has been comparatively little research on the arms control aspects of conventional forces. It is reasonable to assume that more and more countries are becoming aware, through experience, of the essential predictability of the armament process. However the arms control aspects of conventional forces are more complex than those of the nuclear forces. There are several reasons for this: the far greater diversity of conventional weapons, the fact that virtually every country in the world supports conventional forces and, perhaps most important, the strong possibility that possessing adequate conventional forces will at some time be of the highest importance to the nation. It follows that a deeper understanding of the factors determining the proliferation process in various regions and the development of more sophisticated and realistic techniques for comparing conventional forces and assessing the 'balance' of forces would be of great value to future attempts at regional arms control. It would, for example, reduce the fear that, due to a miscalculation, an arms control agreement might lead to a military disadvantage that would endanger a nation's security.

Two remarks can be made in conclusion. The trade in conventional armaments has become a phenomenon of major international importance. It has ceased to be merely a reflection or a by-product of the main East-West arms race. As such it warrants serious attention as a separate problem. At the same time the non-arms producing nations of the world cannot be expected to restrain rigorously and confine their military capabilities unless the major powers take determined steps to move in the same direction.

FOOTNOTES

1. Some of the research for this study was done while the writer was still with the Stockholm International Peace Research Institute. It is used here with permission.
2. For in excellent discussion with a historical perspective see Harkavy, R.E., *The Arms Trade and International Systems*, Ballinger, New York, 1975.
3. United States Arms Control and Disarmament Agency, *World Military Expenditure and Arms Trade 1963–73*. (This was the first in ACDA's annual series to include arms trade data), Washington, 1973.
4. Kende, I., *Local Wars in Asia, Africa and Latin America, 1945–1969*, Studies on Developing Countries No.60, Centre for Afro-Asian Research of the Hungarian Academy of Sciences, Budapest 1972.
5. For the purposes of this study the Third World is defined as the world excluding NATO, Warsaw Pact and other European countries, Japan, Australia and New Zealand.
6. There are various reasons for this choice. Unlike ACDA, SIPRI publishes its arms trade register annually. In addition SIPRI's valuation methodology has been spelled out and the price list is available on request.
7. SIPRI, *World Armaments and Disarmament*, Yearbook 1976, Stockholm 1976, pp.65–66.
8. Over the same period FMS orders from other members of the Organisation of Petroleum Exporting Countries (OPEC) amounted to $254.5 million. Commercial transactions with OPEC totalled $436.5 million.
9. According to SIPRI the design range of the Jericho has been increased from 500 kilometres to 1,000 kilometres.

10. These include: aircraft, MD450 Ouragon, Mystère IVA, Super Mystère Alizé, Mirage III and F-I: missiles SS-10, AS.30, Crotale and Exocet.

11. The full development program is reported to be in jeopardy due to excessive cost increases. It is noteworthy, however, that the Iranian tanks will be the first to be fitted with the new Chobham armour which its developers claim provides greatly enhanced protection against all existing anti-tank weapons.

12. The development of the Crotale missile was funded predominantly by South Africa.

13. One possible exception is the 1650 Maverick missiles for some 90 F–5E/F aircraft, or more than 15 per aircraft.

14. Subcommittee on Foreign Assistance of the Committee on Foreign Relations, United States Senate, *Foreign Assistance Authorisation–Arms Sales Issues*, Washington 1975, pp. 41–42.

15. Jordan had on order F–5As from Iran, F–5Es from the U.S.A. and was negotiating with the U.S.A. for the Hawk surface-to-air missile system and Vulcan anti-aircraft guns.

16. SIPRI, *Southern Africa: the escalation of a conflict*, Stockholm 1976, p.154.

17. Experience suggests that even under optimum conditions licence production is 20–30 per cent more expensive than direct import. F–15 Eagles, if licence-produced in Japan, are expected to cost between 39–76 per cent more than imported aircraft. *International Defence Review*, 1/1977, p.158.

18. The figures are taken from an unpublished paper by Michael Kidron presented at a Pugwash symposium on the problems of military-oriented technologies in developing countries, Feldafing, F.R. Germany, November 1976.

19. Another program, the Military Industrial Complex at Isfahan, is of interest in that the foreign contractors are drawn from NATO (the U.K.), the Warsaw Pact (Czechoslovakia) and a neutral country (Sweden).

20. The assembly and partial manufacture of approximately 100 F–5Es in Taiwan is worth an estimated $235 million to Northrop whereas the sale of the same number of aircraft would yield $225 million. See Clare, Michael T. 'America Exports its Know-how', *The Nation*, 12 February 1977.

21. Pengelley, R.B. 'The Singapore Military/Industrial Scene', *International Defence Review*, 4/1976, pp. 657–660.

22. 'Israeli Arms Exports Spur Concern', *Aviation Week and Space Technology*, 13 December 1976, p.14.

23. Early in 1977 the U.S.A. blocked the sale of 24 Kfirs to Ecuador. At about the same time there was a short-lived controversy over the sale to Honduras of surplus Israeli Super Mystère fighters (acquired from France in 1959) because the aircraft had been refitted with U.S. engines and Israel had neglected to secure prior U.S. approval for the sale.

24. Committee on Armed Services, House of Representatives, *Hearings on Military Posture and H.R. 3689 [H.R. 6674] Department of Defense Authorization for Appropriations for Fiscal Year 1976*, Washington 1976, Part I, pp.1826–1829.

25. *International Defence Review*, 1/1977, p.158.

26. *Budgetary Cost Savings to the Department of Defense Resulting from Foreign Military Sales*, Congressional Budget Office, Washington, 24 May 1976. Savings in connection with the export of some specific weapons have been documented. The U.S. Navy expects foreign sales of the Harpoon anti-ship missile to reduce the program costs of this weapon by $60–70 million, and the Iranian purchase of 80 F–14A Tomcat fighters is expected to save the U.S.A. $302.8 million. *Aviation Week and Space Technology*, 5 July 1976, p.28. Committee on Armed Services, House of Representatives, *Hearings on Military Posture and H.R. 11500 for Fiscal Year 1977*, Washington, 1976, Part 2, p.102.

27. In that year the International Logistics Negotiation Office (ILN) was established in the Department of Defense with the express objective of minimising the balance of payments deficit attributable to U.S. military activities.

28. This is a convenient point to comment on British arms exports in the immediate post-war period. In many ways the U.K. was first off the mark as an arms supplier. With war-inflated defence industries, a full-range of technologically-advanced weapons either in production or under development and a desperate economic situation, the U.K. had both motive and opportunity to seek export markets for armaments. Thus, over the decade 1945–55, British export sales of armaments totalled £600 million (over $2.0 billion at current prices), excluding the sales of naval vessels. *Export of Surplus War Materials*, Cond. 9676, HMSO, London, January 1956. Two features of this export program are worth emphasising. First, the U.K. was exporting its latest weaponry, particularly aircraft. Second, markets were found all over the globe, in Europe, the Middle East, South Asia, Latin America and Africa. The catalytic role of these early British exports probably cannot be over-emphasised. It can be noted, for example, that of the 60 Third World countries that have acquired jet combat aircraft over the post-war period 23 first acquired them from the U.K.

29. Clare, M. 'The Political Economy of Arms Sales', *Bulletin of Atomic Scientists*, November 1976, p.18.

30. Even in the U.S.A. with its very large domestic demand for armaments, such arguments are being more strongly advanced to support the Foreign Military Sales program. To quote former Secretary of Defence, Rumsfeld, 'Production for export assists the U.S. by helping to maintain a warm mobilization base, by avoiding idle or underutilized industrial capacity, and by providing reserve capacity for emergency use. Export demand also results in more readily available skilled and experienced labor. Export demand may yield lower unit cost, and in some cases makes the production of equipment economical when it

would not be justified by U.S. requirements alone'. Secretary of Defense Donald H. Rumsfeld, *Annual Defense Department Report FY1977*, Washington 1976, p.245.

31. Subcommittee on United States Security Agreements and Commitments Abroad of the Committee on Foreign Relations, United States Senate, *United States Security Agreements and Commitments Abroad,* Washington, 1971, Vol.II, Parts 5–11, p.1837.

32. *World Stock of Fighting Ships,* Ocean Yearbook Volume 1, October 1977 (forthcoming).

33. The following figures for Iran, though scarcely typical, are indicative of the manpower requirements:
   (a) 80 F–14A Tomcat air superiority aircraft—by 1981 an estimated 6,500 personnel will be required to support the aircraft of which 2,650 must be technically trained.
   (b) 221 F–4D, F–4E and RF–4E fighter-bomber/reconnaissance aircraft—personnel requirements will level off at about 25,000 in 1978 of which 7,000 will be aircrew and maintenance personnel.
   (c) 169 F–5E/F light fighters—about 6,000 personnel required.
   U.S. Military Sales to Iran, a Staff Report to the Subcommittee on Foreign Assistance of the Committee on Foreign Relations, United States Senate, Washington, July 1976.

34. Kaldor, M., *The Military in Development—World Development,* 1976, Vol.4, No.6, p.459.

35. 'Carter Moves to Cutback Sales of U.S. Arms Abroad', *International Herald Tribune,* 21–22 May 1977, p.1.

36. 'Cut in U.S. Arms Sales Seen Unlikely to Hit World Traffic', *International Herald Tribune,* 13 July 1977, p.3.

37. When extra-regional considerations are important the situation is made much more complicated. In South Asia, for example, India clearly looks beyond Pakistan to China as a potential threat and perhaps to Iran as a challenger to India's prevailing status as the major naval power on the Indian Ocean littoral. However, Pakistan would be inclined to discount these determinants of India's force posture and increase its military effort accordingly, should India increase her own forces to counter such threats.

Appendix 1. Current Military Development and Production Programs in Developing Countries in the Indian-Pacific Ocean Region.

Item	Licence or Indigenous	Licensee	Description/Comment
SOUTH AFRICA			
Aircraft			
MirageF–1	licence	France	Supersonic combat aircraft, assembly and partial manufacture of components, engine imported.
MB–326K/M	licence	Italy	Trainer/lightstrike, predominantly locally produced, engine imported, 50 'K' ordered.
C4M Kudu	indigenous	—	Light observation/transport, probably derived from Italian AM–3C (licence-produced in S.Africa as 'Bosbok') which in turn is derived from the Lockheed AL–60.
Missiles			
Whiplash	indigenous	—	Air-to-air infrared homing, reportedly in production since 1972. A surface-to-air missile is also claimed to be under development and some reports suggest that the Crotale surface-to-air system was manufactured under licence.
Ships			
Reshef	licence	Israel	Missile-armed patrol boats, first warships to be constructed in South Africa. This program will probably be followed by frigate construction. Extensive facilities exist at Simonstown for the overhaul and modernisation of naval ships including an enclosed yard for submarines.
Frigate	licence	France/ F.R. Germany	Total of 6 to be built armed with Israeli Gabriel missile
Armoured vehicles			
Eland	licence	France	Armoured car (Panhard AML–60/90), well-established program, virtually 100 per cent indigenous, current production model incorporates local refinements.

SOUTH AFRICA
Other

South Africa is virtually self-sufficient in small arms and ammunition. Series production of a locally-designed tank is reported imminent.

PAKISTAN
Aircraft

Alouette III	licence	France	Utility helicopter being assembled from imported components.
Hughes 500	licence	U.S.A.	Light helicopter, agreement concluded late in 1975.
Cessna –1	(licence)	(U.S.A.)	Light observation aircraft, built from local components, imports, accumulated spares; no formal licence.
Cessna T–41D	licence	U.S.A.	Primary trainer, licence acquired late 1975.

Missiles

BO–108 Cobra	(licence)	F.R. Germany	Anti-tank, production sustained locally since embargo in 1965; no formal licence.

Ships

—	—	—	Limited naval construction is undertaken in local yards including for export.

Other

—	—	—	Target is self-sufficiency in small arms, some Chinese technical and industrial assistance. Reports of agreement with China for licence production of surface-to-air missiles.

INDIA
Aircraft

HF–24 Marut	indigenous	—	Light fighter, production of about 125 will end 1977; strike fighter in design stage; jet trainer, in production since 1968; a COIN version is in the flight test stage.
HAC–33	indigenous	—	Civil/military light transport, under development.
—	indigenous	—	Primary trainer, scheduled for series production mid-1978.

INDIA

—	indigenous	—	Light armed helicopter; prototype flight planned for 1981.
MiG–21M	licence	U.S.S.R.	In production since 1972, approx 90% indigenous components; an advanced version of the MiG–21M went into production late 1976. prior assembly of about 100 MiG–21FL.
Gnat	licence	U.K.	Light fighter, production completed in 1974. Local development (Aject) now entering production.
SA.315 Cheetah	licence	France	Light helicopter, increasing indigenous production of components.
Alouette III	licence	France	Utility helicopter, in production since 1965; an armed version (Chetale) is under development.
HS–748	licence	U.K.	Medium transport, production will end in 1978.

Missiles

—	indigenous	—	Ship-to-ship, tested in 1975.
SA–6 Gainful	licence	U.S.S.R.	Licence production is planned.
K–13A Atoll	licence	U.S.S.R.	air-to-air missile for MiG–21.
SS–11	licence	France	Anti-tank, complete production rights acquired in 1974.

Ships

Patrol Boat	indigenous	—	First launched late 1976.
Corvette	indigenous	—	In early design stage.
Frigates	licence	U.K.	'Leander'-class; 6 on order, 3 completed. India has also negotiated with France for A.69 frigates.
Submarines	—	—	Negotiations have been held with Sweden for the A–14 type.

Armoured Vehicles

Tank	indigenous	—	Production scheduled for 1980
APC	indigenous	—	Prototype trials in 1973, production probably underway.
Tank	licence	U.K.	Vickers design, in production since 1967, nearly 100 per cent indigenous. Called Vijayanta.

INDIA

APC	licence	Czechoslovakia	OT–62/64.
Other			
—	—	—	India is nearly self-sufficient in small arms. Wide-ranging R&D effort in aero-engines, electronics, rockets.

THAILAND

Ships

—	—	—	Initial agreement with U.S.A. on construction of $275 million naval shipyard near Bangkok reached late 1976. Construction of missile patrol boats planned.
Other			
—	—	—	Small-scale production of West German rifles is underway.

MALAYSIA

Ships

—	(licence)	—	Local contractor (Hong Leong) in affiliation with F.R. Germany firm (Lürssen) may have won contract for 150-foot fast patrol boats. First launched late 1975, 4 more under construction for delivery 1976–77.
Other			
Sharikat Explosives —		—	Ammunition plant. In addition to Malaysian government shareholders are Oerlikon, Dynamit Noblag and 3M.
Aircraft			
—	—	—	32 A–B/C Skyhawk attack aircraft re-built to advanced A–45 configuration A–4B to TA–4 trainer conversion underway.

SINGAPORE

Ships

—	licence	F.R. Germany	Type 148 missile patrol boat; 4 built for local navy, 3 now being delivered to Thailand.

SINGAPORE
Other

—	—	—	M–16 rifle (U.S.A.) produced under licence; 60 mm, 81 mm, 120 mm mortars (Tampella, Finland) produced under licence. New facility established 1974 for repair and production of military optics including tank periscopes for export.

INDONESIA
Aircraft

CASA.212	licence	Spain	STOL light transport, assembly to be followed by licence production, 25 ordered.
BO–105	licence	F.R. Germany	Utility helicopter; assembly, possible licence production.
LT–200	licence	U.S.A.	Primary trainer local derivative of Pazmany PL–2, now entering production.

Ships

Patrol boats	indigenous	—	'Mawar'-class, 147-ton.
Missile boats	licence	(South Korea)	South Korea is producing modified 'Ashville'-class (U.S.A.) under licence; 4 ordered by Indonesia, may be followed by Indonesian production under licence.

Other

—	—	—	Well-established ordnance factories producing machine-guns, rifles, pistols with and without formal licences.

PHILIPPINES
Aircraft

BO–105	licence	F.R. Germany	Utility helicopter; assembly began 1974.
BM–2 Islander	licence	U.K.	Light transport; assembly and subsequent local production of components.
Super Pinto	licence	U.S.A.	Jet trainer/COIN; licence production planned.

Ships

—	—	—	Local construction of 50–foot patrol boats planned.

PHILIPPINES
Other

—	—	—	Substantially self-sufficient in small arms. M16 rifle (U.S.A.) produced under licence.

Aircraft

T–CH–1A/B	—	—	Primary trainer/COIN, in production since 1975.
XC–2	indigenous	—	STOL light transport, prototype under construction.
F–5E	licence	U.S.A.	Light fighter, assembly has been followed by progressive local manufacture of components, 180 ordered.
UH–1H	licence	U.S.A.	Utility helicopter. In production since 1973, 118 ordered.

Missiles

Coral	—	—	A 960-kilometre range surface-to-surface missile is reported to be under development.

Other

—	—	—	Production of small arms is underway, also R&D in electronics

KOREA NORTH
Aircraft

—	—	—	Aircraft industry established in 1975, licence production of MiG–21 planned for 1978.

Ships

Frigates	(indigenous)	—	Apparently of indigenous design but some armaments and electronics probably imported from USSR and/or China. First laid down in 1971/72.
Submarines	licence	(China)	'Romeo'-class, local production following imports from China in 1974 and 1975.
Torpedo boats	licence	U.S.S.R.	'P–6'-type, In production since 1972.

Other

—	—	—	Local production of artillery and small arms.

KOREA SOUTH

Aircraft

—	—	—	Establishment of local aircraft industry planned; licence production of F–5E is possibility. Also Hughes 500 MD helicopters.

Missiles

—	—	—	The purchase of the plant and equipment of the Lockheed Propulsion Division suggests a missile program will be initiated.

Ships

Missile boats	licence	U.S.A.	Construction underway of modified 'Ashville'-class boats armed with Standard missiles.

Other

—	—	—	Local R&D effort commenced 1975 to provide basis for indigenous defence industry. M–47/48 tanks are re-built and modernised locally; 155mm and 105mm howitzers, 81mm mortars, anti-tank rocket launchers and associated ammunition are produced locally.

Appendix 2. Imports of Selected Major Weapons, Indian-Pacific Ocean Region, 1970–76

Country	Type	No.	Supplier	Outstanding orders, comments
COMBAT AIRCRAFT				
South Africa	Mirage III	23	France	32
	F–1	16	France	32
Tanzania	F–4 (MiG–17)	24	China	
	F–6 (MiG–19)	8	China	
	F–8 (MiG–21)	16	China	
Kenya	BAC Strikemaster	6	U.K.	
	Hawker Hunter	3	U.K.	12 F–5E/B (U.S.A.)
Somalia	MiG–15	(6)	U.S.S.R.	
	MiG–17	(18)	U.S.S.R.	
	MiG–19	(6)	U.S.S.R.	
	MiG–21	24	U.S.S.R.	
	IL–28	3	U.S.S.R.	
Pakistan	F–6 (MiG–19)	(120)	China	
	Mirage V	28	France	10 + 10 Mirage III-R.
	F–5A	(50)	Iran	Possibly on loan. (110) A–7 (U.S.A.) or 100 Jaguar (U.K., France).

India	MiG–21	57	U.S.S.R.	
	Su–7B	(80)	U.S.S.R.	
	BAC Canberra	22	U.K./N.Z.	
	Hawker Hunter	5	U.K.	50 TS–11 Iskra (Poland) (MiG–23) (U.S.S.R.)
Bangladesh	MiG–21	10	U.S.S.R.	(50–60) (China)
Burma	SF–260W	—	Italy	
Thailand	OV–10 Bronco	32	U.S.A.	
	AU–23 Peacemaker	33	U.S.A.	
	A–37 Dragonfly	(16)	U.S.A.	(16) F–5E (U.S.A.)
Malaysia	F–86 Sabre	6	Australia	
	F–5E	14	U.S.A.	
Singapore	Hawker Hunter	34	U.K.	
	BAC Strikemaster	6		(12) (Oman)
	A–4 Skyhawk	43	U.S.A.	21 F–5E/F (U.S.A.)
Indonesia	F–86 Sabre	16	Australia	
	F–51 Mustang	14	U.S.A.	
	A–7 Corsair	16	U.S.A.	
	OV–10F Bronco	16	U.S.A.	
Philippines	SF–260W	16	Italy	F–5E (U.S.A.)
Vietnam North	MiG–21	(50)	U.S.S.R.	
	MiG–19	80	U.S.S.R. or China	
	MiG–17	(30)	U.S.S.R.	
Vietnam South	F–5A	(120)	U.S.A.	
	A–37B	90	U.S.A.	Most will be non-operational.
	A–1 Skyraider	20	U.S.A.	Some flown out prior to fall of Saigon.
Taiwan	F–5A	45	U.S.A.	
	F–100 Super Sabre	34	U.S.A.	
	F–5E	(40)	U.S.A.	
Korea, North	MiG–21	(55)	U.S.S.R.	
	Su–7	28	U.S.S.R.	
				(20) MiG–23, (USSR)
Korea, South	F–5E	72	U.S.A.	60
	F–4D/E	55	U.S.A.	18
				24 OV–10G Bronco

HELICOPTERS

South Africa	SA–330 Puma	25	France	
	Super Frelon	15	France	
	Alouette III	(40)	France	
	Wasp	6	U.K.	
Tanzania	Bell 47	2	Italy	
	AB 206B	2	Italy	
Somalia	Mi–4	3	U.S.S.R.	
	Mi–8	5	U.S.S.R.	
Pakistan	Mi–8	(6)	U.S.S.R.	
	Sea King	6	U.K.	
	Alouette III	(70)	France	Assembled from imported components. 4 Super Frelon (France)

India	Sea King	12	U.K.	
	Hughes 300	10	U.S.A.	
	Mi–8	20	U.S.S.R.	
	Alouette III	8	France	
Bangladesh	Alouette III	6	India	
	Mi–8	4	U.S.S.R.	
Burma	Bell 205–A	18	U.S.A.	
Thailand	Bell 205	(62)	U.S.A.	
	CH–47 Chinook	4	U.S.A.	
	FH–1100	16	U.S.A.	
Malaysia	S–61	6	U.S.A.	6 (U.S.A.)
	Bell 47	6	U.S.A.	
	Bell 205	5	U.S.A.	(20) (U.S.A.)
	Bell 212	(5)	U.S.A.	
	Alouette III	8	France	
	Gazelle	3	France	Deliveries continuing
Singapore	Alouette III	(5)	France	
Indonesia	S–55	10	U.S.A.	
	Bell47	3	U.S.A.	
	Bell 206B	2	U.S.A.	
	Bo–105	—	F.R. Germany	Being assembled from imported components
Philippines	Bell 205	17	U.S.A.	(18)
	FH–1100	8	U.S.A.	
	AL–47A	12	U.S.A.	Helicopter gunship
	BO–105	5	F.R. Germany	
Vietnam				
North	Mi–6	6	U.S.S.R.	
South	Ch–47 Chinook	40	U.S.A. ⎫	Most would be non-operational; some flown out prior to fall of Saigon.
	Bell 205 (UH–1)	(900)	U.S.A. ⎭	
Taiwan	Hughes OH–6	6	U.S.A.	
Korea, South	Bell 212	2	U.S.A.	34 Hughes 500 armed helicopters (U.S.A.)

TRANSPORTS/MARITIME RECCE AIRCRAFT

South Africa	C.160 Transall	(5)	France	
	Piaggio P. 166	9	Italy	
	CL–215	3	Canada	
				A–300 Airbus tanker/transport
Tanzania	DHC–4 Caribou	8	Canada	
Kenya	DHC–4 Caribou	4	Canada	[4 DHC–5D Buffalo (Canada)]
Somalia	An–24	—	U.S.S.R.	
	An–26	—	U.S.S.R.	
	IL–18	—	U.S.S.R.	
Pakistan	C–130 Hercules	—	Iran	
	Breguet Atlantic	3	France	
India	IL–38 May	4	U.S.S.R.	3

Bangladesh	An–24	1	U.S.S.R.	
	An–26	(3)	U.S.S.R.	
	DHC–4 Caribou	1	India	
	DHC–3 Otter	4	India	
Burma	C–45	4	U.S.A.	
Thailand	C–123	7	U.S.A.	
	HS748	2	U.K.	
	Skyvan	3	U.K.	
	S–2F Tracker	8	U.S.A.	
Malaysia	DHC–4 Caribou	6	Canada	
	F–28	2	Netherlands	
	C–130H	3	U.S.A.	3
	HS Heron	1	U.K.	10 Nomad (Australia)
Singapore	Skyvan	6	U.K.	
Indonesia	C–130B	3	U.S.A.	
	Nomad	6	Australia	
	Skyvan	3	U.K.	
				8 F–27 (Netherlands)
				6 C.212 (Spain)
Philippines	C–130	4	U.S.A.	
	C–123K	15	U.S.A.	
	Nomad	12	Australia	
	BN–2A	(9)	U.K.	Delivered prior to Licence production
	F–28	2	Netherlands	
Vietnam				
North	An–2	12	U.S.S.R.	
South	AL–119	36	U.S.A.⎫	Most non-operational;
	C–123	48	U.S.A.⎬	some flown out prior to
	C–130	32	U.S.A.⎭	fall of Saigon.
Korea, South	S–2 Tracker	10	U.S.A.	
	HS 748	2	U.K.	

MISSILES[1]

S.Africa	Cactus SAM	3 batt.	France	
	Tigercat SAM	55	Jordan	
	Plagic AAM	—	France	Deliveries continuing.
	AS–12/12 ATM	—	France	Gabriel SSM-N (Israel) MM.38 Exocet SSM-N, (France) AM.39 Exocet ASM (France) Milan ATM (F.R.G./France)
Mozambique	SA–7 Grail SAM	—	U.S.S.R.	
Kenya				Sidewinder AAM
Somalia	Guideline SAM	—	U.S.S.R.	
	Styx SSM-N	—	U.S.S.R.	
Pakistan	SA–6 SAM	—	China	
	AS–11/12 ATM	—	France	
	R.530 AAM	—	France	AM.39 Exocet ASM (France) Crotale SAM, 6–12 batt. (France) TOW ATM, 200 Launchers (U.S.A.)

India	Styx SSM-N	—	U.S.S.R.	
	SA–6 SAM	—	U.S.S.R.	
	Seacat SAM-N	—	U.K.	
	Tigercat SAM	—	U.K.	
				SS-N–9, SSM-N, (U.S.S.R.) SA–7, SAM (U.S.S.R.)
Bangladesh	Atoll AAM	—	U.S.S.R.	Arming MiG–21's?
Thailand	Hawk SAM	36–40 Laun- chers	U.S.A.	
	Sidewinder AAM	—	U.S.A.	
	Seacat SAM-N	—	U.K.	
	Gabriel SSM-N	(15)	Israel	
				MM.38 Exocet SSM-N (France)
Malaysia	SS.12 SSM-N	—	France	
	MM.38 Exocet SSM-N	—	France	Will arm 4 new missile-boats
	Seacat SAM-N	—	U.K.	
	Sidewinder AAM	—	U.S.A.	
Singapore	Bloodhound II SAM	56	U.K.	
	Rapier SAM	—	U.K.	
	Gabriel	—	Israel	
	Sidewinder AAM	—	U.S.A.	Will also arm F–5Es on order
Indonesia				Missile-armed frigates and partrol boats on or-der: Exocet (France) will arm frigates.
Philippines				Sidewinder AAM to arm F–5Es
Vietnam				
North	SA–2 Guideline SAM	—	U.S.S.R.	
	SA–7 Grail SAM		U.S.S.R.	
	SA–9 Gaskin SAM	—	U.S.S.R.	
	Atoll AAM	—	U.S.S.R.	
	Styx SSM-N	—	U.S.S.R.	
	Sagger ATM	—	U.S.S.R.	
South	TWO ATM	—	U.S.A.	
Taiwan	Shafrir AAM	—	Israel	
	Sidewinder AAM	—	U.S.A.	Continuing deliveries
	Gabriel SSM-N	—	Israel	Continuing deliveries Improved Hawk SAM (U.S.A.) Chaparral SAM (U.S.A.)
Korea, North	Styx SSM-N	—	U.S.S.R.	Continuing deliveries
	Atoll AAM	—	U.S.S.R.	
	Frog 5/7 SSM		U.S.S.R.	
	SA–7 Grail SAM	—	U.S.S.R.	

Korea, South	Honest John SSM	1 batt.	U.S.A.	
	Nike Hercules SAM—		U.S.A.	Transfer of additional U.S.-operated batteries begun 1977
	Sidewinder AAM	—	U.S.A.	Deliveries continuing, 733 AAM–9J–1
	Sparrow AAM	—	U.S.A.	Deliveries continuing
	Standard SSM-N	—	U.S.A.	
				TOW ATM (U.S.A.) 120 Harpoon SSM-N (U.S.A.) 200 Maverick ASM (U.S.A.)
SHIPS[2]				
S. Africa	Daphne/SS	3	France	2 Agosta, SS (France) 2 A.69, MSS (France) 6 MSS-M (Spain?)
Tanzania	Shanghai/PB	6	China	
	PB	4	U.K.	
Kenya	PB	(2)	U.K.	2
Somalia	Osa/PB-M	2	U.S.S.R.	
	P–4/PB	4	U.S.S.R.	
	P–6/PB	2	U.S.S.R.	
Pakistan	Daphne/SS	3	France	1
	Shanghai/PB	9	China	2 Whitby/MSS (U.K.) frigates and submarines reported delivered by China late 1976.
India	Foxtrot/SS	6	U.S.S.R.	(2)
	Osa/PB-M	8	U.S.S.R.	Deliveries continuing (7)
	Petya/MSS	5	U.S.S.R.	8 Nanuchka/PB-M (U.S.S.R.)
Bangladesh	PB	2	India	
Thailand	MSS-M	1	U.K.	
	MSS	2	U.S.A.	
	PB-M	2	Singapore	(2)
	Swift/PB	6	U.S.A.	2 PN-M (Italy)
Malaysia	MSS-M	1	U.K.	
	La Combattante/ PB-M	4	France	(4) 4 Spica-M/PB-M (Sweden) 1 MSS (U.K.)
Singapore	Type 148 PB-M	2	F.R. Germany	Additional 4 built in Singapore
	PB	2	U.K.	Additional 4 built in Singapore
Indonesia	Claud Jones/MSS	4	U.S.A.	6
	Attack/PB	2	Australia	4 MSS (U.K.) 3 MSS-M (Netherlands) 4 PB-M (South Korea) 2 Type 209/SS (F.R. Germany)

Philippines	Sewart/PB	6	U.S.A.	
				2 PB (Australia)
Vietnam				
North	Komar/PB-M	4	U.S.S.R.	
	P–6/PB	3	U.S.S.R.	
South	MSS	9	U.S.A.	At least 2 vessels remained after the fall of Saigon.
	PB	2	U.S.A.	Both remained in Vietnam plus hundreds of lesser craft delivered before 1970.
Taiwan	Sumner/MSS	6	U.S.A.	
	Gleaves/MSS	1	U.S.A.	
	Fletcher/MSS	2	U.S.A.	
	Gearing/MSS	6	U.S.A.	Some units reportedly being equipped with Gabriel SSM-N.
	Guppy/SS	2	U.S.A.	
Korea, North	Osa/PB-M	4	U.S.S.R.	New deliveries may be underway
	Komar/PB-M	(4)	U.S.S.R.	
	Whiskey/SS	2	U.S.S.R.	
	Romeo/SS	7	China	
Korea, South	Gearing/MSS	2	U.S.A.	
	Paek Ku/PB-M	3	U.S.A.	
	PB	2	U.S.A.	3

ARMOURED VEHICLES[3]

S.Africa	Centurion tank	42	Jordan	
Mozambique	T–34 tank	—	U.S.S.R.	
Tanzania	T–59 tank	20	China	
Kenya	AML–60/90 AC	(15)	France	
				Fox AC (U.K.)
Somalia	T–54 tk	(100)	U.S.S.R.	Deliveries may be continuing
	BTR–152 APC	(200)	U.S.S.R.	
	BTR–50 APC	(30)	U.S.S.R.	
	BTR–40 APC	(60)	U.S.S.R.	
Pakistan	PT–76 lt tk	(10)	U.S.S.R.	
	T–59 tk	(370)	China	
	M–113 APC	300	U.S.A.	
				100 M–48 tk (Iran)
India	T–55 tk	(500)	U.S.S.R.	
	T–54 tk	(200)	Czechoslovakia	
	OT–62/64 APC	—	Czechoslovakia	Some delivered prior to licence production B M P – 1 A P C (U.S.S.R.)
Bangladesh	T–54 tk	30	India? U.S.S.R.?	

Thailand	Shorland AC	(32)	U.K.	
Malaysia	Ferret AC	600	U.K.	More APCs, ACs on order
	Commando AC	(200)	U.S.A.	
	AML/M-3 APC	(140)	France	
Singapore	AMX-13 lt tk	(50)	Israel	
	V-100 AC	30	U.S.A.	
	V-200	250	U.S.A.	
	[M.60 tk	—	U.S.A.]	
Indonesia	V-150 AC	58	U.S.A.	100+ AC, APC reported on order
Philippines	Scorpion lt tk	21	U.K.	7
	M-113 APC	35	U.S.A.	Deliveries continuing
Vietnam				
North	T-34 tk	—	U.S.S.R.	Approx. 900, mostly delivered since 1970
	T-55 tk	—	U.S.S.R.	
	T-59 tk	—	China	
	PT-76 lt tk	(100)	China	
	BTR-50 APC	(50)	U.S.S.R.	
	JSU-122 SPG	(50)	U.S.S.R.	
	SU-76 SPG	(50)	U.S.S.R.	
South	M-41 lt tk	(300)	U.S.A.	Available spares plus
	M-48 tk	(107)	U.S.A.	cannabilisation will
	M-60 tk	(85)	U.S.A.	probably make some of
	M-113 APC	(1100)	U.S.A.	this equipment
	M-109 SPG	24	U.S.A.	operational for
	M-109 SPG	24	U.S.A.	several years
Taiwan	M-48 tk	—	U.S.A.	
Korea,	T-54 tk	—	U.S.S.R.⎫	Probably several hun-
North	T-55 tk	—	U.S.S.R.⎬	dreds
	T-59 tk	—	China ⎭	
Korea,	M-47 tk	—	U.S.A.	
South	M-48 tk	—	U.S.A.	421 (U.S.A.)
	M-113 APC	(350)	U.S.A.	
	M-107 SPG	(50)	U.S.A.	
	M-110 SPG	(50)	U.S.A.	

1. Code for types: SAM-N = surface-to-air (Naval), ASM = Air-to-surface, ATM = Anti-tank, SSM-N = surface-to-surface (Naval), AAM = Air-to-air.
2. Code for types: MSS-M = major surface ship—(missile armed) (displacing more than 900 tons), PB-M = patrol boat—(missile-armed), SS = submarine.

Appendix 3. Combat Aircraft and Missile systems in Production and Under Development and Available or Potentially Available for Export

Designation Name	Country	Year operational	Exported or on order for export, 31 December 1976
AIRCRAFT			
Heavy fighter/attack			
F–4E Phantom II	U.S.A.	1968	Yes
A–7E Corsair II	U.S.A.	1969	Yes
F–14A Tomcat	U.S.A.	1974	Yes
F–15 Eagle	U.S.A.	1976	Yes
A–10	U.S.A.	1978	No
F–16	U.S.A.	1979	Yes
F–18/A–18 Hornet	U.S.A.	1982	Yes
F–18L	U.S.A.	(1982)	(Yes)
AU–8B	U.S.A.	1984	No
MiG–25 Foxbat A/B/D	U.S.S.R.	(1971)	No
MiG–23 Flogger B/D/E	U.S.S.R.	(1971)	Yes
Su–15 Flagon E	U.S.S.R.	(1971)	No
MiG–21 Fishbed K	U.S.S.R.	(1971)	Yes
Su–17/20/22 Fitter C	U.S.S.R.	(1972)	Yes
Su–19 Fencer	U.S.S.R.	(1974)	No
Forger VTOL	U.S.S.R.	1976	No
F–6 (MiG–19)	China	(1962)	Yes
F–8 (MiG–21)	China	(1974)	Yes
F–9 (Advanced MiG–19)	China	(1974)	No
Mirage III/V	France	1961	Yes
Harrier	U.K.	1969	Yes
F–104S Starfighter	Italy/USA	1969	Yes
AJ. 37 Viggen	Sweden	1971	No
Mirage F–1	France	1974	Yes
JA.37 Viggen	Sweden	1978	No
MRCA Tornado	U.K., FRG, Italy	1979	No
Sea Harrier S/VTOL	U.K.	1979	No
Mirage Delta 2000	France	(1981)	No
Mirage Delta Plus	France	(1982)	No
MRCA ADV	U.K.	(1984)	No
A.20 (Advanced JA.37)	Sweden	(1985)	No
Kfir	Israel	1975	No
Light fighter/attack/trainer			
A–37B/T–37C Dragonfly	U.S.A.	1968	Yes
T–2E Buckeye	U.S.A.	1976	Yes
A–4 M/Y Skyhawk	U.S.A.	1970	Yes
F–5E/B Tiger II	U.S.A.	1973	Yes
BAC.167 Strikemaster	U.K.	1968	Yes
Jaguar	U.K./France	1973	Yes
MB.326 K/L	Italy	1973	Yes
J–1 Jastreb	Yugoslavia	(1973)	Yes

L–39 Albatross	Czecho-slovakia	1974	Yes
T–2	Japan	1975	No
HS.1182 Hawk	U.K.	1977	Yes
Super Elendard	France	1978	No
Alfajet	F.R.G./France	1978	Yes
MB.339	Italy	1978	No
Orao	Yugoslavia/Romania	1978	No
FS-T2 Kai	Japan	1978	No
C–101	Spain	1980	No
HJT–16 Kiran	India	(1969)	No
Ajeet	India	(1978)	No
HF.33	India	(1981)	No

MISSILES
Surface-to-surface

MGM–52 Lance	U.S.A.	1972	Yes
SS–1C Scud B	U.S.S.R.	1963	Yes
Frog–7	U.S.S.R.	1965	Yes
Jericho	Israel	?	No
Coral	Taiwan	?	No

Surface-to-surface, naval

RGM–66D Standard	U.S.A.	1973	Yes
RGM–84 Harpoon	U.S.A.	1977	Yes
SSN–3D Shaddock	U.S.S.R.	(1963)	No
SSN–11	U.S.S.R.	1968	Yes
SSN–9	U.S.S.R.	1969	Yes
SSN–10	U.S.S.R.	(1969)	No
SSN–12	U.S.S.R.	(1976)	No
CSS-N–1 (SSN–2)	China	(1976)	(Yes)
Penguin I	Norway	1970	Yes
Sea Killer II	Italy	1972	Yes
MM.39 Exocet	France	1973	Yes
Otomat I	France/Italy	1973	Yes
Otomat II	France/Italy	1976	(Yes)
Penguin II	Norway	(1977)	Yes
Sea Killer III	Italy	(1977)	No
MM.40 Exocet	France	1978	(Yes)
Gabriel I	Israel	1970	Yes
Gabriel II	Israel	1974	(Yes)
Gabriel III	Israel	(1978)	(Yes)
	India	(1978)	No

Surface-to-air, land

MIM–72C Chaparral	U.S.A.	(1970)	Yes
MIM–23B Hawk	U.S.A.	1972	Yes
FIM–92A Stinger	U.S.A.	1977	(No)
Shorads (Roland II)	U.S.A.	(1980)	Yes
SAM-D Patriot	U.S.A.	(1981)	No

SA.2 Guideline	U.S.S.R.	1958	Yes
SA.3 Goa	U.S.S.R.	1961	(No)
SA.7 Grail	U.S.S.R.	(1966)	Yes
SA.6 Gainful	U.S.S.R.	1970	Yes
SA.9 Gaskin	U.S.S.R.	(1974)	Yes
SA.8	U.S.S.R.	(1975)	(Yes)
CSA–1 (SA–2)	China	(1975)	(Yes)
Tigercat	U.K.	1970	Yes
Rapier	U.K.	1971	Yes
Crotale	France	1971	Yes
Blowpipe	U.K.	(1973)	Yes
Indigo	Italy	(1973)	No
Roland I	France/F.R.G.	1974	No
Rbs–70	Sweden	1977	Yes
Roland II	France/F.R.G.	(1978)	Yes
Spada system	Italy	(1978)	(No)
Chahinn (Crotale)	France	(1978)	Yes
Tan Sam	Japan	(1978)	No

Surface-to-air, naval

RIM–66/67 Standard I	U.S.A.	1969	Yes
Standard II	U.S.A.	(1977)	No
SAM–3 Goblet	U.S.S.R.	1968	No
SAM–4	U.S.S.R.	(1971)	Yes
Seacat	U.K.	1962	Yes
Sea Sparrow	U.S.A./Europe	(1973)	(No)
Sea Dart	U.K.	1973	Yes
Hirondelle system	France	(1977)	(No)
Sea Wolf	U.K.	(1977)	No
Albatross system	Italy	(1977)	(Yes)
Crotale, naval	France	(1978)	(No)

h*Air-to-surface/ship*

AGM–45 Shrike	U.S.A.	1964	Yes
AGM–78 Standard ARM	U.S.A.	1968	No
Paveway laser-guided bombs	U.S.A.	1968	Yes
AGM–62B Wallege II	U.S.A.	(1972)	(Yes)
AGM–65A Maverick	U.S.A.	1973	Yes
AGM–68B Maverick	U.S.A.	1975	(Yes)
GBU–15 (V) guided bombs	U.S.A.	(1976)	No
AGM–84 Harpoon	U.S.A.	1977	(No)
AGM–65C Maverick	U.S.A.	(1978)	No
AGM–65D Maverick	U.S.A.	(1979)	No
Hellfire	U.S.A.	(1980)	No
AGM–88 HARM	U.S.A.	(1981)	No
AS–4 Kitchen	U.S.S.R.	(1981)	(No)
AS–5 Kelt	U.S.S.R.	(1981)	Yes
AS.7 Kerry	U.S.S.R.	(1975)	No
AS-X8	U.S.S.R.	(1975)	No
AS-X9	U.S.S.R.	(1975)	No

AS-X10	U.S.S.R.	(1975)	No
AS.12	France	(1963)	Yes
AS.30	France	1961	Yes
Rb 05A	Sweden	1972	No
Martel	U.K./France	(1972)	No
Rb 04E	Sweden	(1975)	No
AM.39 Exocet	France	(1977)	Yes
AS.34 Kormoran	F.R. Germany	1977	No
Airtos	Italy	(1977)	(No)
Marte system	Italy	(1978)	(No)
Rb 05B	Sweden	(1978)	No
Sea Skua	U.K.	(1980)	No
Ariel (AS.30 laser)	France	(1981)	No
ASM-1	Japan	(1980)	No
Luz	Israel	(1980)	(No)

Air-to-air

AIM-9H Sidewinder	U.S.A.	(1971)	Yes
AIM-54A Phoenix	U.S.A.	1974	Yes
AIM-7F Sparrow	U.S.A.	(1976)	(No)
AIM-9L Sidewinder	U.S.A.	(1976)	Yes
Brazo	U.S.A.	(1976)	No
Sidewinder replacement (ASRAM)	U.S.A.	(1981)	No
AA-2 Atoll	U.S.S.R.	(1960)	Yes
Awl	U.S.S.R.	1968	(Yes)
AA-6 Acrid	U.S.S.R.	(1975)	No
AA.7 Apex	U.S.S.R.	(1975)	(Yes)
AA.9 Aphid	U.S.S.R.	(1975)	(Yes)
(AA-2 Atoll)	China	(1975)	Yes
R.530	France	1963	Yes
R.550 Magic	France	1975	Yes
Super 530	France	1978	(Yes)
XJ521 Skyflash	U.K.	(1978)	(No)
Aspide	Italy	(1978)	(No)
Type 372	Sweden	(1979)	No
AAM-2	Japan	(1978)	No

Anti-tank

BGM-71 TWO*	U.S.A.	1970	Yes
FGM-77 Dragon	U.S.A.	1975	Yes
Copperhead CLGP	U.S.A.	(1980)	No
Lance TGSM	U.S.A.	(1981)	No
AT-2 Swatter	U.S.S.R.	(1960)	Yes
AT-3 Sagger*	U.S.S.R.	(1961)	Yes
SS-11*	France	1958	Yes
Cobra 2000	F.R. Germany	(1963)	Yes
Bantam*	Sweden	1963	Yes
Swingfire	U.K.	1969	Yes
Mamba	F.R. Germany	1975	Yes

Milan	France/F.R.G.	1975	Yes
Beeswing	U.K.	(1976)	(Yes)
Hot*	France/F.R.G.	1976	(Yes)
Hawkswing*	U.K.	1977	(No)
Sparviero	Italy	1977	No
Kam–9	Japan	(1977)	No

* Also deployed on helicopters.

3

The Proliferation of Maritime Weapon Systems in the Indo-Pacific Region
Michael MccGwire

The purpose of this chapter is to review the general trend in the proliferation of maritime weapon systems and to assess the implications. It starts by establishing what is meant by the proliferation of maritime weapon systems, and why such proliferation may be a matter for concern. It goes on to review the geo-strategic elements of the Indo-Pacific region, and to survey the various weapon inventories in the area. It then turns to consider the implications of this developing situation and their impact on Western policies.

General Trends

Maritime weapons are taken to include land-based systems which can be brought to bear at sea, and sea-based systems which are targeted on land. The proliferation of maritime systems can be looked at in terms of 'force capability' and 'systems capability'. In the case of force capability, proliferation is taking place at three different levels, which can be labelled continguous, regional and world-wide. There has been a progressive spread of maritime weapons among coastal states, giving them some capability to prevent the use of their contiguous waters. There is the gradual emergence of regional forces, which are developing some capability to project maritime force into non-adjacent sea areas. And we have the presence of world-wide forces, whose concerns are both regional and related to the global strategic balance.

'Systems capability' addresses the type of proliferation inherent in the advance of weapons technology, which has enabled quantum jumps in such fundamental weapon characteristics as range, accuracy, payload and systems reliability. These have been matched by an exponential increase in the capabilities of sensor and surveillance systems. The effect of these advances (sometimes referred to as 'vertical proliferation') pervades the whole spectrum of capability, but the single most dramatic improvement has been the introduction of the terminally-guided cruise missile. This weapon allows a patrol craft to pack the punch of a battleship, and can be fitted to surface ships, aircraft, submarines or coastal defence installations. As important as the accuracy and payload of the cruise missile weapon is its range. This not only extends a coastal state's reach to seaward, but the greater the range, the smaller the number of weapon-platforms needed to cover a given sea area or stretch of coast. The next major advance of this kind is likely to be the proliferation of precision guided munitions (PGM), which enable shells and bombs to home on designated targets. PGMs have the particular attraction of upgrading the capability of existing gun and aircraft systems by several orders of magnitude.

The cruise missile and PGM are universal weapons which are likely to be seen at all three levels of force capability. There are other weapons whose cost and operational complexity are such that they are only likely to be found at the world-wide level. A long-standing example is the sea-based strategic nuclear delivery capability, which allows an opponent's territory to be targeted from distant sea areas; this was first embodied in carrier-borne strike aircraft and subsequently in submarine-launched ballistic missiles (SLBM). This capability, itself a form of weapons proliferation, evoked two further types. The first took the shape of reactive naval deployments by the target countries. The second involved the development of new weapons and surveillance systems, intended to provide a more effective counter to this qualitatively new threat.

As a byproduct of these developments, new global surveillance systems have simplified the problem of ocean interception by naval forces. They can also provide the target location data which allows long-range weapon systems to be brought to bear. Tactical systems with ranges from 300 miles (cruise missiles) to 1500 miles (aircraft) have been in service since the end of the 1950s, but the emerging capability to strike moving targets at sea with ballistic missiles at intercontinental ranges is introducing a new dimension to maritime warfare.[1] We are entering an era where maritime warfare can be fought as much by land- as by sea-based weapon systems in which it is becoming necessary to distinguish between the 'reaches' of different weapons, and to think in terms of 'global' and 'local' systems.

If we now turn back to 'force capability', we get a clearer idea of proliferation at the three levels. The general trend is suggested by the index to *Jane's Fighting Ships*, which listed 67 navies in 1958–59, 91 in 1966–67 and 135 in 1976–77. Some of this increase can be explained by changes in editorial policy, but the greater part reflects the emergence of newly independent states. In 1976 some 30 navies were operating motor torpedo boats; 33 navies had fast patrol craft armed with anti-ship homing missiles; and there were 71 different types of naval missile in service throughout the world. Between 1966 and 1976 the number of navies with submarines rose from 31 to 36 (with two more having units on order), and nuclear-powered forces rose from three to five.

But at the 'contiguous' level of capability, such forces are only part of the story and there are a whole range of shore-based systems such as aircraft, coast-defence missiles and artillery, and fixed obstructions such as mines, which can be brought into play. There are also the traditional gun-armed surface units, which can range from purpose-designed new procurements, through hand-me-down surplus units to small craft fitted with army recoilless weapons. Their effectiveness at preventing the use of the sea has been demonstrated on countless occasions during the last 30 years, the *Pueblo* and *Mayaguez* incidents being two notable examples.

Proliferation of maritime weapons at this level of capability is likely to continue, for two main types of reason. On the one hand, we have the coastal state's own assessment of its requirements. These will be influenced by the usual factors such as national perceptions of threat and of the role of military power in promoting and protecting national interests, but four additional elements will exert an effect: (1) the new awareness of the sea's potential, the institution of the concept of an exclusive economic zone, and (particularly in the newly independent states) the ideological impulse to claim and attempt to enforce some kind of sovereignty over the zone; (2) the recent use of the sea by subversive forces for access to their target areas, as for example to Guinea Bissau, Malaysia and Oman; (3) the wish to raise the cost of coercive intervention by non-adjacent powers; and (4) the demonstration effect of the development of other maritime forces.

On the other hand, there are the interests of the arms supplying countries: (1) commerical profit, whether it be the corporation, the national balance of payments, or the reduction of unit procurement costs; (2) political and economic influence-building achieved by providing training programs, maintenance teams, advisory groups and the supply of parts and replacements, and, of course, by meeting the client state's requirements; (3) the maintenance of position within the world balance of power; and (4) the strategic defence of the homeland. The dividing line between the last two categories of interest is sometimes hard to distinguish, but it can be illustrated by three examples. The Soviet supply of naval arms to China in the second half of the 1950s, was part of an unsuccessful attempt to set up a joint air defence system in the Far East. The provision of arms to Egypt and Algeria in 1963 was made in order to offset the threat posed to the U.S.S.R. by the U.S. Sixth Fleet, rather than to meet the requirements of the two recipients. By contrast, the supply of arms to Indonesia between 1958 and 1962 was probably directed at eroding Western maritime supremacy in the area, even though it did have the effect of drawing British strike carriers away from their NATO commitments.

A large part of Soviet arms supply appears to be directed towards shifting the world balance of power in their favour. Although this shift is seen by the Soviets as an inevitable historical process, it can, however, be delayed by Western military intervention in support of reactionary forces. By providing newly independent states with a military capability, the Soviet Union has hoped to raise the costs of such intervention, and thereby reduce its likelihood. A large part of Western arms supply is similarly aimed at preserving the present imbalance of power in favour of the West. Outside the NATO area (and perhaps Japan), it is hard to identify cases where the supply of arms can be directly tied to the defence of the U.S. homeland.

While the commercial motivation is less prominent in Soviet arms supply than in the West, there is a comparable dynamic for the continual upgrading of a client state's weapon systems. It appears that a fixed share of industrial resources is allocated to Soviet defence production and that weapon design, development and procurement is a continuous process whereby new, improved versions are introduced at regular intervals. This results in the periodic replacement of all equipment, the older models becoming available for supply to other countries. In this context, the Soviet SS–N–3 300-mile surface-to-surface anti-shiping cruise missile is now being superceded by the SS–N–12, and may become available for selective supply to client states for coast defence purposes.

Much of what has been said about the proliferation of maritime weapons at the contiguous level of capability applies equally to the regional level. The difference between these two types of capability stems as much from the political purpose which generates the requirement for each, as from the different types of systems needed to achieve the higher level of capability. There are, however, certain additional distinctions to be made. First, the attempt by one power to achieve a regional capability must raise fears amongst its neighbours of hegemony, and encourage the growth of maritime forces in the region, either in competition or in self-defence. Second, a regional capability implies less reliance on shore-based systems and a greater emphasis on the seaborne components of a maritime force. And third, a regional force achieves the worst of both worlds once it moves out from its own waters; when facing a world-wide force, it foregoes the advantages of close proximity to its own territory, and when dealing with a contiguous force, such proximity to land favours its opponents. Nevertheless, the emergence of regional maritime forces is already taking place, and the process is likely to continue and spread. It stems from a number of causes including the acquisition by regional powers of a greater economic capability, the waning of Western naval hegemony, and the balancing effect of the Soviet naval presence, which combine to allow the pursuit of traditional national aspirations. While most of the putative regional forces continue to buy the bulk of their weapon systems abroad, several are seeking to develop some indigenous capacity for such production.

Moving on to proliferation at the world-wide level of capability, we see that while overall force levels have dropped and the number of units deployed away from homewaters has progressively declined, the effect has been distorted by other developments. First, we have the shift to sea-based strategic delivery systems; this change prompted the reactive deployment of counter forces, and turned various sea areas into arenas for the continuous discharge of what are essentially wartime tasks. Second, the co-operative monopoly of world-wide naval power which the West enjoyed for the twenty years after 1945, has been replaced by an adversary relationship with the Soviet Union, which is also concerned about the possibility of war with China. These antagonistic relationships have engendered new interest in overseas bases to support maritime operations in distant theatres. And third, we have the appearance of global systems which on the one hand provide the means for world-wide real-time surface surveillance and on the other can bring land-based weapons to bear on non-adjacent waters; both of these capabilities could be used in local or regional conflicts, the current intelligence being particularly useful to client states, giving them a capability for ocean interception which they would otherwise lack.

The overall effect of these advances in weapons technology and of the proliferation of sophisticated systems is to make the sea a much more complex and potentially hostile operating environment. The reach of coastal states is being progressively extended, regional navies are beginning to emerge in various parts of the world, and superpower competition flourishes. But we are left with the questions . . . does it matter? . . . and if so, in what way? These cannot be addressed until the weapon inventories throughout the area have been reviewed; but first, it is necessary to establish the structure of the ensuing analysis.

Analytical Structure

There are two ways in which the proliferation of maritime weapon systems could provide cause for concern. One involves the effect of such proliferation on the likelihood of conflict within the region. The other, which is of more immediate concern to this analysis, involves the capability of maritime weapon systems both to secure the use of the sea for one's own purposes and to deny its use to an enemy.

Man has a twofold interest in using the sea: first as a means of access; and second, as a natural resource. This second interest is best seen as a maritime extension of normal commercial activities carried out on land, like agriculture or mining, and as such it involves issues of domestic jurisdiction and territoriality. The right to exploit some other state's coastal resources is acquired through commercial negotiation, diplomatic pressure or military intervention; it is no different to any other commercial involvement with a foreign country.

The use of the sea to gain access to non-adjacent areas is, however, *sui generis*, and it is this which endows the sea with its strategic quality. Maritime strategy is about using the sea; using it for one's own purposes and preventing its use to one's disadvantage. This navigational type of use includes two main categories: the conveyance of goods and people; and the projection of military force against targets ashore.

The first category covers seaborne trade, which in a strategic context spells maritime communications. It also covers the movement of military cargoes in merchant ships, although this use shades into the second category, particularly when a war is actually in progress. The shading is inevitable, since the military and commercial uses of the sea form a continuum. While we can identify what is purely military, there are few commercial cargoes which have no military value.

The second category of navigational use has two forms: the traditional one of bringing force (actual or latent) to bear on coastal states; and the deterrent form of targeting distant land areas with nuclear weapons. At present only four countries can do the latter, using this capacity in the deterrent role through missile-armed submarines, with units continually on station. The projection of traditional military force covers a much broader range of activity, and may involve the landing of troops, or be restricted to standing offshore and striking targets with shipboard weapons such as guns, missiles and aircraft. And the scale of such operations can range from insignificant harassment to full-scale invasion. However, capability falls off sharply with range, and very few countries can project substantial military force to any distance from their coasts. Only the U.S.A. has a world-wide capability to project force ashore against appreciable land-based opposition, and without some measure of local support. Excluded from this category is the use of naval forces as an adjunct to territorial conflict between neighbouring states, since this activity is better dealt with in terms of land-warfare systems.

The ease with which use of the sea can be *prevented* depends on maritime geography and the type of use involved. Focusing first on the navigational use of the sea, we have to think in terms of waterways (defined as any stretch of sea used for passage), which can be described in terms of their geographic characteristics as lying somewhere on a continuum between narrow shallow waters and the deep ocean. Narrow waterways, where ships must pass close to shore-based weapons, are relatively easy to obstruct, particularly if they are shallow and hence mineable. It is far harder to prevent passage along an ocean waterway, out of range of land and with opportunities for evasive routing. By the same token, different types of use involve different capabilities and lengths of time at risk. It is usually easier to interrupt a flow of merchant shipping than to prevent the passage of a heavily armed naval task force.

As a general rule, it is easier to *prevent* the navigational use of the sea than it is to *secure* such use. In the case of resource exploitation, the imbalance is even greater, because the use is tied to a particular location. Where coastal resources are involved, this imbalance is accentuated by the preventive advantages which go with narrow waters. To *prevent* the use of the sea requires an appropriate military capability, whether it be physical obstruction or the means of sinking ships. However, military force is only one of several ways of *securing* the use of the sea against such opposition, which include diplomatic pressure, economic sanctions and navigational diversion.

The Indian Ocean Region

The Indo-Pacific region divides naturally between the Indian Ocean and the Asian-Pacific region, two very different areas which are separated by the archipelagic barrier stretching from Malaysia to Australia.

The importance of the Indian Ocean region as a source of oil and raw materials, and as a waterway for the shipment of these goods, is well known. In 1975, the proportions of total oil imports which came by sea from the Middle East were: Japan and Australasia—74 per cent, Western Europe—70 per cent, Canada —63 per cent and the U.S.A.—19 per cent. As a proportion of total oil consumption this represented for Japan—74 per cent, Western Europe—66 per cent, Australasia—35 per cent, Canada —32 per cent and the U.S.A.—7.5 per cent.[2] Raw materials are shipped from Africa and India to Japan and Europe, and about 40 per cent of all Japanese imports cross the Indian Ocean.

The region as a whole serves as an arena for the competition between the U.S.S.R., China and the U.S.A. for world influence. The northern part is, however, particularly important in terms of Sino-Soviet rivalry, with the U.S.S.R. concerned to counter physically Chinese expansion, while protecting herself from being outflanked to the south. The Indian Ocean is also important to the U.S.S.R as a waterway. In peacetime, the Asian provinces are supplied by rail, but in the event of war with China, the trans-Siberian railway would be cut and military supplies to the Far Eastern front would have to move by sea. If possible, these would pass via the Suez Canal, but if that were closed, they could be moved overland to the Persian Gulf or the Arabian Sea. And finally, the Indian Ocean remains an optimal area from which to target the Soviet Union with SLBMs; countering the threat of strikes from the sea continues to be a mission of the Soviet armed forces and of the navy in particular, although there is some argument as to the relative priority now accorded this mission.

However, in strategic terms, the Indian Ocean is not a self-contained region in the sense that military developments in Southern Africa need not affect the situation in Sri Lanka or Australia. This would not be true of comparable situations in the Mediterranean, or (for very different reasons) the North Atlantic, both of which are coherent strategic regions. For purposes of analysis, the Indian Ocean is therefore best thought of in terms of first the main axes of movement, and second the different littoral areas.

Shipping routes across the Indian Ocean trace out the perimeter and both diagonals of a trapezoid, the base running from Cape Town to Fremantle. The north-west half of this figure is by far the most important, and the main axes of movement in the region form a triangle which joins the Cape of Good Hope, the Arabian Sea and the Indonesian Straits. The countries bordering the Indian Ocean can be divided into four main groups: Southern Africa, including Kenya; the Middle East, extending from Somalia to Iran; the Indian subcontinent; and South-east Asia and Australia.

Southern Africa

The littoral of Southern Africa comprises the Republic of South Africa, Mozambique, Tanzania, Kenya and the island of Malagasy. Of these five countries, only South Africa has any distant water capability, and although in world terms this capability is limited, South African maritime forces outrank their northerly neighbours by several orders of magnitude. Kenya has some seven 33m. patrol craft, armed with two 40 mm. guns and the Malagasy navy is about the same size. Tanzania has a more numerous force supplied by China, but it is still a coastal navy and includes 11 motor torpedo boats and six Shanghai class gun boats and perhaps another six on order. The situation in Mozambique is unclear, but one would expect the Soviets to provide them with some kind of coastal naval force (perhaps including missile craft and coast defence units), since President Machel is known to be concerned about the threat from the sea in the event of conflict with South Africa over Rhodesia.

For a long time South Africa's naval forces were seen as a way of binding the country to the Western alliance by preserving wartime links, and they were therefore configured to contribute to the general anti-submarine effort in defence of sea lines of communications. The bankruptcy of that policy became clear in the mid-1960s, since when naval procurement has been related directly to the Republic's own requirements. It appears that initially, the primary concern was to discourage the imposition of U.N. sanctions, enforced by naval blockade; hence the purchase of three Daphne class 850 ton submarines in 1970–71. In the last few years concern seems to have shifted towards a more generalised maritime defence capability, and new forces on order include two frigates, six corvettes and six fast patrol craft (the last two types being armed with the Gabriel SSM), and two of the 1500 ton Agosta class submarines. Add these to the existing units, which include five World War II destroyers/frigates and three Rothesay-type frigates, and there is a sizeable force which will have the reconnaissance support of seven Shackleton LRMP aircraft, plus 18 Piaggo 16S Albatross aircraft with a range of 1300 n.m. When operating under shore-based aircover, with close support by ground attack aircraft in the surface strike role, this force has an appreciable capability to both prevent and secure the use of South Africa's contiguous waters in the face of all except U.S. carrier forces, or a concentrated campaign by submarines.

The South African Navy also has some capability to project force northwards along the neighbouring coasts of Southern Africa and, given the likely opposition, the lack of specialised assault lift would not seem to be important. The Navy has not, however, been developed for such a role and to that extent it cannot be seen as a regional force, despite its over-whelming local superiority. This preponderence derives mainly from the inadequacies of the other indigenous maritime forces, which are not favoured by geography; they lack the capability to prevent the use of the sea to any distance from their shores, or to defend their coastline against seaborne assault. Mozambique, flanking the channel of that name, may in due course develop some capability in this regard, but the channel is very broad and in any case can be easily circumvented.

The Middle East
Moving north to the Middle East, we come first to the Red Sea and its approaches. The Red Sea is 100–200 miles wide and some thousand miles long, narrowing to the Straits of Bab el Mandeb. These open into the 500 mile funnel of the Gulf of Aden, with the island of Socotra lying out in the Indian Ocean, about 150 miles beyond the Horn of Africa.

The Egyptian Navy is the only sizeable force in the Red Sea. Except for Israel, all the other countries, North and South Yemen, Ethiopia, Sudan, Saudi Arabia and Jordan, each have a few lightly armed patrol craft, while North and South Yemen and Saudi Arabia also have two or three torpedo boats apiece. Israel has a force of 18 missile-armed fast patrol craft, including six 400-tonners with a range of 1500 n.m., and six more of the latter with twice the range are on order; she also has an ex–T class oceangoing submarine and is acquiring three 420 ton units. These forces have to be shared between the Mediterranean and the Red Sea, as does the Egyptian Navy. The latter comprises eight World War II design destroyers/frigates, 12 W– and R–class submarines, 16 missile-armed fast patrol craft and 26 torpedo boats, and at present Egypt has the advantage of the Suez Canal for redeploying these forces as necessary.

During the last two Arab–Israeli wars, the Israeli Navy has acquitted itself well, and if operating under air superiority with close air support and given sufficient numbers, Israeli missile units should be able to establish limited command of the northern end of the Red Sea including both Gulfs. However, if Egypt continues to enjoy a favourable air environment and friendly coastlines elsewhere in the Red Sea (i.e., assuming that the Arab alliance remains intact), then Egyptian naval forces should be able to establish command over the rest of the sea and its approaches. It is relevant that in October 1973 the Egyptian Navy established a surface ship patrol in the Straits of Bab el Mandeb to discourage support and supplies from reaching Israel by this route. This may explain why Israel is now acquiring a force of small submarines suitable for operating in the confined waters of the Red Sea. It may also explain the acquisition of missile-armed craft having ranges of 1500–3000 n.m., although they might have a long-distance role in the Mediterranean, given favourable weather conditions.

As one departs the Red Sea for the Indian Ocean, to the north of the Gulf of Aden lies South Yemen, whose Soviet-supplied Polnocny landing craft were used to ferry support to the Dhofari rebels in Oman. To the south lies Somalia, which possesses three Osa class missile craft and four torpedo boats; together, these units have the potential to prevent the use of the sea in the approaches to the Straits of Bab el Mandeb.

Somalia also plays host to substantial Soviet base facilities at Berbera. The complex includes alongside berthing, refit and repair facilities, missile storage and maintenance shops, a fuel tank installation with ship re-fuelling points, and extensive communication facilities. A Soviet repair ship and barracks ship are permanently berthed in the harbour and there are accommodation trailers ashore. An airfield for medium-range aircraft is already in use, two other existing airfields are being extended to handle all types of Soviet aircraft, and a fourth large airfield is under construction at Uanle Uen. A separate base facility is being developed at Mogadiscio on the Indian Ocean, which includes a missile facility capable of handling any of the tactical systems fitted in Soviet ships.[3] A Soviet naval squadron operates from Berbera. The force usually comprises one or two destroyer/cruiser-sized units, two escorts, two diesel submarines, two minesweeper/submarine rescue ships and one landing craft, but numbers are increased in reaction to U.S. deployments and in response to crises. Soviet long-range reconnaissance and ASW aircraft have operated from Somali fields, but are not permanently based there. It appears that the facilities are designed to support a bigger force than the present squadron, with a much larger missile inventory.

The northern half of the Middle East littoral encompasses the Persian Gulf, which is linked to the Arabian Sea by the Straits of Hormuz and the Gulf of Oman. Iran, with more than a thousand miles of coast, occupies the whole northern shore of both gulfs. The southern shore is divided between Oman, the United Arab Emirates,

Qatar, Saudi Arabia (which straddles the Arabian peninsula), Kuwait and the Island of Bahrein, with a sliver of coast at the head of the Gulf giving access to Iraq. Of these eight countries, only Iran and Iraq possess substantial naval forces, the others having varying numbers of gun-armed patrol craft, ranging in size from six to 45m., and in numbers from Bahrein's five to Saudi Arabia's 70; the latter also has three torpedo boats and eight hovercraft. Although many of these vessels are more properly border patrol than naval forces, the restricted waters of the Gulf and the type of cargo being shipped gives them a potential for preventing use by merchant ships which they would lack elsewhere. Three of the countries have ground attack aircraft which could be used in the anti-shipping role, and mines can be laid from most kinds of craft, including dhows.

The great bulk of the Iraqi Navy comprises 10 Osa missile units and 12 P6 torpedo boats; it also has three SO–1 sub-chasers. This represents a substantial kill capability, but the Navy is gravely disadvantaged by its location at the very head of the Gulf with no proper coastline, and the radius of operation of these units would be limited by the extent to which they could be provided with air cover. With Iran and Saudi Arabia on either flank such provision could be difficult and the Iraqi force is likely to be effective only in the waters at the head of the Gulf. It does however have the potential to prevent the use of those waters and would, for example, pose a major threat to naval forces deployed to help Kuwait defend itself against an Iraqi attack.

The Iranian Navy is the most substantial force in the Gulf, but it is more interesting for what it will be than for what it is now. At present it has three modernised World War II destroyers carrying Seacat or Standard SAM, four new Vosper frigates fitted with Seakiller SSM and Seacat SAM, four ex–U.S. patrol frigates, seven ex–U.S. patrol craft, four minesweepers, some amphibious units, and 14 60–knot hovercraft, four of which are armed with SSM; these forces are backed by six P–3F Orion LRMP aircraft and six ASW helicopters. By the early 1980s, it is intended to double the size of the force, with naval personnel rising from about 20,000 to 40,000, and the following units are already on order: three ex–Tang class submarines, four Spruance class destroyers fitted with ASROC and Standard SAM, 12 missile-armed fast patrol craft and another six ASW helicopters. The Navy will have a twofold mission:[4] first, to secure the use of the Persian Gulf using helicopters, hovercraft and fast patrol craft; and, second, to secure the use of the sea for merchant shipping along the main axes of movement in the Arabian sea and beyond if possible. For this second mission, Iran is seeking to develop a balanced force comprising submarines, destroyers, frigates and ASW helicopters, backed by underway replenishment units, maritime reconnaissance aircraft and long-range air cover. The full capability is not expected to be operational before 1990.

This naval program is part of a general buildup of the Iranian armed forces whereby the Air Force will be increased by half and the Army by a third, accompanied by a general updating of equipment. This expansion reflects a growing concern for the long-term security of Iran, stemming from two separate sources: on the one hand Iran is faced with an assertive U.S.S.R., apparently more willing to take risks, while U.S. resolve and her reliability as an ally is becoming increasingly suspect; and on the other hand Iran is faced with a growing possibility of conflict within the sub-region, stemming from changes of regime in the Arab states or instabilities in Pakistan. Iran aims to become self-sufficient in respect of sub-regional conflicts, but will still need U.S. support in the event of major aggression by the U.S.S.R.

Assuming that the Navy and Air Force can assimilate their new equipment, Iran should be able to gain and maintain command of the sea in the Gulf if required, and deploy a strong maritime capability in its approaches. Given Iraq's disadvantageous position, it seems unlikely that the U.S.S.R. will seek to build up a counter-capability in the Gulf. However, Soviet naval units have had access to shore facilities at the Iraqi port of Umm Qasr, and it is possible that at some time in the future the U.S.S.R. might seek to maintain an inhibiting presence in the Gulf, although it would be extremely vulnerable. Meanwhile, the U.S. Navy is relinquishing its facility at Bahrein this year.

The Indian Sub-Continent
Moving on to the Indian subcontinent we come to the Pakistani, Sri Lankan and Indian Navies, the last being the largest force in the whole region. Sri Lanka, with over 700 miles of coastline has a small force comprising five Shanghai class gunboats and one Stenka torpedo boat (all supplied by China), plus one World War II frigate. Given the geography of Sri Lanka this force has a very limited capability, although anything armed with torpedoes should be able to sink an unarmed ship. Pakistan has a relatively large navy and the loss of Bangladesh has allowed her to concentrate this force in the Arabian Sea. However, the majority of her larger units are old, namely a Dido class cruiser and five World War II

destroyers/frigates. Besides these she has two Whitby class frigates, 12 Shanghai class gunboats and six motor torpedo boats; she also has three Breuget Atlantique LRMP aircraft and six ASW helicopters. By regional standards this is a substantial force, particularly in relation to Pakistan's 500 mile coastline. Unfortunately for Pakistan her opponent is the Indian Navy.

That force comprises an aircraft carrier, two World War II cruisers, seven World War II destroyers/frigates, 11 post-war British frigates (including four Leander class, with another two on order), 10 Soviet Petyas, eight Soviet F–class submarines and a depot ship, eight Osa missile units and seven landing craft. The ex-British light fleet aircraft carrier which was modernised in 1973–74 can embark 25 aircraft, including 18 Sea Hawk fighter-bombers, four Alizé fixed-wing ASW aircraft and two ASW helicopters. In total the naval air force comprises 25 Sea Hawks, six LRMP aircraft (three Super Constellation and three Il–38 May), 12 Alizé fixed-wing ASW aircraft, and 36 ASW helicopters. This is a relatively powerful force, backed by support facilities ashore and, like the Pakistan Navy, its operational experience as a contemporary ocean-going fleet reaches back to the inter-war years. There seems little doubt that the Navy is seen in India as a regional force, but while one can expect a continual upgrading of its capability, the final objective is not clear. Following the threatening deployment of a U.S. carrier strike force to the Bay of Bengal during the Bangladesh crisis in December 1971, there must have been those who urged the need to acquire the means of countering such a force; others may have argued that the task was best left to the Soviet Navy. If India does decide to develop an anti-carrier capability, one would expect her to follow the Soviet example of relying on cruise missiles launched from submarine and aircraft. It is possible that at this stage the Soviet Union would be willing to supply such systems, and it is perhaps relevant that India is the only country to have been provided with the F–class submarine and that the initial supply was from current production.

The Eastern Littoral
Turning next to the eastern rim of the Indian Ocean, we find a disparate group of countries, comprising Burma, Thailand, Indonesia and Australia. Burma has almost a thousand miles of indented and archipelagic coastline, but her Navy has a negligible capability. The four major units are all World War II vintage (one frigate, one ocean minesweeper and two patrol escorts), besides which there are two patrol craft and about 30 gunboats, with speeds of only

12–15 kts. Thailand to the south focuses her main attention on the South China Sea and is only marginally an Indian Ocean state, although she is now building a naval base on her west coast. Moving on to Indonesia, we see that most of the units which Russia supplied to Sukarno at the beginning of the 1960s have gone for scrap. The Navy now comprises three W–class submarines (two newly refitted), nine frigates (all nearing obsolescence), six ocean minesweepers, 25 patrol craft (of which 11 are obsolete), plus five motor torpedo boats and 12 Komar, whose missiles may no longer be serviceable; three new corvettes are on order. Indonesia also has nine landing craft and 11 coastal minesweepers. The air element comprises three helicopters and five flying boats. This force is a far cry from the Soviet-sponsored Navy which appeared to be emerging in the early 1960s, when Sukarno bragged of his nation's maritime tradition and changed the name of the Indian Ocean to the Indonesian Ocean. Given the sea area covered by this 3000 mile long archipelagic state, the force is small and not particularly well balanced.

Coming finally to Australia, we have another substantial force comprising an aircraft carrier, three Adams class guided missile destroyers carrying Ikara ASW missiles, three Daring class destroyers, six River class frigates fitted with Seacat SAM and Ikara ASW, and four Oberon class submarines. The carrier embarks a mixed load of attack and ASW aircraft from a total inventory of 16 A–4G Skyhawk, 19 S–2 Tracker fixed wing ASW aircraft, seven ASW Sea King helicopters and 19 Wessex utility helicopters and there are some 22 landbased LRMP aircraft, all of which will be P–3 Orion in due course. The R.A.N. also has a destroyer tender and a fleet replenishment ship, and 12 Attack class coastal patrol craft. Two Perry class patrol frigates and two more Oberon class submarines have been ordered and contracts are pending for a class of fifteen large patrol craft, a landing craft and a new fleet replenishment ship. This is a well balanced fleet with a true distant water capability, which can operate effectively in a hostile maritime environment on its own, or as a component of a larger force.

The Region as a Whole

If we now turn back to survey the Indian Ocean as a whole, we see a growing concentration of naval strength in the north-west quadrant of the region, and localised concentrations in South Africa and Australia. But the distances between them are immense and strategic interaction occurs only when they lie on the same axis of movement. For that reason, the Iranian Navy is establishing links with the South Africans, but Australia is virtually an external power.

The situation in the Arabian Sea is complex, with all the makings of a naval arms race, the outcome of which will depend as much on the aspirations of the main actors as on the level and nature of any threats. In the Red Sea and Persian Gulf a local capability to prevent the use of these waters is emerging. The situation in the area is further complicated by the presence of external powers. Soviet installations in Somalia are intended for long term use and are designed to support a more substantial capability than is deployed at present. The periodic deployments of a U.S. carrier task force brings even greater military power into the area, and the activation of the Diego Garcia facility will increase this capability. Besides the superpowers we also have the occasional deployment of small British and Netherlands forces, and the presence of French naval units.

The Arabian Sea is the nexus of many divergent interests: the West's concern for their energy supplies; the U.S.S.R.'s concern over China; Iran's concern to achieve military security and India's concern for her regional aspirations. The whole is overlaid by superpower competition for world influence in accordance with their perceptions of the global balance of forces. However, despite these divergences, there is no reason in principle why the interests of India, Iran and the West could not all be served through a common policy which concentrates on ensuring the flow of oil, with responsibility for securing the use of the sea being divided between the Iranian, Pakistani and Indian Navies. Unfortunately, this is unlikely to serve Soviet interests since, in the event of war with China, she may have to insist on moving military supplies across Iran or even Baluchistan for shipment by sea to her Far Eastern front.

The Asian-Pacific Region

The Pacific Basin is very different to the Indian Ocean, but it too can be usefully discussed in terms of major axes of movement and three main areas. The east-west axis of movement across the Pacific is made up of multiple shipping routes which link the two sides of the basin in trade and influence relationships. Japan is overwhelmingly dependent on the U.S. market and in 1974, 35 per cent of her trade was with North America,[5] with South America becoming increasingly important. The U.S.A. competes with Japan for the lion's share of trade with non-communist Asian countries and Australia.[6] This axis also provides the means for the U.S.A. to sustain her western defence perimeter based on the offshore chain of Asian islands, and to project U.S. military power in the Asian-Pacific region. The other major axis runs north-south for the length of the region, serving as the major means of intra-regional communication, and giving East Asia access to the Indian Ocean, via the Indonesian archipelago.

East Asia
The three main areas are East Asia, South-east Asia and Australasia. In East Asia, the territories of three of the world's most important powers come together, and a fourth power, the U.S.A., maintains substantial forces on the mainland in Korea. The area bristles with long-standing enmities and disputes, to which has now been added argument over sea-bed resources. Table 1 below gives some impression of the concentration of naval assets in this area, although it does *not* indicate relative capabilities since the crude type-categories are based on size, and do not distinguish between age, armament, propulsion and primary function; both nuclear and diesel powered units are included under 'submarines', and torpedo- and missile-armed units are included with 'coastal craft'. While all the six states located in the area have a primary concern to secure their maritime frontiers, the emphasis given by the Communist states to coastal units in this role is notable, particularly in comparison with the preference shown by the Western-oriented navies for ocean-going vessels. This difference is accentuated by

Table 1

East Asian Waters: Approximate Order of Battle

Country Type	North Korea	South Korea	Taiwan	Japan	China	Soviet Pac.Flt.	U.S. Pac.Flt.
Carrier	—	—	—	—	—	—	6
Submarine	13	—	2	15	80	75	35
Cruiser	—	—	—	—	—	6	15
Destroyer	—	7	18	30	8	27	28
Frigate	2	9	14	17	23	25	33
Coastal Craft	200	60	20	40	850	100	—
Mine Warfare	2	12	22	37	30	100	—

Sources:
1. Soviet and U.S. Pacific Fleets—Working paper prepared by Dr. F.J. West et al., Center for Advanced Research, U.S. Naval War College, April 1977.
2. Chinese Submarines—based on building rates.
3. Remainder—based on *Jane's Fighting Ships* and *The Military Balance*, IISS, London.

Japan's long-range air reconnaissance capability which is matched only by the U.S.S.R. and the U.S.A.

The Chinese submarine force clearly provides a capability to attack shipping at sea but it is probable that its primary role is still to prevent the use of the sea for the projection of military force against the homeland. In this respect it is interesting that China has supplied North Korea with 9 R–class submarines to help secure the Yellow Sea. The Japanese have a substantial ocean-going force but their island chain extends over 1500 miles and occasions numerous disputes about fishing rights, offshore resources and the ownership of islands. Her World War II experience left Japan sensitive to the dangers of maritime blockade and she is faced by a major submarine threat. Hence her navy is biased towards ASW, and has a general capability for effective operations within range of shore-based air cover. Japan is not at present seeking to develop the capability to project military force, and she relies on bilateral trade agreements, long-term contracts and joint ownership at the point of extraction to safeguard her sources of raw materials.

The concentration of maritime forces in this area goes back eighty years or more, with some changes in the naval cast. It is not dissimilar to the situation which now pertains in European waters and force levels are likely, if anything, to grow. There are obvious sources of conflict in the area, Taiwan and Korea being the most likely to involve maritime forces. This situation does not however mean that conflict is inevitable. The four-power involvement in the area and the fact that most of East Asia comprises great power territory imparts a certain political rigidity to the situation.

South-east Asia

Such rigidity is not in evidence in South-east Asia, which is made up of a large number of disparate and relatively weak states, whose governments have to balance external pressures while guarding against internal collapse. The diversity of language, race and religion has contributed to instability as different forms of government have striven to become established in the aftermath of colonialism and war. The political situation is inherently fluid, and great-power rivalry in the area is of a quasi-colonial, influence-building nature. In strategic terms, the area has two foci of interest: the South China Sea; and the international waterways through the archipelagic barrier which divides the Pacific and Indian Oceans.

The South China Sea provides strategic coherence to the area. It is four-fifths the size of the Mediterranean and there are certain resemblances between them: both are major waterways; the opposite coasts have different political complexions and there is a degree of instability among littoral states; in both areas the Soviets and the Americans have supported opposing sides in a local war; and a U.S. carrier force operates in each of the two seas. It is therefore all the more noticeable that, unlike in the Mediterranean, the U.S.S.R. did *not* seek to establish a naval presence in the South China Sea, despite the political importance of her seaborne supplies to North Vietnam at the time of the Soviet Navy's shift to forward deployment. The fact that she chose instead to establish a naval presence on the far side of the Indian Ocean, a much more difficult task with high political and economic costs, gives some indication of Soviet geostrategic priorities; it supports the hypothesis that the pattern of peacetime naval deployment is primarily determined by the Soviet Union's war-fighting requirements, with influence-building being seen as an ancillary activity.

The dominant maritime force in the South China Sea is the U.S. Navy and its bases in the Philippines are an important component of its strength. The loss of Subic Bay would greatly increase the costs of forward deployment, while restricting operational flexibility, and the loss of Clark Field would deprive the Seventh Fleet of important shore-based air support. The second most important force is the Chinese Navy. There seems little doubt that China will gradually extend her defence perimeter to take in a large part of the South China Sea, and as she does so, her (disputed) possession of the four deep-water island groups (particularly the distant Spratlies) will prove an asset, and the control of Taiwan (particularly its airfields) could become important. Except for her submarine force, China at present lacks a true distant water capability, but the naval forces of the other littoral states are relatively weak.

Starting with the five ASEAN countries, the Philippines has 10 World War II vintage ex–U.S. frigate-sized units, about 22 patrol craft and numerous inshore craft, plus about 30 landing craft. The balance of forces reflects the U.S. bias towards ocean-going units which we noted in the East Asian area, but given the spread of islands, this particular capability has its uses. Understandably, the Philippines has tended to rely on the protection of her defence treaty with the U.S.A., backed by a permanent U.S. naval presence. But even allowing the geographic advantages of relatively narrow (if not usually shallow) waters, her maritime forces have a somewhat limited capability to prevent the use of the sea within the archipelagic area.

Indonesia's maritime forces have already been described.

Malaysia, its eastern and western parts divided by sea which is strewn with small Indonesian-owned islands, has two frigates (one modern Yarrow type fitted with Seacat SAM, the other a World War II Loch class), eight missile craft (four carrying two Exocet SSM and four with eight SS–12), plus 24 patrol craft, six inshore minesweepers and two landing craft. Singapore has six missile-armed craft (five with Gabriel SSM) and six motor gunboats. The primary significance of these forces is their capability to prevent the use of narrow shallow waters in their vicinity, and this is discussed further below.

The fifth ASEAN country is Thailand whose main force comprises three World War II vintage frigates and three modern ones; one Yarrow type carrying Seacat SAM and Limbo, and two ex–U.S. patrol frigates. The Thai Navy also has three missile units (five Gabriel with SSM), 13 patrol craft and 26 motor gunboats, plus 14 landing craft and 18 minewarfare vessels. These are backed by a squadron of 10 S–2F Tracker ASW aircraft. Like the Philippines, Thailand tended to rely on the U.S. military presence but is now beginning to bestir herself. The Gulf of Siam is something of a backwater, but the Thais recall that in 1941 the Japanese came by sea, and know that the shallow waters of the Gulf are vulnerable to mining.

Of the two remaining non-ASEAN countries, the Khmer Republic has only some 25 small coastal craft, but these were the forces which took over the *Mayaguez*. Newly united Vietnam has two ex–U.S. frigates, about 45 patrol craft, four missile-armed Komar, 12 motor torpedo boats and 30 coastal patrol boats, plus 13 landing ships and 40 odd landing craft. Given the length of the Vietnamese coastline, this force is insubstantial but they are backed by a relatively powerful air force, which in most circumstances should be able to ensure air superiority for a hundred or more miles out to sea, and which can also be used in the anti-shipping strike role. Past practice led one to expect that the Soviet Union would build up Vietnam's naval forces, but this does not appear to have happened as yet.

Looking at the South China Sea as a whole we see that the eight littoral states have a localised naval capability and only the U.S. Navy, with the air cover provided by its carrier forces, has the capability to operate throughout the area within range of shorebased opposition, and to project military force ashore in the form of air strikes or amphibious assaults. The Chinese submarine force could, however, mount an effective anti-shipping campaign throughout the area. The geography of the area and the widespread availability of amphibious vessels facilitates the limited projection of force by neighbouring states, in support of the many disputed territorial claims.

Shifting focus southwards, we have the Indonesian archipelagic barrier, stretching from Malaysia to Australia, with the Philippines directly to the north. The five major passages through this inter-oceanic barrier are (west to east): Malacca, between Malaya and Indonesia, with a governing depth of 23m. and a minimum width of 8 n.m.; Sunda (Indonesian, about 37m. and 12 n.m.), Lombok (Indonesian, over 180m. and 11 n.m.), Ombai-Wetar (Indonesian, over 180m. and 12 n.m.) and Torres (Australia/Papua New Guinea, 12 m. and 10 n.m.). The Malacca Straits suffer from traffic congestion and the governing depth means that laden tankers over 250,000 tons have to use Sunda; neither strait is suitable for submerged transit by large submarines.

The strategic significance of these waters stems from the comparative ease with which they can be physically obstructed and the legal arguments currently raised about the status of archipelagic seas and rights of free passage. Lombok and Ombai-Wetar have deep water approaches, but involve a 700–1000 n.m. passage through relatively constricted archipelagic waters, where ships are vulnerable to submarine attack. The other three straits involve a 200–300 n.m. passage in less than 45 m. of water and are particularly vulnerable to mining. All are vulnerable to shore-based systems and missile-armed craft. As we have seen, local forces in the area can already deploy a total of three submarines, five motor torpedo boats, and 22 units armed with Gabriel or Styx SSM plus another five carrying the SS–12 anti-tank system. This is in addition to 13 frigates armed with 75–100 m.m. guns and about 30 gun-armed patrol craft. There are also fighter-bombers to be contended with, and Indonesia is reputed to have a relatively large stock of mines supplied by the Soviets.

Australasia

The third area of the region comprises New Zealand, Australia, Papua New Guinea and the slew of islands lying to the north and east. Australian maritime forces have already been described and the New Zealand Navy is the only other of any serious account. It consists of four post-war frigates (two Leander, two Rothesay), and four coastal patrol craft; these are backed by five P3–B Orion LRMP aircraft. Papua New Guinea has five ex-Australian Attack class patrol boats. The Australasian area has two kinds of strategic significance. First, it can provide access to the Asian mainland at the maximum distance from the home-territories of the Asian-Pacific powers; this was its strategic utility in the Second World War. And second, it lies on the great circle route between the U.S. west coast and the Tasman Sea; to be more precise, the shortest route between Washington State and Bass Strait passes between the Fiji Islands and New Caledonia, and not far from either. The U.S. Trident class SSBN are to be based at Bangor, Washington, and Congressional testimony justifying this choice implied that the Indian Ocean would be an SSBN operating zone.[7] It is therefore likely that the Soviet Union would perceive this as an area where it would be extremely useful to develop some kind of submarine surveillance capability.

The fact that Australia was first discussed as a littoral state of the Indian Ocean, that it is now seen to be the key country of the Australasian area, and that it also forms the southern wall of the archipelagic barrier separating the Pacific and Indian Oceans, highlights the difficulties of formulating a defence posture which is within the economic capabilities of the country. This continental island has a periphery of some 6,500 miles. Its industry and population are concentrated in the south-eastern sector, facing the South Pacific, yet half the country's trade crosses the Indian Ocean. To the north lies whatever threat there is of physical encroachment, into a sparsley settled territory which is mainly unappealing to Australians of European descent. Western Australia is so distant from the south-eastern concentration that it is almost a separate country. But enormous mineral resources have been discovered in the inhospitable north-western part of that State, and these are exploited and shipped by Japan. Given such circumstances, it is not surprising that in the past, Australia has tended to place her main faith in defensive alliances.

The Region as a Whole
If we now turn back to survey the Asian–Pacific region as a whole, we see that the Western-oriented states form a loose alliance structure which is well placed strategically along what could be called an island defence perimeter. The U.S. maritime forces provide the mainstay of this capability, but it is anchored in the north by a sizable and modern Japanese force, with base facilities strung along a 1,500 mile island chain. In the south there is a smaller but reasonably well balanced Australian-New Zealand force, which has a true distant water capability, either on its own or as a component of a larger force. Airfields along the main north-south axis of movement allow the provision of shore-based air

support throughout most of the region. In East Asian waters (the northern part of the region), there is a sizable concentration of maritime force and the situation is not unlike that obtaining in European waters, with all that that implies in terms of preventing and securing the use of the sea. In South-east Asia, maritime forces are relatively sparse, but they do have the capability to prevent the passage of merchant ships through the archipelagic waterways linking the Pacific and Indian Oceans. And, in the narrower, shallower straits, these forces could offer serious opposition to naval forces seeking to secure such use. China has the capability to wage commerce war in the South China Sea, but shipping routes could be diverted well to the east of the Philippines. The U.S. Navy has the capability to operate throughout the area, but would find it costly to secure the use of the sea in shallow, narrow waters. Although the Soviet Pacific Fleet is not all that much smaller than the American force, their activity is mainly concentrated in the northern and oceanic parts of the region, and in support of the Indian Ocean deployment. Apart from the latter, little has been seen of them in the South China and Philippine Seas.

Compared to the Indian Ocean, the pattern of maritime forces in the Asian-Pacific region is notable for its relatively coherent strategic structure. While the region lends itself to being treated as a whole, the tidy result largely reflects U.S. defence requirements, and her earlier emphasis on physical containment and the need to establish a firm defence perimeter off the Asian mainland. American advice and military aid played an important role in the shape and composition of her allies' forces, as indeed did Soviet opinion and arms supply in the early stages of the Chinese and North Korean navies. In contrast, the impulse behind the different navies in the Indian Ocean has been varied, and their size and composition more closely reflect the perceived requirements of the states concerned, rather than an external power's idea of what was needed.

Assessment

We can now make some assessment of the implications of the proliferation of maritime weapon systems in the Indo-Pacific region, using the framework established in the earlier parts of this chapter. For convenience, the effects of proliferation at the contiguous and regional levels of capability will be considered first, the world-wide level being treated separately.

In reviewing general trends, we noted that modern weapon systems made it easier to prevent the use of the sea. But the existence of a generalised capability is one thing and its effective application another, and in this context, maritime geography plays a crucial role in determining a coastal state's ability to prevent the use of its waters. It requires an experienced submarine commander to bring a diesel boat within torpedo range of a target in open waters. And while target range is not so great a problem to missile-armed patrol craft, they are very exposed to counter attack when away from the cover of land, and the state of the sea affects their operational performance. Mines are a cheap and simple way of preventing use, but they can be laid only in relatively shallow depths, and are effective only if they cannot be circumvented or swept, factors which depend largely on the breadth of the waters.

We have the example of the build up and decline of Indonesia's Navy, and the limited effectiveness of the Egyptian force, both nations with a sea-faring tradition. The rapid deterioration of the Indonesian Navy was mainly a failure of maintenance, the lack of spare parts being a subsequent cause, and this underlines the problems of keeping complex equipment operational, particularly in hot and humid climates. When this is coupled with such evidence as the apparent superiority of Israeli pilots over their Egyptian opponents, one begins to ask whether a country requires some minimal technological base in order to make effective use of the latest weapons. On the other hand, North Vietnamese air defence units inflicted heavy casualties on the latest American aircraft, which suggests that perhaps it is as much a matter of priorities and commitment, as of innate capability. Meanwhile, the trend in weapon design appears to be towards increasing internal sophisti-cation, matched by a greater simplicity in operation and main-tenance, and this may come to compensate for the technological constraints.

Turning now to specific uses of the sea, we start with the exploitation of marine resources. The introduction of the exclusive economic zone not only gives the coastal state a mix of exclusive and preferential rights to such resources, but obligates it to manage them and regulate their exploitation. This requires the use of maritime units in a constabulary role, as an extension of domestic jurisdiction. To the extent that maritime weapon systems contribute to the effective discharge of these responsibilities, they are to be welcomed.

Next, we have the navigational use of the sea; first, the conveyance of goods and people. The capability to hamper or prevent the passage of merchant ships is now fairly widespread, both on the ocean waterways and in narrow, shallow waters. But how likely is such action, outside the circumstances of war? The diffuse nature of seaborne trade provides a strong measure of self-protection, since most nations have an interest in the principle of safe passage for merchant ships in peacetime. Moreover, as the number of national merchant fleets grows, so too does the extent to which all ships are in hostage to each other. Meanwhile, straits states which have the greatest capacity to prevent use also have the greatest interest in the continuous flow of trade and shipping through their waters, and their economies would be damaged by a prolonged diversion.

It is, of course, possible that littoral states might wish to use their monopoly power to extract rent from a geographical asset, and might threaten various restrictions if their demands were not met. But so far their position in this regard has been moderate, reflecting reasonable concerns for the dangers inherent in the passage of very large crude oil carriers and comparable ships through narrow waters, and the devastation a major spillage could cause to their shores. In this they can expect a fair amount of international support; but there would be little backing for a general toll on all types of cargo, because most countries now have a vested interest in lower shipping costs. An unprovoked attempt to hold the international community to ransom by preventing use of such waterways would be bound to leave the littoral states worse off than they started, and undoubtedly they appreciate this. We should also bear in mind that maritime weapon systems can be used to secure use, as well as to prevent it. The emergence of regional forces belonging to states with a vested interest in the unhindered passage of shipping, is another factor which militates against the disruption of international trade.

The shipment of military supplies is a different matter. So far, the convention has been observed that attacks on the lines of supply are limited to the territory and coastal waters of the primary belligerents or client states. With the growing number of states possessing submarines, it is not certain that this convention will hold. The U.S.A. went close to breaching it during the Cuban missile crisis, but this could be justified on the grounds that Cuba was within the American national security zone. But the same justification can be claimed by China in its adjacent sea areas, and it now has a force of some 80 submarines. While the mid-ocean interdiction of military supply lines remains unlikely, the probability is increasing that they will be liable to attack or other forms of interference as they near the terminal areas. It is also possible, although much less likely, that attempts will be made to prevent the passage of such supplies through international straits, on the grounds of group solidarity. We have seen the use of the oil weapon to bring pressure on Western nations during the Arab–Israeli war of 1973, which had tactical as well as strategic consequences. Denial of passage through strategic waterways could be used in the same way. Whether it would be is another matter. Turning off the oil did no damage to the supplying countries; rather the reverse. But a littoral state which sought to prevent the passage of a superpower's military supplies, would have to allow that its territory might be attacked. While it is true that when international passions are aroused, reactions tend to be unpredictable, that would still be a heavy price to pay in support of a distant state and the diffuse aims of a loose ideological bloc.

Moving on to the second category of navigational use, we see that with the emergence of regional navies the capability to project traditional force has spread. This is, however, still limited, and there is no capability for long range coercive intervention at the regional level. Meanwhile, the capability to prevent the use of the sea for the projection of force has also spread, and depends on shorebased systems as well as naval forces. In terminal areas this new capability is mainly restricted to narrow shallow waters, while open coastlines remain uncomfortably exposed. But military force has to reach the terminal areas and can be interdicted en route. There is little new capability to attack ocean waterways, but passage through shallow waters is vulnerable. However, for the reasons given above it would not be in the interests of the straits states to deny passage to military forces transiting their waters, since the likelihood of retribution would be even higher in such circumstances. Nevertheless, the use of passive systems such as mines cannot be excluded, since responsibility could be disclaimed.

We can now focus on three international waterways in the region where it would be relatively easy to prevent use, and consider the implications of such measures. The Straits of Bab el Mandeb control the entrance to the Red Sea. For the greater part of international shipping this passage is significant only as the gateway to the Suez Canal, which is itself far more vulnerable to closure. Meanwhile, world trade has shown in the past that it can make do without this route.

Second, we have the waters of the Persian Gulf, including the Straits of Hormuz; not only are these waters vulnerable to mining, but this is a terminal area and cannot be circumvented. However, one of the main reasons why Iran is building up her maritime forces is to give her the capability to *secure* the use of the sea for the shipment of oil, on which her economy depends, as do the economies of other states in the area. It is true that these same forces could prevent the use of the Persian Gulf by tankers, but if the objective is to prevent the flow of oil, then that is more easily done at source than at sea. Oil supplies will always be liable to interruption from a range of causes, but the emergence of regional naval powers in the Persian Gulf–Arabian Sea area would seem to reduce the vulnerability of the maritime-passage link in the chain of supply.

Lastly, we have the straits through the Indonesian Archipelago. These are the most international of all these waterways, consequently the general constraints against impeding passage are at their strongest. There are other factors. First, Singapore depends heavily on the entrepot trade and servicing of ships which use the Sunda and Malacca Straits, and would be reluctant to support a closure. Second, the five main straits span some 1200 miles and Indonesia would be hard put to maintain an effective preventive capability in each. Third, and perhaps most important, it is possible to bypass this potential barrier by rounding Australia or going west-about through Panama. If we take Japan as the destination for goods and people, this would increase the length of passage by 30 per cent–80 per cent, depending on the port of origin (See Table 2).[8] Port terminal expenses are fixed, so direct costs will perhaps rise about 25 per cent–75 per cent, and if we take 15 per cent as a rough but fairly generous average of the direct share of shipping in total import costs, we are talking of an increase of 4 per cent–11 per cent in the cost of about 40 per cent of Japanese imports. Even if we double the price of shipping to allow for the rise in demand, the effect would only be equivalent to something like an 8 per cent shift in the terms of trade, and foreign trade is only 10 per cent of Japanese GNP. If the diversion of traffic was from Malacca to Lombok Straits, 1,000 miles to the south-east, this would add only about 0.5 per cent to the price of oil shipped by 200,000 ton tanker

Table 2
Relative Distances to Yokohama

From Via	Persian Gulf	Capetown	Mombassa	Calcutta	N.W. Cape (Aust.)	Rotterdam	Black Sea
Malacca	100	102	100	100	—	100	100
Sunda	109	100	104	118	—	—	—
Lombok	118	104	112	127	100	—	—
Ombai	123	106	116	132	—	—	—
Bass	180	130	132	222	175	—	—
Panama	—	—	—	—	—	111	147
CapeGH	—	—	—	—	—	—	164

(June 1975 prices). These figures are necessarily crude, but they give some idea of the costs involved in bypassing the Indonesian archipelago, and suggest that they are no greater than those caused by normal fluctuations in the price of raw materials. The overall economic effect is even harder to forecast. In times of shipping glut and world recession, an increase in the demand for shipping which reached back into the shipyards could be positively beneficial.

For the projection of U.S. military force from the Pacific into the Indian Ocean, the diversion round Australia would add over 3,000 miles to the passage from Guam to Diego Garcia, increasing the transit time for ballistic missile submarines by some 8–10 days. This loss of time-on-task could be absorbed in various ways such as increasing the length of individual deployments, reducing the time in rest and maintenance between them, and changing crews in the operating area; alternatively, the pool of submarines could be increased by 20 per cent or a new forward base could be established closer to the patrol areas. For reactive deployments, the penalty would be much more severe. From the U.S. base at Subic Bay in the Philippines, the diversion would more than double the distance, and a carrier force would be 12–14 days on passage to the central Indian Ocean. The closure of the Indonesian straits would be even more serious for the U.S.S.R., in the event of war with China. Supply of the Far Eastern Front is a time-critical operation, where the initial shipments must arrive before the stockpiles run out. Diversion round Australia could increase transit time by as much as 80 per cent.

As we seek to reach some conclusions concerning the proliferation of maritime weapon systems at the contiguous and regional levels, it may help to clarify the central issues if we consider the nature of a country's interest in the use of the sea. These are of two kinds: *purposive* interests, when a country is concerned to use the sea for its own purposes; and *preventive* interests, when the concern is to prevent the sea being used to one's disadvantage. In very general terms, we can say that in peacetime, most countries have a purposive interest in the use of the sea for conveying goods and people, and a preventive interest in its use for the projection of military force against their own territory. A very few countries also have a *purposive* interest in its use for the projection of force against other states.

On this basis, we may conclude that on balance, the proliferation of maritime weapon systems at these levels is generally beneficial in terms of using the sea. The exploitation of the sea's resources and its use for the conveyance of goods and people should be rendered more secure by the improved military capability of the coastal states. They now have some capacity to regulate their offshore resources, to secure the passage of ships through their waters, and to raise the cost of coercive intervention by nonadjacent powers.

It is true that these same weapons give certain states the capability to hamper the flow of shipping. There are, however, only a very few situations when it would be in their interest to do so, and the structure of international trade imposes powerful constraints on such adventures short of war. But in the unlikely event that the use of such waterways were prevented, in most cases it is possible to accept diversion at relatively little cost. The Persian Gulf is a crucial exception, but here we see the emergence of a regional maritime force which already has some capacity to secure the use of the sea against limited opposition and has a strong interest in doing so.

There remains the question of whether the proliferation of maritime weapon systems will increase the likelihood of conflict in the region. At the contiguous level of capability, the effect of maritime systems as a cause of conflict between neighbouring states is likely to be marginal compared to the proliferation of land-based systems used in territorial warfare. Similar arguments apply at the regional level, since the capability to project coercive force in nonadjacent areas is still extremely limited, the ability to project supportive force would seem to be beneficial. Of course, this begs the question of whether there is any causal relationship between force levels and neighbourly conflict. However, the existence of secure frontiers is generally considered to reduce the likelihood of conflict, and there is no reason why this should not apply to maritime as well as land frontiers.

On balance therefore, it would appear that the proliferation of maritime weapon systems at the contiguous and regional levels serves the interests of international peace, stability and equity, as well as the interests of the countries directly concerned.

This cannot be said of proliferation at the world-wide level. The use of the sea to project deterrent force evokes counter-deployments, introducing superpower competition into distant sea areas and increasing the level of interaction. The Trident submarine and missile system will double the range of the Polaris–Poseidon systems, hence (to quote a 1974 article by Admiral Gorshkov), 'the front of operations will be expanded accordingly ... [and] the corresponding growth in the spatial dimension of operations against naval strategic nuclear weapon systems is also quite clear'. Many types of weapon and sensor systems will join in 'the battle against strategic nuclear weapon platforms including those from other branches of services'.⁹ The deployment of such systems outside the protection of home waters generates its own form of weapons proliferation. The introduction of the Tomahawk submarine launched cruise missile (SLCM) is likely to evoke a further response. Meanwhile, the presence of these maritime forces in distant areas provides the opportunity for the political exploitation of their presence, and increases the possibility of superpower confrontation in support of client states or factions.

Finally, if we look at the significance of these developments in terms of Western policy, it may appear that the increased reach of coastal states and the spread in the capability to prevent the use of narrow shallow waters must work against the West's maritime interests. I, however, would argue the opposite to be the case. The emergence of regional forces is to be welcomed, since their interest in the free passage of shipping in peacetime is matched by a legitimacy in employing force to secure such use, which external powers must lack.

Meanwhile, the coastal state's improved capability does not prevent the West's use of the sea to project traditional military force. What it does, is to raise the possible costs of projecting such force in certain circumstances. This development should encourage Western leaders to be more selective in their choice of this instrument of policy, whose casual use can produce the opposite effects to those desired. For example, it was the deployment of the USS *Enterprise* to the Bay of Bengal during the Bangladesh crisis of 1971 which prompted India's acceptance of a permanent Soviet naval presence in the area, as the only means of countering the threat posed by U.S. carrier strike forces. The utility of coercive force beyond a country's national security zone is increasingly in doubt, and it is relevant that the American naval presence has a 'legitimacy' in the Asian-Pacific region which it appears to lack in the Indian Ocean.

We may therefore conclude that the proliferation of maritime weapon systems at the contiguous and regional levels of capability is to be welcomed. The implicit assumption that such proliferation must threaten the peaceful use of the sea reflects ethnocentric attitudes, stemming from centuries of Western maritime domination, most of which were not at all peaceful! Proliferation at the world-wide level is not beneficial in world terms and, where strategic delivery systems are concerned, is of questionable utility in Western terms. It is arguable that the theoretical benefits of Western

initiatives in this field are, in the long run, outweighed by the costs
to the West of the inevitable Soviet response.

Footnotes

1. As long ago as 1972, the Soviet Union claimed that 'naval groupings'
   were targeted by the Strategic Rocket Forces (A.A. Grechko, 'A
   Socialist, Multinational Army', *Krasnaya Zvezda*, 17 December 1972).
   The SS–N–X tactical SLBM is reported to have a range of more than
   300 n.m. and is equipped with mid-course guidance, can vary its initial
   aiming point by up to 30 miles, and has terminal homing. This missile
   began testing in 1969 and was expected to be deployed in 1975,
   although this did not eventuate. There are no technical reasons why
   a similar guidance system should not be fitted to longer range missiles.
   See K.J. Moore 'Developments in Submarine Systems' in *Soviet Naval
   Influence: domestic and foreign dimensions*, M. MccGwire and J.
   McDonnell (Eds), Praeger, New York, 1977, pp. 172–73, also Dr.
   Currie's testimony in Senate Armed Forces Committee, *Appropriations Hearings, FY 1976*, p. 2816. It is now widely accepted that U.S.
   carrier strike groups are targeted by land-based ballistic missiles when
   within strike range of the Soviet Union.
2. *Statistical Review of the World Oil Industry*, British Petroleum,
   London.
3. B. Crozier, *The Soviet Presence in Somalia,* Institute for Conflict
   Studies, London, February 1975; *Defence Space Business News,* 13
   November 1975; E.B. Atkeson, 'Hemispheric Denial', *Strategic Review,* Washington D.C. Spring 1976, p.33; Seminar on the Indian
   Ocean, University of California at Berkeley, 19-21 May 1976.
4. Shahram Chubin, *Iran's Security in the 1980's*, a paper presented at
   the International Studies Association meeting at St. Louis, U.S.A. in
   March 1977.
5. J. Simons, 'Japan's "Ostpolitik" and the Soviet Union', *The World
   Today*, April 1974.
6. T.B. Millar, Unpublished paper given at seminar on the Indian Ocean
   at the University of California, Berkeley, 19–21 May 1976.
7. In justifying this basing (in preference to East Coast), a Department
   of Defense official made specific reference to the advantages of
   conducting patrols in the Indian Ocean from the U.S. west coast. U.S.
   Congress, Senate Armed Services Committee, *Appropriations Hearings FY 1974*, p.728.
8. The data in this section is extracted from my article 'The Geopolitical
   Importance of Strategic Waterways in the Asian-Pacific Region' in
   Orbis, Vol. 19, No. 3, Fall 1975, pp. 1069–70.
9. S. Gorshkov, 'The Development of the Art of Naval Warfare', *United
   States Naval Institute Proceedings*, June 1975, pp. 56, 59, 60,
   translated and reprinted from *Morskoj sbornik*, December 1974.

4
The Proliferation of New Land-Based Technologies: Implications for Local Military Balances
Steven J. Rosen

Will the proliferation of new land-based weapons systems, including tactical ground weaponry, land-based air power, sophisticated early warning and target acquisition systems, and surface-to-air and surface-to-surface artillery and missiles, significantly affect the political stability of recipient countries and their regions? The global arms traffic now consists of larger quantities of equipment moving to smaller powers at an accelerated rate, as well as technologically more advanced weapons being introduced to Third World countries and other states outside the compass of the great powers earlier in their production and deployment life cycles. The purpose of this chapter is to review briefly some implications of the proliferation of land-based systems for regional politico-strategic relations.

The Centre and the Periphery
The global arms production and distribution network can be characterized as a flow system having a centre and a periphery, with the United States, the Soviet Union, and the major European arms producers (the centre) accounting for over 90 per cent of production and distribution[1] and the 110 states of the periphery depending primarily on imports from the metropolitan powers for the greater part of their essential military requirements.[2] Moreover, the driving forces of military research and development are the perceived strategic, economic, political, and bureaucratic imperatives of the countries of the centre, rather than the periphery. New technologies are developed primarily to affect the European military balance and the global strategic balance between the superpowers. The subsequent introduction of these technologies into the peripheral regions is often an incidental byproduct or a mere spillover effect of the Eurocentric system. In short, the global system is characterised by patterns of structural *strategic* dependency not

unlike the relationships of structural *economic* dependency that
have been described by students of world trade and capital flows.

The fact that research, development, production, and distribution
are dominated by the Europeans and the superpowers and that the
spillover effects to the Third World countries are secondary and
often uncoordinated and unanticipated is in one sense quite
irrational for the contemporary world. There have been over fifty
substantial wars in the peripheral countries since 1945, depending
on how one counts, but not a single instance of large-scale fighting
in Europe or between the superpowers since the end of the World
War. Today, the stability of the European balance is reinforced
by redundant levels of deterrence and military equilibrium, including substantial inventories of conventional arms making it unlikely
that an aggressor could achieve a theatrewide superiority or even
sustain a local breakthrough; backed up by thousands of tactical
nuclear weapons acting both to strengthen the correlation of forces
in the central theatres and to provide a signalling device linking
the conventional deterrent to the strategic nuclear deterrent; and
finally the panoply of strategic atomic weapons themselves including
submarine-launched ballistic missiles, land-based ICBMs, long-
range strategic bombers, and the new strategic cruise missiles.
Central war in the European theatre or between the superpowers
is highly unlikely in the foreseeable future. On the other hand,
further rounds of active fighting in the peripheral areas are only
too easy to predict, including the ongoing insurgency in Eritrea;
potential Somali irredentist actions in the Ogaden district of
Ethiopia, the Northern Frontier district of Kenya, and possibly
Djibouti; eruption of large-scale fighting in Rhodesia–Zimbabwe;
the increasing possibility of renewed conflict in Korea; the struggle
between Morocco, Mauritania, Algeria, and the Polisario in the
former Spanish Sahara; the recrudescence of the Arab–Israeli
conflict; possible Guatemalan actions against Belize; instability on
the South Asian subcontinent; conflict between Thailand and the
new Communist powers of Indo-China; and many other cases. A
survey of world conflicts conducted in 1969 identified no fewer than
160 significant disputes having some potential to erupt into large-
scale violence within fifteen years—and of these, the vast majority
were in the peripheral areas.

We have, then, technologies developed primarily in response to
perceived European needs with only incidental attention to the
implications for the Third World, but technologies whose most
direct and important effects are likely to be seen in these peripheral
countries rather than the centre. What are the consequences of this

Asymmetrical Proliferation and Regional Stability

First, as I have already argued, the periphery should not be viewed as a world of settled political relations and recognised borders, but rather as a collection of simmering conflicts and potential wars involving separatist and irredentist territorial claims, competition over geopolitical assets and natural resource deposits, internal challenges to incumbent regimes, and other disputes. In many areas, such peace as exists has been achieved not because the regional actors have become reconciled to the existing political relations or regard them as equitable or optimal, but rather the equilibrium that has been achieved depends on delicate balances of power that dissuade challenges to the status quo. In situations where stability is fragile, large-scale changes in relative military capabilities or perceived capabilities may tempt those dissatisfied with the existing situation to resort to a trial of strength.

The redundancies of the European balance make it unlikely that marginal additions of new technologies or augmented quantities of combat equipment can upset the basic balance of power there within short periods. But in many peripheral areas, existing inventories of tanks, artillery, advanced combat aircraft, missiles, and other hardware are small, and relatively minor shipments of equipment can produce rapid and decisive changes in the local correlation of forces. Two recent examples are the Soviet shipments to the MPLA in Angola, which are credited with the decisive victory of that faction in the civil war, and the bolstering of the Dergue regime in Ethiopia. Similarly, the reliance of many peripheral states on technologically obsolescent equipment means that the local balance of power can be affected rapidly by the sudden introduction of an off-the-shelf system closer to the frontier of technological possibility, such as a superior anti-tank system to neutralise a neighbour's preponderance in armour or the provision of night vision equipment to one side only. Thus, local balances in the periphery are more sensitive to fluctuations in the arms trade than are the central balances in Europe and between the superpowers. The uncontrolled traffic in arms has the potential to unhinge the delicate deterrence relationships on which the stability of political arrangements in many regions depends.

Moreover, there are gross asymmetries in the capacities of various neighbouring states in peripheral areas to acquire, deploy, and effectively use various systems. The ability to acquire weapons may be affected by a state's balance of payments position; by the degree of support it enjoys from great power allies or petrodollar-endowed sponsors; by its geopolitical position in relation to the perceived interests of potential suppliers; by the indigenous technological base limiting a state's ability to absorb arms; by the level of inventories available in the supplier states with whom the consumer is politically associated; by the degrees of restriction placed on arms exports by the principal supplier state; by the lead times required to obtain a given system from a certain source; and by other factors. Neighbouring states may be favoured quite unequally by these factors. A thorough analysis of the contemporary flow of arms from the centre to the periphery would show many cases of asymmetry in the quantities of equipment going to each side in various regional conflicts, altering the respective balances of forces.

One of the types of asymmetry that deserves special note is the subclass of regional balances in which one side is supplied by the United States or the West Europeans and the other side is supplied by the Soviet Union. In most of these cases, it is becoming painfully apparent, the Soviet Union has demonstrated a capability to deliver larger quantities of tanks, armoured personnel carriers, and artillery pieces out of existing inventories on schedules that could not be achieved by the Western countries even if they had the will to do so. For example, Libya, Syria, Egypt, and Iraq, four secondary allies of the Soviet Union, have received almost 5,000 tanks from the U.S.S.R. since 1970, a number half as large as the total NATO armoured forces in the central European theatre. United States armour production during this period for all purposes, domestic and foreign, major allies and minor, was less than 3,000. The Soviet export advantage is rooted in the higher levels of output of general purpose land forces produced by Soviet military industries in recent years. According to former United States Secretary of Defense Rumsfeld's final report to Congress, the following were the average annual production rates of selected general purpose forces from 1972–1976:[3]

Average Annual Output 1972–76[4]

	Tanks	*APCs*	*Artillery*	*Tactical Fighters, Bombers and Interceptors*
USSR	2770	4990	1310	1090
USA	469	1556	162	573

It might be objected that this comparison excludes the production of America's European allies, several of whom are major suppliers. But a comparison of NATO aggregates with those of the Warsaw Pact yields substantially similar results. The following figures are from a statement by Congressman Les Aspin, a leading critic of military spending in the U.S. House of Representatives:[5]

Average Annual Output 1972–75

	Tanks	*APCs*	*Artillery*	*Tactical Fighters, Bombers and Interceptors*
Warsaw Pact	2800	4350	1400	938
NATO	983	1678	330	821

It may even be argued that the primary relationship between the Soviet Union and the Third World is one of arms supply. The U.S.S.R. is not a major non-military trading partner of the developing countries—the entire Eastern block typically absorbs less than 5 per cent of LDC exports and provides just over 5 per cent of their civilian imports.[6] Nor is the Communist superpower a major source of economic aid (it accounted in 1975 for only 10 per cent of agreements and 3 per cent of aid actually delivered)[7] or cultural influence (most Third World elites and media being oriented to Western languages, educational influences, films and publications). This means that the Soviet Union's one major concrete form of influence in the Third World is its ability to deliver arms in quantity and when they are needed, particularly to states and insurgencies whose purpose in acquiring arms is to challenge the existing political status quo. In material terms, the Soviet Union's status as the world's largest conventional arms producer gives her a unique role as a supplier and an identifiable interest in the maintenance of tense conditions in regional conflicts. It also means that in quantitative terms, friends of the Soviet Union will tend to enjoy some significant advantages over neighbours who tie their interests to the West. For example, Somalia received from the Soviet Union some 250 tanks and 310 armoured personnel carriers by the end of 1976; neighbouring Kenya with four times the population and eight times the GNP had no tanks and 13 armoured cars and Ethiopia with nine times the population and eight times the GNP had 62 tanks and 50 APCs before Soviet supplies started rolling in this year. It should also be noted that, should war erupt in the Horn of Africa, the most likely battlefields (Ogaden, Djibouti and the Northern Frontier District of Kenya) are soft-surfaced open areas where tracked vehicles will be important. Peru, during its long years of association with the U.S., accumulated 60 M–4 medium tanks. In the few years it has been associated with the Soviet Union, it has received an estimated 200 T–55s, while neighbouring Ecuador has 40 American and 41 French light tanks. Island Cuba has over 600 tanks. Angola has more tanks (over 200) than South Africa (160). Even the

Israelis have received from the Russians in the form of captured equipment half as many usable tanks as they have got from the United States—615 compared to 1250.[8]

On the other hand, Western equipments continue to outperform many Soviet items on a unit comparison basis, and in most categories of hardware the technologically superior Western supplies are preferred by many Third World consumers. It is true that Soviet research and development expenditures now exceed those of the United States by margins of 25 to 50 per cent, and that, if these trends continue indefinitely, the U.S.S.R. could eventually compound its preponderance in quantities with superior quality as well.[9] But the present Western advantage in computers and microelectronics, in radars and sensors, and in precision guidance technologies would take some years to overcome even if Western research and development efforts stopped altogether or failed to respond to the stepped-up pace of Soviet investments. Assuming that the West retains its qualitative lead, the theoretical possibility exists that in areas where the Soviet Union provides larger quantities of weapons to one side the West could react to restore the military balance by providing offsetting technologically superior equipment to the other side. Whether such a rational system of counterbalances can be sustained and whether quality can always offset quantity are of course arguable, but it is clear that without such compensatory actions the system of regional deterrents is in peril. There will even be some states (Libya, Iraq, and Kuwait providing current examples) who will have the best of both worlds by shopping 'brawn' in the East and 'brains' in the West.

Of course, it is possible to take the view that the sensitivity of regional balances to the introduction of greater quantities of arms will be reduced over time as local inventories accumulate and further increments have a smaller percentage effect on the correlation of forces. Such a condition of relative immunity to numbers has probably already been achieved in the Arab–Israeli case, where the stocks on hand are so large as to reduce the significance of additional acquisitions. For example, the 4,600 tanks fielded by the Arab armies against Israel in 1973 represented a number two thirds as large as the entire peacetime inventory of NATO in the vast northern and central European theatre (7,000) and the 1,225 combat aircraft of the Arab confrontation states was again nearly two thirds of the 2,050 combat aircraft in north-central NATO. It seems unlikely that additional numbers of tanks or aircraft would fundamentally alter the balance in this region unless the new equipments also had performance capabilities significantly greater than the old ones. Similarly, there may be a self-correcting element in the qualitative-technological side of the arms trade. As the inventories of the peripheral states are improved to incorporate new technologies and advance closer to the existing state of the art in military equipment and aircraft, the possibility that a regional balance will be disturbed by the sudden introduction of a technologically new system will be to that degree reduced though never eliminated. After a certain point is passed in the arms proliferation, the global system of local deterrents may achieve a dynamic equilibrium and resilience that will insulate it to a degree from the destabilising effects of further arms transfers, though it is unlikely that any regional balance will be able to keep pace with all developments in technology.

The problem with this view is the long unstable period during which the low-technology, low-inventory states will be transitioning to high technologies and high inventories. Moreover, the new balances of forces achieved at the end of the transition may be qualitatively different from the balances that existed before the proliferation process began, so that the comparative capabilities of the parties will have been altered in the evolution from one relatively stable force ratio to another. In many cases, this can mean that states enjoying new military advantages will insist on significant border alterations or they may even supervene neighbouring states in their entirety. Separatist and autonomist peoples who happen to be favoured by the changed balance of power may insist on secession. In short, even if proliferation finally results in a new military equilibrium, it may well mean increased political turbulence and a heightened possibility of war in many peripheral areas, particularly during the transitional decades, if states and movements dissatisfied with the political status quo that existed before the large-scale arms transfers happen to emerge in a more favourable position than before. Relatedly, the chances for war can also increase during the transitional period if some actors believe that their own military positions are deteriorating rapidly because of their adversaries' mounting accumulation of weapons, and they choose to resort to preventive war before their military positions are eroded completely.

None of this is to argue that the proliferation of tanks, armoured personnel carriers, artillery, missiles, and land-based aircraft necessarily and invariably will lead to political instability, but rather to develop the theme that periods of rapid change in capabilities have this potential unless the relative balance of forces between contentious neighbours is managed with care. There are some circumstances of course, under which the supply of arms to recipients in areas of tension can make the outbreak of war *less* likely. Furnishing a status quo power with a sizeable and unambiguous superiority in military strength may help regional rivals with anti-status quo aspirations to recognize the futility of starting a war. Examples here might include the effects of the Shah's massive arms imports in dampening down the expansionist ambitions of Iraq against Kuwait and other neighbours. Another example might be Korea, where the strengthening of the South seems to be effective in deterring Kim Il Sung from exercising military options for reunification. Sometimes, arms transfers can reinforce stability by altering the position of a threatened state from one of military inferiority to one of parity with its potential adversaries, thus making it a less tempting and vulnerable target for attack. However, these are exceptional cases. In most regions, there already exists some correspondence between the present balance of military forces and the distribution of territory and other valued assets. More often than not, alterations in these existing military balances will not serve to correct unstable force ratios but rather will tend to undermine such stability as has been achieved.

The Effects of New Technologies
Beyond these general remarks, it is worthwhile to single out a number of particular new technologies most likely to proliferate widely and to assess their effects on regional stability in areas of the periphery. Are there some technologies that are inherently favourable to the defence, and hence will tend to reinforce existing military balances, versus others that are favourable to the offence and are destabilising? I will deal with four systems, three of which (anti-tank weapons, surface-to-air missiles, and airborne and over-the-horizon radar early warning systems) have the prima facie image of favouring the defence and one (surface-to-surface medium-range weaponry) which seems offensive in character, to show that the actual pattern of offensive/defensive interaction that might result from the proliferation of these systems will be more complex than first impressions indicate. Following this selective examination of new hardware, I will relate the systems to the aspect of 'human technology'—the effects of the equipment in relation to existing levels of technological competence in the affected countries, and the effects of training programs and technological cooperation in altering the relative competence of manpower in various regional adversary relationships.

A. Anti-tank guided weapons.

Probably the most benign of the new land-force technologies from the offence/defence point of view are the anti-tank guided weapons, including missiles and artillery shells with terminal guidance capabilities and vastly improved single-shot kill probabilities. Large and costly offensive systems like tanks and armoured fighting vehicles are becoming more vulnerable to detection and targeting by relatively inexpensive anti-systems that can be proliferated to defensive forces in large numbers and operated by personnel with relatively low levels of technical skill. These are labour-intensive intermediate military technologies that are well-suited to developing countries and have been evaluated as inherently defensive in nature by many commentators. Offensive forces entering areas where the defence has been well-planned in advance will tend to suffer very substantially in the lethal hail of fire. For example, a tank that betrays its location to a small defending force of missile-armed infantrymen whose own positions are concealed by ground cover or terrain undulations has a high probability of being hit and destroyed. The difficulty of assaulting prepared positions on the ground was already evident in the October Middle East War, where every offensive or counteroffensive by either side against fully mobilised and alert enemy strongholds found unexpectedly fierce resistance and sustained higher loss rates than had been expected even when the local force ratios strongly favoured the attacker. Small defending units will not only be able to threaten and destroy larger armoured units in more situations, but they themselves will be more survivable because of their lower all media signatures, that is, their lower visual, radar, electronic, thermal and acoustical contrasts with the surrounding environment. A great premium will be attached to hiding, blending with background, and remaining motionless, and this premium will tend to serve the defender, who can play a more passive role while the attacker is obliged to move aggressively forward often over open terrain in unfamiliar territory.[10] Against such anti-tank defences, the aggressor will require much larger amounts of suppressive supporting fire, artillery barrages, organic mechanised infantry attached to the armoured corps, and other elements of the combined arms offensive. The scale of mobilisation and concentration required to achieve a break-through against even relatively small defending units armed with precision guided munitions will raise the costs of offensive operations considerably, both in terms of the numbers of men and equipment necessary to execute a given operation and in terms of the levels of battle attrition that will have to be tolerated. Another new anti-tank technology worth mentioning in this connection is a cluster munition fired by rockets or artillery or dropped from aircraft and consisting of a canister of small minelets which are scattered over a relatively wide area instantly upon impact. Disbursable minelets do not destroy tanks, but they do immobilise armoured vehicles passing over them by destroying the tracks. Effectively, they are instant area-denial weapons that can be used to close certain approaches to an aggressor, to force him to concentrate his forces and expose them to attrition by precision-guided fire, or to canalise his movements into certain routes rather than others. Here again, countermeasures are available to the offensive forces, but the net effect of this technology is to slow the enemy advance and to raise the scale of the operation required to achieve a breakthrough.

There are a few special cases in which the tactically defensive orientation of anti-tank guided weapons could be used to support the strategic offence rather than the defence. One is an adversary relationship in which the attacker depends primarily on guerrilla foot soldiers and the defender depends on highly mobile fighting vehicles (tanks, armoured personnel carriers, mechanised infantry fighting vehicles, or even wheeled vehicles). Here, the high hit probabilities of the new PGMs might serve to enhance the effectiveness of the guerrilla units and at a minimum force a change in tactics by the defenders. Depending on the nature of the terrain and the political orientation of the surrounding civilian population, anti-tank guided weapons could change the balance of forces in some regions in favour of the insurgents.

The other exception that should be noted with regard to anti-armour weapons is the class of cases in which an aggressor successfully seizes a piece of territory and then turns the PGMs to his own advantage to hold it against counterattack. More generally, it may sometimes be necessary for an army which is oriented defensively in the political and strategic senses to adopt offensive means in a particular tactical engagement—to carry the way to the territory of the enemy, to strike along the line of least expectation, to execute a pincer operation to isolate and encircle an enemy unit that has managed to achieve a breakthrough, to force the diversion of enemy battalions from areas of weak defence to more favourable positions, or for other reasons. The defensive army may be forced to use offensive tactics, and the anti-tank missiles, by making such operations more difficult, may in particular cases actually work against the strategic defender and in favour of the aggressor.[11]

However, these are exceptional cases and circumstances, and the net effect of the proliferation of anti-tank guided weapons in the majority of cases should be to enhance the ability of small states to defend themselves at relatively low cost, in some cases against adversaries whose preponderance in armour might have been much more threatening in the past.

B. Surface-based air defences

Another relatively benign class of weapons whose proliferation is often regarded as favourable to the defence is the new generation anti-aircraft artillery with sophisticated fire control and very high rates of fire, such as the Soviet ZSU–23 quad guns, and a wide array of surface-to-air missiles with radar and infrared terminal guidance. In theory, the effect of these systems is similar to that of the anti-tank guided weapons: they make it difficult for offensive strike aircraft to enter a certain lethal envelope without risking high rates of attrition. Protective measures against the surface-to-air systems, such as evasive manoeuvres and electronic countermeasure jamming pods, can reduce sortie loss rates for the aircraft, but only at the cost of system degradation by displacing part of the ordnance-carrying capability of the aircraft or reducing its mission performance capability by forcing it to fly at unusual altitudes or in non-optimal flight profiles and to lose some accuracy in weapons delivery. As long as the surface-to-air systems are operative, their effect is to raise significantly the active attrition of enemy aircraft or to degrade the system effectiveness of the attacker's equipment (sometimes called passive attrition). Ron Huisken has shown the speed with which these systems are being introduced in a large number of Third World countries. Those possessing surface-to-air missiles, for example, grew from 8 in 1965 to 26 in 1976 (though during the same period the number of Third World countries possessing supersonic combat aircraft increased even more rapidly: from 14 to 44).[12]

However, it is somewhat less clear that there is an organic link between surface-to-air weapons and the defence than in the case of anti-tank guided weapons. In addition to the caveats noted already for the anti-tank weapons (strategic defence versus tactical offence; seize and hold operations; guerrilla forces) effective surface-to-air weapons may be used to construct a defensive umbrella protecting offensive ground forces moving aggressively forward from aerial interdiction.[13] In cases where the offensive side is preponderant on the ground and the defence leans on its air force to restore the balance, this has the net effect of enhancing the offence. This argument might apply especially to the class of cases mentioned earlier in which one side is supplied by the Soviet Union, and therefore is likely to possess larger numbers of tanks and field artillery as well as surface-to-air missiles and guns, while the other side depends on the West and therefore tends to be air-intensive.

C. *Relatively long-range air-to-surface and surface-to-surface weapons*

Surface-to-air missiles and artillery may affect the offence/defence balance in another way: by forcing the enemy air force to acquire long-range standoff defence suppression weapons such as air-to-surface missiles and glide bombs with terminal guidance, surface-to-surface ballistic missiles with ranges in excess of 40 miles such as the Lance, and perhaps eventually tactical cruise missiles. Combined with precision radar emitter location systems, RPV reconnaissance, and other means of acquiring SAMs as targets, these weapons can be highly effective in suppressing the larger and longer range radar-dependent surface-to-air defences, though they cannot eliminate infantry-portable missiles proliferated on the battlefield in huge numbers.[14] After the defence suppression missions are completed, the air force will have relatively wide freedom of the skies at altitudes above two miles (the approximate limit of effectiveness of infantry SAMs and smaller anti-aircraft artillery). At this altitude, the aircraft will require terminally guided missiles and bombs effectively to support friendly ground forces, interdict enemy units, and conduct strikes against enemy targets in the interior. For these reasons, the net effect of the proliferation of SAMs may be to accelerate the proliferation of longer-range air- and surface-based missiles and bombs of an unambiguously offensive character.

Delivery vehicles that enable an attacker accurately to strike fixed and mobile targets relatively deep within his adversary's interior while firing from platforms within the attacker's own territory and air space are among the most offensive of the new weapons because they mean that the defender's army can no longer act as a shield against attacks on the homeland even if it is superior to the attacking forces. Fixed targets whose locations are known, such as factories, refineries, generating and pumping stations, communications facilities, and bridges, will be particularly vulnerable, as will the civilian population unless extensive civil defence measures are undertaken.

It is important to distinguish here between the older beyond-the-battlefield weapons such as the Scud surface-to-surface missiles with long ranges but low accuracy (circular error probability of the Scud is estimated to be several hundred metres) and the coming generation of surface-to-surface and air-to-surface weapons combining range with precision terminal guidance. While the former systems could have a psychological effect, they were not efficacious in the performance of primary military tasks unless armed with nuclear warheads. Moreover, their psychological effect was often the reverse of that intended. The Germans fired over 10,000 V–1 buzz bombs and V–2 rockets against Britain late in the Second World War, carrying warheads as large as 1000 kilograms, only to find British resistance stiffened by the 'hail of blows', as it had been by smaller air raids in 1940–41, rather than weakened.

However, the new generation of medium-range weapons, including tactical cruise missiles, terminally guided submunitions carried by tactical ballistic missiles, kamikaze drones and RPVs, rocket-assisted artillery shells with extended ranges, and air-launched glide bombs and missiles with ranges in excess of fifty miles, will enable the attacker to be far more selective and effective in his choice of targets. Moreover, the unit costs of the new systems are coming down as research and development outlays are spread over longer production runs, modular guidance and propulsion systems are adapted to a multiplicity of weapons, micro-miniaturised electronic components reduce both weight and cost, and economies of scale are achieved in production. The United States is now developing a 500 pound buzz bomb with its own booster engine and a simplified laser guidance system with a range in excess of 50 miles and a unit cost of only $6,500.[15] The GBU–15 glide bomb is expected eventually to have a unit cost under $50,000,[16] as is the tactical range cruise missile.[17] Expendable attack RPVs and kamikaze drones are expected to reach a unit cost in full production of $10–20,000—with ranges of 200 miles and more.[18] Unguided rocket-assisted artillery projectiles with ranges in excess of 30 miles are already in production at unit costs of $500 to $1000.[19] Cannon-launched guided projectiles will soon be available for a few thousand dollars per round. Taken altogether, these systems, should they become off-the-shelf items, will be affordable by many peripheral countries in substantial quantities.

If both sides in a regional adversary relationship possess the means to strike each other's interior, the possibility exists that a system of deterrents may operate within war if reason can restrain the temptations to action. Referring to the Scuds in his possession, President Sadat addressed a warning to the Israelis at the height of the October War:

We realise the responsibility of using certain kinds of weapons and we control ourselves. But the Israelis have to remember what I have said: an eye for an eye, a tooth for a tooth, and interior aggression for interior aggression.[20]

Following the 1973 war, Israel proposed an agreement through the International Red Cross under which she would join Syria and Egypt in a pledge to refrain from striking at each other's population centres if another war erupts.[21] It is conceivable that, if standoff and beyond-the-battlefield weapons do proliferate to peripheral regions, tacit and explicit restraints on deployment may follow.

However, historical analogies suggest that rational interest alone can fail to arrest the escalation from limited to total war, even when there is a highly developed process of signalling and tacit bargaining. There are bound to be some factions who will call for the use of a prohibited weapon to turn the tide of battle, to bring a more decisive victory, to end the war earlier, or to break the morale of the enemy. The advocates of escalation will play upon the belief that eventually the other side intends to use beyond-the-battlefield weapons anyway, or, conversely, that it has only a limited means to do so. Accidental violations of limiting principles by the enemy may be misread as intentional acts signalling the end of restraint. As the distance between 'allowed' and 'disallowed' weapons and targets narrows, as both sides try to bring within their disallowed sanctuaries an increasing number of targets regarded as legitimate military objectives by the enemy, and as the 'fog of war' thickens, the boundaries between permissible and impermissible actions will be eroded. There may be a sequence of small escalatory steps whose end result the leaders are unable to foresee, but which will lead incrementally to unlimited warfare. And, in the heat of battle, restraint may fail under the pressure of anger demanding expression. Once the hounds of war are unleashed, the decision-makers may be overwhelmed by the social forces that they have activated.[22] Once long-range weapons are in the hands of belligerent states, it may be more difficult to restrain their use through mutual deterrence than a purely rational theory of behaviour would suggest. On the other hand, the number of states manufacturing and aggressively marketing aircraft with weapons fits capable of delivering standoff ordnance and the wide variety of standoff systems being introduced will make an effort to arrest the proliferation of these weapons exceedingly difficult to realize in practice.

D. Early warning systems.
Early warning surveillance systems are not in themselves weapons

systems at all, but large-scale reconnaissance aids designed to provide near real-time information on enemy deployments, . Two principal types are of interest here: airborne early warning aircraft, and over-the-horizon radars. The principal mission of airborne early warning aircraft is to loiter in a holding pattern over a particular region, and by the use of long-range radars and other sensors to conduct surveillance well beyond the limits of ordinary ground-based radars lacking over-the-horizon capabilities. In the case of the Hawkeye E–2C, the effective surveillance cylinder has a radius of about 250 miles and extends from the surface to 100,000 feet altitude. AEW aircraft also enhance interception capabilities; in the case of the Hawkeye, the system is capable of following the movements of as many as 300 enemy aircraft at a time and can vector in intercepting aircraft or missiles against as many as 30 simultaneously. Its greatest appeal is the possibility to act as a force multiplier for the defender, enabling him to oversee the entire area of the enemy's potential attack and based on the 'big picture' of the enemy's deployments to allocate his own scarce military resources earlier and far more effectively than was formerly possible with piecemeal intelligence and without downward-looking radars and real-time communication. Grumman claims that the Hawkeye can enable a fighter force to reduce friendly losses by 400 per cent and increase enemy attrition by 200 per cent at the time that full-scale hostilities are initiated. It makes surprise attack harder to achieve and increases the losses that the attacker will have to be willing to sustain while reducing those of the defender.[23]

The problem with this seemingly benign system is that it also has the potential to assist one's fighters and ground attack aircraft operating on the enemy's side of the front line, by identifying and locating lucrative targets in the air and on the ground. Hawkeye's Passive Detection System, for example, can identify emitting SAM radars out as far as 400 miles, facilitating air defence suppression, while its radars can acquire and locate enemy tank and artillery concentrations over a large area. In summary, while the primary mission of airborne early warning is defence, it can very substantially enhance the offensive capabilities of air and ground forces as well. This kind of system is going to be very attractive to reasonably well-heeled armed forces, and both Grumman and Hawker Siddeley will be happy to have export orders to take up idle capacity in their Hawkeye and Nimrod production lines, respectively. The British firm is said to be looking to the Middle East, the Persian Gulf, Australia, and Japan, expanding the capabilities of the Nimrod by outfitting it with the avionics suite of the E–2C and especially by adapting the APS-125 overland radar.[24] The Soviet Moss is an airborne warning and control system with capabilities an order of magnitude below the U.S. Hawkeye or AWACS, but its effectiveness in defence and offence was evident during the December 1971 Indo-Pakistani war when it was on loan to India. Flying at night, Indian strike aircraft repeatedly succeeded in making low-level penetrations of up to 160 kilometres into Pakistani air space, locating and attacking targets with great precision, while at the same time providing gap-free detection of aircraft incoming to India.[25] As in the case of anti-tank guided weapons and surface-to-air missiles, the implications of proliferation of AWACS aircraft for offensive/defensive interaction in particular regions are more complex than initial impressions may indicate.

Ground-based over-the-horizon radars are an alternative means of performing many of the early warning functions of airborne systems, but at the present time they do not appear to have the same degree of bonus offensive potential. Recent 'backscatter' radar developments make it possible to bounce high-powered signals off the ionosphere to detect targets at ranges between 800 and 3200 kilometres or even further around the curvature of the earth and to 'mirror' the signals back to separately located receiver stations in the home country. Aircraft, large cruise missiles, and some types of surface shipping can be detected and, with some refinements now under development, intercepted by defensive systems vectored into a general envelope by the ground radar. The early warning range of over-the-horizon backscatter radar is much longer than that of present airborne systems, enhancing the defensive function, but at the same time OTH has several limitations that make its offensive potential less threatening: (1) The known capabilities of OTH to acquire targets on the ground are considerably less than the comparable capabilities of Hawkeye and AWACS. (2) Aircraft detected by the system are not, as yet, located with the precision that is possible with existing airborne early warning systems. (3) While some writers have suggested further developments of OTH radar that would enhance its offensive applications, these are probably beyond the ability of less developed states to realise and exploit on their own. However, the possibility exists of providing some peripheral states—particularly those with deep interiors and long frontiers—with an alternative to airborne early warning systems that is less expensive, has wider coverage, and with fewer offensive temptations.[26] OTH is also likely to gain in importance with the adoption of the 200 mile economic zone.

The Human Factor

This highly selective and cursory examination of a few technologies confirms what is already common knowledge: that there are no hard and fast distinctions between offensive and defensive weapons and systems, and much depends on the particular strategic and tactical applications for which the hardware is used. Another factor at least as important is the unequal capacity of military personnel in different recipient states of the periphery effectively to maintain, operate, and obtain the greatest combat utility from given sets of equipment. Differences in social and cultural environment, prevailing levels of human technological competence, past combat experience, the quality of officer cadres and the political leadership, and other human factors will impact greatly upon the effectiveness with which different technologies are adapted to the particular needs of recipient states. While differences in manpower are less quantifiable than differences in equipment, a considerable body of historical evidence points to the conclusion that sound training, well-considered tactics, and the individual competence of personnel have a much *greater* effect on combat outcomes than any normal differences in weapons hardware.[27]

This is illustrated by the experience of U.S. Navy pilots in Indo-China, who during the first phase of the air war (1965–68) achieved kill ratios in air combat of F–4s against MiG–21s of 2.3:1. This was considered unacceptably low by Navy officials, who sought to correct it during the bombing pause of 1968–1970 by instituting the so-called Dissimilar Air Combat pilot retraining program (nicknamed Topgun). When intensive air combat was resumed in the 1970–73 period, Topgun pilots flying essentially the same planes against the same adversaries improved their kill ratios to 12.5:1 —a 500 per cent improvement based primarily on improved human performance.[28] Similarly, the air combat superiority of the Israelis, evidenced by dogfight kill ratios of 20:1 in 1967 and 40:1 in 1973,[29] is explained far more convincingly by differences in pilot skill and tactics than by objective disparities between the Israeli Phantoms and Mirages and the Arab MiGs and their respective weapons and avionics fits (indeed, on some measures the Russian platforms were regarded as superior by the Israeli pilots). These and other evidences, as well as many first person accounts, suggest that differences in equipment and hardware technology are swamped by differences in human skill and training in the circumstances of all but the most unfavourable force ratios and technological imbalances.

It follows that even if identical quantities and qualities of equipment were introduced equally to both adversaries in a local conflict, the effective balances of force might be altered simply because one side could absorb and utilise the material better than the other. It also follows that manpower training programs and other forms of 'human technology' transfers from the centre to the periphery may be as important or more important than the arms transfers themselves. Technical skills, systems of military management, methods of logistical planning and operations analysis, strategic and tactical conceptions, and other 'intangible arms transfers' have the same potential to alter local military balances and thereby destabilise regional deterrent relationships as transfers of weapons, though the weapons themselves may be more highly regarded by both the supplier and the recipient, not to mention those who monitor arms flows at SIPRI. Yet military advisory missions and training programs are one of the largest components of the global military flow system. In 1976, the United States alone had military missions and groups in 44 countries, [30] including 132 technical assistance and training teams either contracted for or actually in 34 countries.[31] The Vinnell Corporation, for example, has contracted through the U.S. Army to provide 1,000 U.S. civilians, mostly former military men, to train the Saudi Arabian internal security forces.[32]

The Relationship Between New Technologies and Manpower Competence

In some respects, the introduction of highly sophisticated but simple-to-operate weapons systems will reduce the impact of human skill in military operations. The closer we come to the mythical automated battlefield, with pushbutton 'fire and forget' weapons, the less individual competence and initiative will count. The new systems vary greatly in the expertise they demand of the operators, but they do, with some exceptions, tend to simplify the skills required of the actual users on the front line. For example, the second-generation anti-tank missiles (TOW, Dragon, Milan) come closer to truly automatic guidance than the first generation missiles that they replace,[33] and the coming introduction of laser-homing cannon launched guided projectiles will require even less of the target designators and artillery crews. As the tactical subtlety and technical sophistication required to operate the new systems is on the average lower than for the systems they replace, it may be argued that the revolution in military equipment will reduce the advantage of 'brainpower' in the operation of weapons on the battlefield and act to some degree as an equaliser between armies of unequal skill. This is another way in which proliferation will alter existing military balances.

On the other hand, although many of the systems themselves are easier to operate, the overall effect of the technological revolution will probably be to increase the demands on a core of highly trained personnel and to increase the advantage of an officer corps that can adapt and improvise. Because effective firepower is becoming increasingly light and compact, mobile and relatively independent small units will in the future be used to threaten and destroy larger units in many situations. This is expected to lead to a proliferation of small units and to a molecular pattern of deployment on the battlefield.[34] A larger degree of authority will have to be delegated to lower command levels, and the quality of junior officers and the intermediate ranks from captain to colonel will impact more heavily than before on the effectiveness of the fighting forces. Improvisational tactics and operational flexibility will find their widest scope, and the net effect of the new technologies will enhance rather than reduce the importance of the human qualitative factor. And on the higher levels of strategy and war planning, the very speed of technological change and innovation may reward the side that is able to modify its organisation and force posturing more rapidly and to absorb and integrate new equipments on shorter lead times. The former head of U.S. military research and development, Malcolm Currie, offered the hypothesis that in the coming years, a technological breakthrough or surprise is less likely to take the form of an unforeseen new weapon, per se, than of the innovative use of a known technology on the basis of a superior understanding of its ultimate significance on the battlefield.[35] So the relationship between the new equipment technologies and human technology may enhance the advantage of states favoured by the balance of skills at the higher levels.

Conclusion

The world system of local military balances, like the global ecosystem, is the product of many years of mutation and adaption leading to a delicately tuned equilibrium. The system has some homeostatic resilience, and can tolerate moderate amounts of change introduced at a reasonable pace, but sudden and large-scale changes in the environment run the risk of upsetting the basic equilibrium. Just as rapid and uncontrolled industrialisation can upset the planetary bio-system, the present anarchic and uncontrolled pattern of proliferation of advanced weapons technologies has the potential to upset the ecology of military relationships on which regional political systems rest. In some cases, it may be desirable to alter political relationships and therefore it may be necessary to change the existing military balances. But the present phenomenon of largely indiscriminate proliferation, both quantitative and qualitative, lacks a guiding hand and may well have consequences unforeseen by the principal actors.

This essay reviewed briefly some of the ways in which the present pattern of proliferation threatens to alter the delicate regional balances. Neighbouring states are unequally favoured by the possession of resources with which to pay for arms, by the geopolitical assets they can offer to potential suppliers, and by the degrees of support they enjoy from great power allies or petrodollar-endowed sponsors. States are also unequally affected by the levels of inventory maintained by the suppliers with whom they are associated, by the different restrictions placed on arms exports by the various suppliers, and by the lead times required to obtain particular systems when they are needed. States supplied by the Soviet bloc tend to receive larger volumes of equipment, while those supplied by the West tend to receive technologically more advanced systems. There is no assurance that all these asymmetries will cancel each other out—indeed, in many cases, there are reasons to believe that the asymmetries will worsen over time.

On the qualitative side of the arms trade, some important differences have been noted in the destabilising potential of various new technologies likely to proliferate, but it has not been possible to identify any technologies that are purely defensive in practice. The most benign of the systems examined were the anti-tank guided weapons, but even these could aid an attacker by facilitating seize-and-hold operations, impeding the use of offensive tactics by the strategically defensive side, and enhancing the opportunities for guerrilla incursions. Surface-to-air missiles can aid the attack by degrading the interdiction capabilities of the defending air force, operating offensively to cover the defender's own air space, and by encouraging the proliferation of standoff SAM-suppression weapons which themselves have considerable offensive potential. Medium-range surface-to-surface missiles, rocket-assisted projectiles, standoff air-to-surface missiles and glide bombs have many offensive applications and are likely to become off-the-shelf items from many suppliers and in some cases to be relatively simple technologies for indigenous production. Airborne and surface-based early warning systems have an offensive bonus in their ability to vector attacking aircraft, missiles, and other weapons systems against enemy forces once the latter are located.

Finally, the ability of states to absorb and integrate the quantities and qualities of weapons that become available to them is highly unequal. Military skills are distributed across the globe asymmetrically, and some states will obtain greater net utility from given inputs of equipment than others. Moreover, the distribution of military skills is itself being disturbed, as human technology transfer proliferates in patterns as asymmetric as the equipment flows.

It would be impossible and in many ways undesirable to freeze the global arms system at a certain moment in time solely to stabilise the existing complex of political relations in all parts of the world. But even those who seek large-scale political change cannot be sanguine with the present pattern of arms proliferation, because the actors who come out on top may not be the good guys from their point of view in every case. The world is a picture with some aesthetically pleasing areas and some areas whose arrangement is not delightful to the eye. But the solution is not merely to scramble the pieces of the image in the hope that the new arrangement, randomly arrived at, will be more satisfactory. This, in effect, is what the present pattern of arms proliferation threatens to do. On the other hand, it is not clear that a conventional arms control regime imposed by the exporting states will be any more satisfactory, nor that one can be established effectively.[36]

Footnotes

1. The Soviet Union, the United States, France, and Great Britain alone account for more than 85 per cent of the global arms traffic.

2. The indigenous arms production and co-production industries of such peripheral states as India, South Korea, Taiwan, Singapore, Iran, Israel, and Egypt are growing in scale and importance, and a more detailed analysis would need to distinguish between states that are essentially self-reliant, those which are wholly dependent, and those which depend on a combination of home production and imports. However, it should be noted that the advanced technologies discussed later are still primarily under the control of the countries of the centre.

3. These simplified tabulations aggregate in broad categories equipments with widely varying performance characteristics, such as comparing the U.S. M–113 armoured personnel carrier with the more sophisticated Soviet BMP mechanised infantry fighting vehicle or classing the MiG–21 with the F–15. It is virtually impossible to quantify in a simple and comprehensible way the wide array of systems under production without comparing incommensurables. For example, tanks vary in mobility, protection, accuracy, range, and rate of fire, target acquisition and location aids, etc. Fighters differ from ground attack aircraft and themselves vary in acceleration, manoeuvrability, range, payload, avionics, and weapons fits. Obviously, aggregate comparisons can be

highly misleading. However, available evidence based on more detailed and exhaustive studies tends to support the broad point made by Tables I and II: that Soviet production of these land-based general purpose forces has in the net assessment exceeded that of the West in recent years.

4. Donald H. Rumsfeld, Secretary of Defence, *Annual Defence Department Report FY 1978*, Government Printing Office, Washington 1977, p.11. For trends in U.S. and Soviet production of ground force equipment 1966–1976, see Rumsfeld p.27.
5. Statement of Congressman Les Aspin, 'Comparing Soviet and American Defence Effort', reprinted in *Nato's Fifteen Nations*, June–July 1976, esp. p.41
6. United States Department of State, *Communist States and Developing Countries: Aid and Trade in 1972*, State Department Bureau of Public Affairs, August 1973, p.19.
7. United States Central Intelligence Agency, *Communist Aid to Less Developed Countries of the Free World, 1975*, Washington, July 1976, p.5.
8. All figures from *The Military Balance, 1975–76* and *1976–77*, International Institute for Strategic Studies, London 1976 and 1977.
9. See statements of Malcolm Currie, former Director of US Defence Research, Development, Testing, and Evaluation, reprinted in *Aviation Week and Space Technology* 16 Feb. 1976 & 17 May 1976. See also Robert Perry, *Comparisons of US and Soviet Technology,* Rand Report R–827–PR. The Rand Corporation, Santa Monica, California 1973.
10. Future developments may include robotised self-initiating anti-tank missiles which can be prepositioned in areas the enemy is expected to enter and fire automatically when targets whose signatures match pre-coded profiles approach. The possibilities for concealment and camouflage of such systems are endless.
11. Richard Burt makes the case still more generally, arguing that the defender is often required to adopt mobile tactics. Compare *'New Weapons Technologies: Debate and Directions'*, *Adelphi Paper* Number 126, International Institute for Strategic Studies, London, 1976, pp.8–14.
12. See above, Chapter 2.
13. Cf. the Egyptian and Syrian offensives of 6 October 1973.
14. The next generation of medium and long-range SAMs may reduce vulnerability by separating the radar transmitter from the receiver (the bistatic principle) or by replacing radars altogether with passive (non emitting) detection systems dependent on infrared sensors. See S.J. Rosen, 'Surface to Air Missiles and the Future Value of Air Superiority in the Middle East', *Survival*, September/October 1977.
15. However, surface-based laser designation of Smartroc will be limited by the horizon—22 miles at sea. RPV–designators could extend the range.

16. Present unit costs of the GBU–15 are projected at over $150,000.
17. See Kosta Tsipis, 'Cruise Missiles', *Scientific American*, Feb.77, p.25; and Richard L. Garwin, 'Effective Military Technology for the 1980s,' *International Security*, Fall 1976, Vol. 1, No.2, p.61. Both authors are aware that the present unit costs of tactical cruise missiles are vastly in excess of this figure (e.g. $500,000 and more).
18. E.g., the Northrop Low Cost Expendable Harassment Vehicle, which weighs 90 pounds, flies 120 mph, and has a total endurance of five hours including ferry and loiter.
19. See Rumsfeld, *op. cit*, p. 173.
20. Speech 16 October 1973, in Egyptian Ministry of Information, *Speeches and Interviews by President Anwar El Sadat, July–December 1973*, State Information Service, Cairo: 1974, p.207.
21. 'Israel Seeks Pact on Sparing Cities in Any Future War', *New York Times,* 5 April 1975, p.3.
22. On the failure of efforts to limit strategic bombing of cities during the Second World War, see Frederick M. Sallagar, *The Road to Total War*, Van Nostrand Reinhold, New York, 1969. For a more optimistic view, see George Quester, *Deterrence Before Hiroshima*, John Wiley, New York, 1966.
23. See J. Philip Geddes, 'Airborne Early Warning for the U.S. Navy', *International Defence Review*, 1975, Number 5, pp. 679–682, and Philip J. Klass, 'E–2C Radar to Provide New Flexibility'; *Aviation Week and Space Technology*, 12 July 1976, pp.51–53.
24. See David A. Brown, 'Nimrod Early Warning Version Pushed', *Aviation Week and Space Technology*, 14 March 1977, pp. 47–50, and Brown, 'British Order Nimrod AEW Development', *Aviation Week and Space Technology*, 4 April 1977, p.15.
25. See Nikolai Cherikow, 'Moss: AWACS with a Red Star', *International Defence Review*, 1975, Number 5, pp. 677–678.
26. It should be noted that, since OTH-Backscatter is generally reported to be not effective at ranges *less* than 800 kilometres, it is most applicable to island states widely separated from their notional adversaries or to states with territory deep enough to move the emitters a considerable distance inland. For a general description of OTH–B, see Desmond Ball, 'Jindalee: Over-the-Horizon Radar in the Defence of Australia' in *Pacific Defence Reporter*, February 1977, and his 'Some Further Thoughts on Jindalee' in the same journal, May 1977.
27. See Jack N. Merritt and Pierre M. Sprey, 'Negative Marginal Returns in Weapons Acquisition', in Richard G. Head and E.J. Rokke, eds., *American Defence Policy*, Third Edition, Johns Hopkins University Press, Baltimore, 1973, p.491.
28. See Philippe Grasset, 'Dissimilar Air Combat Training', *International Defence Review*, June 1975, pp. 823–827 and Andrew Hamilton, 'Topgun The Navy's "Mig–Killing" School', *U.S. Naval Institute Proceedings*, Volume 102, Number 1, pp. 95–97.

29. Edward Luttwak and Dan Horowitz, *The Israeli Army*, Allen Lane, London 1975, pp. 299, 302, and 347.

30. *International Security Assistance and Arms Export Control Act of 1976*, Report of the Senate Committee on Foreign Relations,U.S. Government Printing Office, Washington 1976, p.23.

31. *U.S. Defense Contractors' Training of Foreign Military Forces*, Hearings of the House Committee on International Relations, U.S. Government Printing Office, Washington 1975, p.5

32. *Ibid*, pp. 51–53.

33. The first generation systems require the operator to align the horizontal and vertical coordinates of both the target and the missile until impact, while operating under fire. Second generation systems either autonomously home in on infrared or electro-optical signals or call upon the operator to fix a single set of cross-hairs on the target alone.

34. See James F. Digby, *'Precision Guided Munitions: Capabilities and Consequences'*, RAND Paper P–5257. Rand Corporation, Santa Monica, California, 1975. Ross Babbage develops the implications of dispersal and concealment of small units in 'Technological Trends on the Conventional Battlefield Till the Turn of the Century', a paper circulated by the Strategic and Defence Studies Centre, Australian National University, 1976.

35. Statement in *Aviation Week and Space Technology*, 16 February 1976, p.38.

36. The author is indebted to Ross Babbage for comments and suggestions on this chapter as a whole.

5
Military Weaponry and North-east Asian Security*
Shinkichi Eto

This chapter proposes to analyse the fundamental security problems of North-east Asia, which is defined as the region which includes Japan, China, and the Korean Peninsula. The author will also attempt to assess how changes in military technology affect the geopolitical configuration in the area.

I. The Han Civilization Region

The most basic ethnic unit in East Asia was the Han Chinese who flourished in the Huang Ho River basin. They were threatened by the incursions of other groups who periodically swooped down on the Chinese over the Asian land mass from the north and west. This pattern began 3,000 years ago and lasted up to the 18th century. The Han Chinese moved southwards when the pressure from the north and west was severe and returned to the north and west in periods when this pressure declined. These groups of nomadic peoples and hunting tribes descended southwards in search of food in the fall and winter months. For the Chinese, who were an agricultural people, the most fundamental security issue of the day was how to deal with this challenge.

In the early 17th Century, the Manchu army swept across the Korean peninsula, subjugated the Mongols, and eventually conquered all territories under Han control. The Tibetans then followed, with Lhasa being occupied. The Moslems in Sinkiang were vanquished after several clashes. To the west, the Pamir Highlands were clearly added to the Manchu sphere of control. To the south, in the 18th century, Vietnam and Burma were defeated and forced to become vassal states. Except for the Mongols at the peak of their power, the Ch'ing court controlled a greater area than any other dynasty in Chinese history. In fact, the area under Ch'ing control was greater than that under the control of the People's Republic of China (P.R.C.) today.

To the west of the Urals, Ivan the Great, the Grand Duke of Moscow, destroyed the Tartar Kingdom of the Golden Horde and unified most of the present Russian land mass. Timofeevich Yermak, the Cossack chieftain, crossed the Urals and subjugated the Tartar Kingdom of Sibir Khan. He then presented it to Ivan the Terrible, who had already been crowned Tsar. The name of this small Tartar Kingdom of Sibir Khan soon came to refer to all of Siberia.

The Russians trapped the fur-bearing animals of Siberia and moved rapidly eastward. They crossed the Yablonoi mountain chain and came into contact with the Ch'ing along the banks of the Amur River. After several battles, the Russians were defeated and in the 1689 Treaty of Nerchinsk, the Argun River and the Yablonoi mountain range were to serve as the boundary line for the two states. Since the Treaty of Nerchinsk prevented the Russians from developing the Amur River basin, they began to march to the distant north instead. The Russians moved into Kamchatka, the islands of the North Pacific and the Aleutians and Alaska. They even began to press down the Pacific coast of the American continent.

In the 19th Century there were striking advances in the nature of Western European weaponry. Thus the Ch'ing army, which relied chiefly on outmoded bows and arrows, and swords and spears, began once again to feel the pressure of the Russian forces, which were equipped with guns this time. By the middle of the 19th Century, the Russians had in fact succeeded in occupying the lower reaches of the fertile Amur River basin.

In 1858, the Russians dealt the Ch'ing court a crushing military blow and the Treaty of Aigun ceded the area to the north of the Amur to the Russians. The Maritime Province to the east of the Ussuri was henceforth to be under the joint control of the two countries. However, in the 1860 Treaty of Peking, the Maritime Province was ceded to Russia.

The original inhabitants of the Korean peninsula were primarily of Ural-Altaic stock and as such were completely distinct from the Han Chinese. However, for over 2,000 years, Korea was heavily influenced by Chinese civilization. It was forced to become part of the Chinese tributary system when China was strong but moved towards greater independence when Chinese power was on the wane. Korea was condemned to repeat this cycle over and over.[1]

A powerful kingdom appeared in western Japan about 2,000 years ago and gradually unified the Japanese archipelago. It expanded in power so drastically that around the 7th Century,

Japan subjugated the southern part of the Korean peninsula. However, Japanese forces were defeated by the mighty T'ang army and lost control of the Korea Strait. It would be a long time before Japan would again become involved in a military conflict with a power on the Asian continent.

China is basically a land power and none of the Chinese dynasties ever plotted to cross the ocean to attack Japan with the one exception of the Mongols. Thus, Japan found itself in the enviable position of experiencing few external threats to its security which helped in creating a culturally homogeneous society.

II. The Impact of Guns, Aircraft, and Missiles

In August 1863, seven British ships under the command of Rear-Admiral Kuper bombarded Kagoshima City. This was Japan's first major battle with a foreign country since it turned back the Mongol naval attack in the 13th Century. The British had 101 guns, which included some of the newest Armstrongs with their rifled bores. Kagoshima, the capital of the Satsuma-han, had 83 guns of an older type. The battle lasted three and a half hours and after the smoke had cleared it was found that 10 per cent of Kagoshima City had been burned to the ground and that all Satsuma ships, including three steam ships, and all batteries had been destroyed. The British suffered only 13 dead and some 50 wounded.[2]

The following year, a joint British, French, Dutch and U.S. expedition of 17 ships, again under Rear-Admiral Kuper, attacked Shimonoseki. The Choshu-han attempted to defend Shimonoseki with 65 guns, but these were soon destroyed and 2,000 foreign troops landed and occupied all the batteries.[3]

The sea power of the Western nations was based on a capitalist mode of production and on superior military technology and shipbuilding techniques. It dealt the previously isolated Japanese stinging blows at Shimonoseki and Kagoshima. Prior to this, the Western powers had fought the Opium War and the Arrow War with China. In response, both the Chinese and the Japanese began to concentrate on creating a strong naval force equipped with guns which had rifled barrels.

In 1895, the Peiyang Fleet of the Chinese, the strongest naval power in Asia, fought with Japan, the second strongest naval power in Asia. The Japanese Navy, with its far more accurate guns, emerged the victor. This experience clearly impressed upon the Japanese the efficacy of large fleets equipped with heavy guns and manned by a carefully trained crew. These Japanese strategic precepts were vindicated by the Russo-Japanese War of 1904–1905.

The Russian Fleet was almost completely destroyed by the Japanese Navy, and Japanese control of the seas in the Far East became virtually absolute. The Japanese Navy continued to cling to these strategic precepts even into the 1930s.

Subsequently, only the Americans would be able to challenge the Japanese in East Asian waters. However, the Japanese themselves doubted their capability when matched against the U.S. Navy, which was based on massive industrial productivity. Thus, while the Japanese Navy drilled hard with the U.S.A. in mind as the hypothetical enemy, it tried at all costs to avoid a conflict with this new Pacific power. From 1907 on, Imperial Navy staff officers did discuss in secret the possibility of fighting with the U.S.A. They felt that the only naval war they could win would be one fought in the waters close to Japan. Since this was seen as their only hope for victory against the U.S.A. they would have to wait patiently for the Americans to advance into the seas surrounding Japan. Because of their limited capabilities in seeking out and destroying the U.S. Fleet, the Japanese never seriously considered this tactic.

In 1941, when the Japanese came to the conclusion that they had to fight the U.S.A., Admiral Yamamoto felt that the first order of priority was the destruction of the U.S. Pacific Fleet. For the first time in history, a task force was formed which was heavily dependent on aircraft carriers. This task force succeeded in its surprise attack on Hawaii. Moreover, H.M.S. *Prince of Wales*, which was considered invulnerable to air attack because of its ability to provide a heavy protective barrage, was sunk in less than an hour off the Malayan coast by Japanese aircraft.

Ironically, however, it was the U.S.A. and not Japan that learned a lesson from this experience. The U.S.A. came to feel that air power was of overriding importance. The U.S. Navy moved rapidly to form new task forces centred on aircraft carriers and in the summer of the following year it dealt the Japanese a serious defeat in the Battle of Midway.

Following that victory, the U.S.A. shifted its emphasis from large fleets and guns to a new strategic philosophy based on air power. The subsequent American task forces, centred on aircraft carriers, were so successful that the U.S.A. was able to maintain control of the seas throughout the world until three years ago.

Now, it seems to the author that a new strategic philosophy dominates military thinking in the Soviet Union. This is based on new developments in missile technology which have made it possible to defend oneself against an air attack through the use of surface-to-air missiles. The might of the SAM–6 in the recent fourth

Middle East War is a good demonstration of this new situation. It appears that the Soviet Union has embarked on the construction of a global naval force which is predicated on the belief that the development of missiles is the key to strategic power today.

On the 36th anniversary of Naval Day in 1975, Admiral N.I. Smirnov stated that the primary focus of the Soviet Navy should be on nuclear submarines armed with long-range ballistic missiles. A secondary emphasis was placed on the importance of anti-submarine aircraft equipped with rockets.[4] In 1976, Admiral Sergei Gorshkov also observed that of all the weapons in its arsenal, the Soviet Union took the most pride in the nuclear powered submarine. He bragged about Soviet global naval power by saying that 'The Soviet Navy which has made tremendous advances through a scientific and technological revolution has made the oceans of the world its own.'[5] Today, as always, a navy is terribly expensive. The Soviet Union is the only nation in the history of the world to rebuild a navy once it had been destroyed. However, a note of caution should be added. There is some room for debate as to whether the Soviet Union has really moved completely to a strategy centred on missiles or whether it does in fact still subscribe to the aircraft centred task force concept with a concurrent emphasis on missiles. The appearance of the aircraft carrier *Kiev* would tend to support the latter proposition.

In any case, in addition to the Soviet impact on the nations of North-east Asia as a continental giant to the north and west, its impact as a naval power has also come to be felt. The Soviet Pacific Fleet does not have a single aircraft carrier but, as can be seen in Table 1, its total tonnage is over 1,200,000 tons and it is thus the foremost naval power in East Asia. As a result, in Admiral James Halloway's analysis, there are sections of the high seas that the United States Armed Forces cannot control today even with the help of its allies. The Sea of Japan would be one such example.[6]

III. Nations of the Region: Their Intentions, Capabilities, and Constraints.

A) The Soviet Union

Admiral Gorschkov summarised the general goals of the Soviet Navy when he stated that,

> The Soviet Navy is completely loyal to the Party of Lenin and keeps a constant vigil over the seas. The Navy splendidly safeguards the national interest of the motherland by joining forces with the other Soviet armed services.[7]

Table 1.

Military Power in the Far East

		Ground Forces *(Divisions)*	Naval Forces *(Tons)*	Air Forces *(Aircraft)*
Soviet: Far East (East of Irkutsk)	1965	170 (M.B.)	700,000	1,400
	1975	30–35	1,200,000	2,000
China	1965	115 (M.B.)	200,000 (J)	2,800 (M.B.)
	1975	142 (M.B.)	350,000 (J)	4,400 (M.B.)
Japan	1965	13	140,000 (J)	500
	1975	13	180,000	445
U.S.A.	1965	3 + 1 MD*	750,800 to 800,000 (125 ships)	more than 600
	1975	2 + 1 MD	600,000 (ca. 60 ships)	more than 423

Note: Figures marked (M.B.) are from *The Military Balance 1976–77,* I.I.S.S., London, 1976. Those marked (J) are from *Jane's Fighting Ships,* Macdonald and Jane's, London, 1976. Others estimated by the Author.
* Marine Division.

(The author will return to a consideration of the term 'national interest', later.)

The core of the present Soviet Pacific Fleet is 57 major surface combatants and 74 submarines which include four or five SSBN-D type submarines. The SSBN-D is equipped with SSN–6s or SSN–8s. The SS–8 has a range of 4,800 miles and can hit the eastern U.S. seaboard from the Sea of Okhotsk. Thus it seems clear that the nuclear weapons of the Pacific Fleet have a second strike capability.

Another major purpose of the Soviet Pacific Fleet is to destroy any naval offensive task force despatched by the enemy. However, a striking feature of the Soviet Navy is that it employs smaller calibre weapons. The Navy is built around missiles. Thus if it were to engage in an actual battle with U.S. aircraft carrier task forces, the result would hinge on the effectiveness of Soviet missiles. Estimates of the effectiveness of the missiles of the Soviet Fleet vary widely: some specialists feel that the Soviets could rapidly increase their naval defensive capabilities and virtually protect themselves completely from U.S. air attack by forming groups of one cruiser and three destroyers, but other analysts disagree.[8]

If the present Soviet Fleet fought the U.S. aircraft carrier task forces, it seems likely that victory would go to the side which first fired an accurate volley. The future strategic balance in North-east Asian waters will obviously be deeply affected by the advances in military technology. For example, new weapons which would enable one side or the other to launch a surprise attack, long-range high-accuracy ship-to-ship missiles, or rapid advances in the ability to search out enemy vessels would all obviously be of enormous importance.

The Japanese Maritime Self-Defence Force would almost surely be destroyed by the Soviet SSN–11s which are armed with ordinary warheads. If for some reason, the Self-Defence Force should withstand a first volley by the SSN—11s, the continuing battle would be waged by guns. Then the Japanese would be in a very good position since their fleet has large guns, ranging in size from five inches and upwards. But it is inconceivable that the Japanese Navy could withstand a Soviet missile attack.

The next question to consider is whether the Soviet Union has any plans to land troops in Japan. At the present time, the Soviet Pacific Fleet does not have the type of landing craft that would be required for such an operation. In addition, the Soviets do not have the large-scale guns which would be needed to bombard the coast, and it would be too costly to use missiles, which also have limited destructive capability. Thus a Russian attack on Japan prior to the landing of troops would have to depend primarily on rockets and bombers; however, there is not the slightest indication that the Soviets are trying to increase the number of their bombers with this goal in mind. Thus it seems that for the present time, at least, the Soviet Union does not intend to attempt a military occupation of Japan. Although there is no immediate indication that the Soviet Union intends to do so, should it decide to develop a landing capacity it could probably do so in less than a year.

Another possibility to consider is whether or not the Soviet Union is likely to use its navy to attack merchant vessels. The use of submarines armed with strategic nuclear missiles would be very expensive and, in addition, would reveal the position of the submarines, thus preventing the submarines from fulfilling their original strategic purpose. For an attack on merchant vessels, the Soviets need a submarine equipped with non-nuclear warheads. However, at the present time, the Soviet Navy in the region has only nine of this type of submarine which could pass through the Tsugaru Strait or the Korea Strait, surface, and attack merchant vessels. Thus it seems clear that the Soviet Union is not intent on preparing to destroy the Japanese merchant fleet at the moment. Needless to say, the Soviet Union could complete rapid preparation for such an attack in a matter of months once it perceived the necessity to do so.

All of the above considerations tend to lead one to the conclusion that the aims of the Soviet Pacific Fleet are two-fold: first, it serves to deter U.S. use of force in the area and second, it serves to exert political influence on the various coastal nations during peacetime.

B)China

The government of the P.R.C. controls one-fourth of the earth's population. As such, it is the focus of much attention. However, since it does not yet have any offensive military capability, its threat is a potential one and is more of a problem for future consideration. The intentions of the P.R.C. are clearer than those of the Soviet Union. In the eulogy following the death of Mao Tse-tung, the Chinese Communist Party publicly proclaimed two foreign policy goals.[9]

The first goal is to adhere firmly to proletarian internationalism and to promote the struggle against 'imperialism' and 'social imperialism' to the fullest. Thus the Chinese have not relinquished their goal of world revolution. The second goal is to make China a powerful socialist nation. With this aim in mind, the Chinese are developing a foreign policy which stresses the maintenance of friendly relations with other states and the active importation of technology from various capitalist countries.

At times these two national goals come into conflict. Friendly relations with Japan are beneficial for China's industrialisation and for building a powerful nation. However, this clearly downplays the goal of world revolution and solidarity with the 'revolutionary people' of Japan. Good relations with the Malaysian government are clearly in China's national interest but result in discarding the goal of world revolution and the abandonment of the revolutionary Malayan Communist Party. The Chinese flow of weapons to Communist guerrillas in Malaysia, the Philippines and elsewhere seems to have completely dried up. For the time being, the Chinese will apparently stress the building of a strong Chinese state while downplaying their revolutionary goals.

For the Chinese, military power is a prerequisite for both the building of a strong Chinese state and the fostering of world revolution. Thus China became the fifth member of the nuclear club. However, the subsequent development of the Chinese ICBMs has taken far longer than most Western specialists predicted, and it is unclear whether or not they are at present ready for use in war. The development of IRBMs has also been lagging and it is estimated that the Chinese have approximately 20 IRBMs with a range of between 2,400 and 4,000 kilometers. The Chinese probably have between 50 and 90 MRBMs.

The main Chinese defensive warplane is reported to be the F6, a copy of the MiG 19, which does not have modern air-to-air or air-to-ground weapons.[10] The Chinese have an army of 3,000,000 with ten armoured divisions, but it is not a fighting force which is capable of striking deep into its neighbour's territory. However, as was demonstrated in the Korean War, the Chinese army is capable of fighting in a restricted geographic area if it is prepared to take heavy losses. It would also seem to be very well suited to guerrilla warfare within China.

The government of Hua Kuo-feng is aiming at the realisation of the 'Four Modernisations'. This refers to the modernisation of agriculture, industry, national defence and scientific technology. In order to fulfil these goals it is necessary to reduce the number of potential enemies while increasing the number of friendly nations. This is obviously doubly true of relations with the advanced industrial nations and is the reason for which Peking has been cultivating friendly relations with the United States, Western Europe and Japan in the years following Nixon's visit to China. The Chinese are trying to learn what they can from these countries while importing their scientific technology. It will be only in the distant future that the Chinese can possess an offensive military capability.

Taiwan is an extremely important political issue. At present, the Chinese have neither the ability nor the will to 'liberate' Taiwan either by peaceful or military means. It is likely, however, that the will to 'liberate' Taiwan would arise if the Chinese were to perceive it to be possible. The 'liberation' of Taiwan actually depends on the U.S.A. If U.S. military aid and the export of weapons to Taiwan were discontinued, it would be only a few years until Taiwan's defensive capabilities plummet. On the other hand, Taiwan lacks the military power to attack the Chinese mainland. This military deadlock in the Taiwan area has continued as long as it has because of U.S. military aid to the Kuomintang government.

The Chinese are pressing the Americans to discontinue this military aid to Taiwan as a precondition for normalising relations. Washington wants to normalise relations with China but does not want to discontinue its military aid to Taiwan. As Secretary of State Cyrus Vance stated in his speech at the Asia Society on 29 June 1977, 'We place importance on the peaceful settlement of the Taiwan question by the Chinese themselves . . . But the progress may not be easy or immediately evident',[11] i.e. it would appear that the problem will remain unresolved for some time to come.

C) The U.S.A.

During the Nixon years, the U.S.A. made a tremendous effort to extricate itself from the Vietnam quagmire. Washington decided to leave the fate of South Vietnam to the Vietnamese themselves. In addition, in order to improve relations with Peking, the U.S.A. pledged in the Shanghai Communiqué to withdraw its troops from Taiwan.

Furthermore, President Carter pledged to pull American ground troops out of South Korea during the presidential election campaign. In his statements, on 9 March and 26 May 1977, President Carter reconfirmed his policy by saying that he would withdraw U.S. ground troops from South Korea within the next four or five years. At the same time, he promised to maintain a firm and undeviating commitment to the security of South Korea. It seems that the U.S. policy will be to diminish its military commitments to countries like Taiwan and South Korea while trying to maintain the status quo in the region.

D) Japan

Table 2 seems to indicate that Japanese economic dependence on trade is not very great. However, Table 3 shows that there is an extremely high level of reliance on foreign sources for key materials necessary for industrial production and survival. In this sense, Japan is economically, geopolitically and historically a maritime nation.

Table 2

Dependence on Overseas Trade

	Export/GDP (%)		Import/GDP (%)	
	1965	1974	1965	1974
Australia	12.7	12.7	14.4	13.i
Belgium–Luxemburg	37.5	53.0	38.1	55.9
France	10.1	17.2	10.3	19.9
West Germany	15.8	23.6	15.5	18.3
Italy	12.2	20.2	12.5	27.3
Japan	9.6	12.2	9.3	13.6
Korea, South	5.9	26.5	15.6	40.6
Netherlands	33.3	47.4	38.8	47.2
Switzerland	21.3	26.6	26.6	32.2
U.S.A.	3.9	6.9	3.1	7.6

Source: *Annual Report of MITI,* Tokyo, 1977.

Table 3

Dependence on Imported Raw Materials—Percentages of Each Commodity Imported

	Japan		*U.S.A.*		*West Germany*	
	1965	*1975*	*1965*	*1975*	*1965*	*1975*
Wheat	73.9	95.9	0.0	0.0	26.4	8.2
Corn	97.9	99.9	0.0	0.0	95.1	84.1
Soybean	88.9	96.4	0.0	0.0	100.0	100.0
Lumber	24.1	62.4	6.9	4.5	35.7	33.4
Iron Ore	88.2	99.4	36.0	37.6	82.2	93.1
Copper Ore	74.9	89.7	33.5	8.3	99.8	99.7
Lead	62.7	73.5	63.7	30.7	81.8	85.6
Coal	20.5	75.8	0.0	0.0	0.0	0.0
Crude Oil	98.9	99.7	13.9	28.5	87.1	94.4
Natural Gas	0.0	64.1	2.8	4.1	0.4	52.7
Energy Resources	65.7	92.5	7.3	16.7	28.0	53.5

Source: *Annual Report of MITI,* Tokyo, 1977.

The Japanese people can survive only if the market mechanism functions freely and if the flow of goods, people and money is unimpeded. In other words, following their defeat, the Japanese gave up the idea of seizing goods and resources for themselves and concluded that they would have to seek prosperity through reliance on the free market system. Therefore, the present Japanese offensive capability is nil. Japan would be completely defenceless in the face of a nuclear attack and it has been estimated that the Japanese could last only a few days if an all-out offensive with conventional weapons was launched against them. Switzerland is only one-ninth the size of Japan but could raise 700,000 troops in two days.

Table 4

Defence Expenditures

	Defence expenditures (million US$)		*Defence expenditure/GNP (%)*	
	1965	*1974*	*1965*	*1974*
Australia	1,130	1,620	4.36	2.66
New Zealand	136	237	2.10	1.75
Japan	1,250	3,670	0.96	0.82
P.R.C.	6,500	17,000	6.76	7.62
Taiwan	360	814	10.70	7.17
Mongolia	15	55	2.50	6.87
North Korea	350	625	14.00	10.20
South Korea	143	642	3.71	4.33
Malaysia	98	295	3.43	3.79
Philippines	64	213	1.35	1.77

Source: Kokubo (National Defence), No. 288, February, 1977 and No. 289, March, 1977.

Including the 38,000 men in the reserves, Japan has only 280,000 men in the Self-Defence Forces.[12]

The next question to consider is whether or not Japan intends to develop military power commensurate with its economic might in the future. One can say with confidence that there is no such intention. In the first place, the strength of the opposition parties in the Diet is growing, and they are proponents of a reduction in the size of the SDF. It is even unclear whether or not the Liberal Democratic Party which advocates light rearmament and reliance on the Security Treaty system, will be able to maintain a monopoly of the government. The author personally feels that the LDP will be able to maintain itself in power. Nonetheless, the domestic political constraints regarding the SDF are so strong that it is virtually inconceivable that Japanese defensive capabilities will be significantly increased.

For the foreseeable future, Japan will not pose a military threat to the members of ASEAN, Australia, or any of its other neighbours. For the U.S.A. and Australia, Japan will be a friendly country but one which will be militarily unreliable. For example, despite the importance of Japan for Korean security, it is impossible for the Japanese to play an active role in the defence of Korea.[13]

If an increase in Japan's military power is out of the question, it is worth considering the likelihood of Japanese sale of weapons abroad. Technologically and economically, there is no doubt that Japan is quite capable of producing large quantities of sophisticated weapons. However, the Japanese people are as opposed as ever to the export of weapons. The government also has three principles concerning the export of weapons.[14] Of course, there is some opposition to this policy from industrial circles and from those who advocate exporting weapons in order to be able to mass produce weapons and thus lower the cost. However, these people are in the minority.[15] Thus for the foreseeable future, Japan will not follow the example of France and become a weapons-exporter.

E) Korea

North Korea has a long-term goal of unifying the Korean peninsula. In April 1975, Chairman Kim Il-sung visited Peking and made the following remarks in a speech at a banquet in his honour.

> If a revolution occurs in South Korea, we, as their brethren, cannot remain on the sidelines. We would actively support the people of South Korea. If the enemy should foolishly launch an attack, we will resolutely wage war against him and crush him to pieces. The only thing we have to lose

through such a war is the military demarcation line. We have the unity of the motherland to gain.[16]

There are three ways in which North Korea could attempt to unify the Korean peninsula. The first is all-out war; the second is the instigation of the civil strife which Chairman Kim referred to in the above remark; and the third is to cause constant political turmoil in South Korea. There are too many constraints on the first method. In the first place, North Korea lacks the developed industrial base necessary to support large-scale war. Therefore, North Korea cannot launch total war without the support of either or both the Soviet Union and the P.R.C. Almost all analysts agree that neither the Soviet Union nor China wants a general war.

As for the second alternative of creating large-scale civil strife, the police system in South Korea is quite elaborate and the people are so anti-Communist that it is virtually impossible for Pyongyang to infiltrate guerrillas into South Korean territory. Furthermore, as long as the political and economic situation in South Korea remains stable, a spontaneous, violent uprising among the people is extremely unlikely. Therefore, the North Koreans are left with the third alternative, i.e. to cause political confusion in the South.

Pyongyang's ceaseless declarations of support for the anti-government students and politicians in the South serves to make the South Korean government more suspicious of anti-government movements. The South Korean government has no way of knowing which of the anti-government activists have links with North Korea and which do not. Thus the government is forced to suppress them all. This, in turn, serves to aggravate the political strife and to increase international criticism of Seoul. Pyongyang can thus isolate the Park regime by indirectly causing this increase in the criticism heaped on Seoul by the U.S. and Japanese mass media.

At present, it looks very much as if this third alternative is succeeding very well. Therefore, the nature of the crisis in the Korean peninsula is not primarily military. It is a crisis of domestic South Korean politics. If the Park regime can handle this problem well, South Korea will return to economic and political stability and peace on the Korean peninsula will be maintained.

The withdrawal of the U.S. ground troops by the Carter administration will result in the South Korean Army attempting to arm itself heavily and to strengthen its chain of command. There are, as a result, some people who fear that South Korea might attack the North of its own volition. However, most of the present leaders in Seoul have personally experienced the Korean War of

1950–53. They have not forgotten the havoc wreaked by war on the small Korean peninsula. Thus it does not seem reasonable to assume that an increase in modern conventional weapons by the South Korean Army will lead to a more dangerous situation on the Korean peninsula.

IV. Prospects for the Future

A) The Proliferation of Nuclear Weapons

The three nuclear powers in the North-east Asian region are the Soviet Union, the United States and China. The Chinese, as observed earlier, are taking much longer to develop nuclear weapons than expected. As long as the Sino-Soviet conflict continues, most of its nuclear weapons will be directed at the Soviet Union.

Taiwan and South Korea are interested in developing nuclear weapons, but their technology and source of raw materials is controlled by the U.S.A. It does not appear, therefore, that they will be able to develop nuclear weapons for the time being. Should they dare to consider going nuclear, they would face many problems such as finding a test site for explosions or devising computer-simulated tests, determining whether a nuclear capability of their own would deter an enemy attack, developing their own delivery systems and so forth. At the same time, a decision to go nuclear would certainly antagonise the American government and people and would culminate in a total trade ban by Washington. This use of economic sanctions would surely asphyxiate their economies easily. Thus the bold decision to go nuclear would in fact be akin to suicide.

Japan is quite capable of producing nuclear weapons but has not the slightest intention of doing so. This policy is not likely to change as long as the international market mechanism is functioning. Japan is extremely interested in arms control in North-east Asia. For example, as early as May 1966, the Japan Socialist Party called for Japanese efforts to create a zone of unarmed neutrality which was to include South Korea, the Philippines, Indonesia, Burma, Thailand, India, Pakistan, Malaysia and Singapore. Furthermore, in March 1972, the Japanese delegate to the Geneva Conference of the Committee on Disarmament stated that

> There is already a treaty in Latin America banning nuclear weapons . . . Last year in Asia there was a similar movement with the proposal to make the Indian Ocean a zone of peace. Japan will actively cooperate to the fullest with this type of regional arms control.[17]

The author has constantly urged that this policy of the Japanese government be worked out in greater detail and be given greater stress. The fact of the matter is that nuclear disarmament will be very difficult to achieve if left solely to negotiations between the U.S.A. and the U.S.S.R. The most that can be expected through these talks are arms control agreements like the NPT or SALT, which do no more than regulate nuclear weapons and benefit only Moscow and Washington. The author believes that the only way that nuclear disarmament can be achieved is through the formation of a strong united front by the non-nuclear nations.

Unfortunately, many Asian nations have been quite uninterested in this problem. However, Soviet and U.S. nuclear-armed submarines are now operating freely in Asian waters and in ten years it is possible that Chinese MRBMs will be pointed at the various Asian nations. Therefore, it seems likely that a clear call for nuclear disarmament in the region would be a great contribution to the future peace of Asia and the world.

Care must be taken, however, to ensure that this movement to control nuclear weapons must not be allowed to serve the interests of any major power. Up to the present time, the Japanese movement against nuclear weapons has been soft on the Soviet Union, and there have even been some factions which have expressed support for Chinese nuclear weapons. This type of biased approach will not serve the cause of peace.

The movement to limit nuclear arms should not be too radical and impractical. For example, the Japanese Diet has declared its support for the three non-nuclear principles, namely that atomic weapons will be neither produced nor installed in Japan and that they will not be allowed into Japan. The first two principles are fine since they are policies which can be decided by the Japanese government alone. However, the third principle poses a problem.

The principle was at first intended to block any country from bringing nuclear weapons into Japan proper, but due to strong pressure from the opposition parties, it was expanded to cover both the Japanese territorial sea and airspace. However, an executive agreement between the U.S.A. and Japan made Yokosuka the home port of the Seventh Fleet. It is inconceivable that vessels of the Seventh Fleet divest themselves of nuclear weapons before entering Yokosuka harbour. This has led to sharp criticism of the Japanese government by the opposition parties. The Japanese government only serves to discredit its non-nuclear commitment by adopting a policy that it cannot implement.

B) The Military Presence of the U.S.S.R. in the Region

As previously mentioned, Soviet naval power in the region is expanding. The Russians now have effective control of the Sea of Japan. According to the Self Defence Force, in 1976 at least 140 Soviet warships passed through the Tsushima Strait, 60 through the Tsugaru Strait and 110 through the Soya (La Perouse) Strait.[18] In 1971, the Air Self-Defence Force was put on alert 345 times. In 1974 there were 323 alerts and in 1975, although there was a slight decline, there were still 281 alerts. Over 80 per cent of these alerts were called in response to the intrusion of Soviet warplanes into Japanese airspace.

The Soviet Union advocates détente but it is felt in some quarters that this is actually a strategy aimed at weakening the U.S.A. and Western Europe militarily. There are some analysts who insist that the Soviet Union will persist in an arms buildup whatever the costs.[19] Should this be the case, caution would be in order.

The U.S.A. used to be the predominant naval power in the region. One of the traditional goals of the U.S.A. has been to guard the freedom of the seas. For example, in Defense Secretary Rumsfeld's words:

> Although we are not so dependent upon the seas as other nations such as Japan and Great Britain, the United States has significant and longstanding maritime interests. Many of the raw materials and energy sources vital to our economy reach us by sea and the seas provide essential links to our allies. The United States, together with its allies, therefore must maintain maritime forces that are capable of ensuring unhampered use of the seas.[20]

There is not the slightest reason to doubt that this is the U.S. goal. However, it is unclear why the Soviet Union is strengthening its arsenal in North-east Asia. The Russian national interest is ambiguous on this point. Some people have said that the Soviet arms buildup in North-east Asia is in response to the Sino-Soviet confrontation. However, Soviet military strategy is clearly not that limited in its goals. Neither is it for the sole purpose of global competition with the U.S.A. In the region, the Soviets are prepared to use their military power to confront the P.R.C., the U.S.A., Japan and the other groupings of states in the area. This determination was voiced repeatedly by the Russians at the 'Japanese-Soviet Specialists' Conference on Peace for Asia' which was held in Kyoto in April of last year.

Although the U.S.A. has been traditionally dependent on the

ocean for trade links, the Soviet Union is fundamentally a land power. Moscow would not hesitate to disrupt sea trade, if it concludes that Soviet national interest demands such action. At present, the Soviet Union's military power is not playing a destructive role in the region, but it will certainly come to exert political influence on the Asian nations. Furthermore, there may come a day when Soviet military power has increased to such an extent that a rapid shift in their assessment of their capabilities occurs. At that point, the Soviet Union may very well exert direct military pressure on some Asian adversary that has aroused its ire. It is impossible to estimate when Soviet military power will reach this critical level, resulting in a qualitative change in the political environment of the region.[21]

There are only two ways of dealing with this uncertainty. The first is the strengthening of the regional military alliances centred around the U.S.A. The enhancement of naval power would be of particular importance. Since it would be difficult to consider the P.R.C. an ally, the key alliance in the region would continue to be that between Japan and the U.S.A. If the U.S.A. continues to withdraw from the Asian region, there would be only Japan to fill the military vacuum. This is why there are some who feel that Japan will embark on a rapid arms buildup in the 1980s.[22]

The second alternative response to the Soviet uncertainty is to deter the Soviet Union by non-military means. That is to say, the major nations in the Asian region should join together and present the Soviet Union with a united front in negotiations. They should strengthen economic ties with the Soviet Union by aiding the exploitation of Siberia and should strive in general to strengthen their bargaining position vis-à-vis the Soviet Union while maintaining friendly relations with it. Close ties with the U.S.A., and a friendly relationship with China would serve this end. In addition, negotiations for the establishment of a non-nuclear zone in the region would also enhance their bargaining position. This second alternative in effect responds to the Soviet challenge with a number of coordinated non-military moves. It is more sophisticated and far more attractive than the first alternative. There will certainly be a number of problems, but there is no question that the second choice is preferable to the first one.

C) The Proliferation of Conventional Weapons

It is often observed that the U.S. withdrawal from Korea is liable to stimulate the proliferation of conventional weapons in the Northeast Asian region. The author does not agree with the proposition that the U.S. withdrawal would automatically cause South Korea and Taiwan to set about rapidly strengthening their own military capabilities. For the defence of Taiwan, the key factor is the control of the airspace over the Taiwan Straits. Taiwan therefore needs planes that are superior to the MiG-21s and it cannot obtain them without U.S. aid. Thus arms proliferation in the Taiwan area will be governed by U.S. policy towards China.

South Korea is in the same position. It has been extremely successful in its plan to build a modern heavy industry and thus assure itself of self-sufficiency in weapons. Nonetheless, it is still dependent on the U.S.A. for all sophisticated conventional weapons. Here again, U.S. policy towards Korea will determine whether or not there will be an arms buildup in the region.

In conclusion, the U.S.A. remains the decisive military power in the region. This is true despite U.S. efforts to withdraw from Asia following the defeat in Vietnam and the emergence of neo-isolationism in the U.S.A. itself. It will be U.S. policy which will determine the fate of South Korea and Taiwan.

Footnotes

* The author is indebted to Ms. Maura Brennan for her help in editing this chapter.

1 Shinkichi Eto, Tadao Miyashita, Shinichiro Sato (ed.), *Higashi Ajia* (East Asia), Tokyo: Daiyamondo-sha, 1970, pp. 4ff.

2. Morinosuke Kajima, *Nihon Gaikō-shi* (A Diplomatic History of Japan) I (1970), pp. 99–100.

3. *Ibid.*, p.100.

4. *Krasnaya Zvezda*, 27 July 1975.

5. *Krasnaya Zvezda*, 11 February 1976.

6. See Congressional testimony of U.S. Navy Chief of Naval Operations, James Halloway III, 2 February 1976 in U.S. Congress, *Hearing of U.S. Congress House Committee on Armed Services, Military Posture H.R. 11500: Part I,* Washington, D.C., 1976, p. 822.

7. *Krasnaya Zvezda*, 11 February 1976.

8. Heihachiro Fujiki, 'Soren Kaigun no Kyōi to Sono Jittai' (Facts about the threat of the Soviet Navy), Kokubō (National Defence), No. 285 November 1976, pp. 19ff. Also cf. S.J. Dudzinsky, Jr. and James Digby, 'The Strategic and Tactical Implications of New Weapons Technologies', Robert O'Neill (ed.), *The Defence of Australia: Fundamental New Aspects,* Canberra, 1977, p. 39ff; and Steven J. Rosen, 'Surface-to-air Missiles and the Future Value of Air Superiority', Desmond Ball (ed.), *The Future of Tactical Airpower in the Defence of Australia,* Canberra, 1977, p.200ff.

9. *Jen-min Ji-pao*, (People's Daily), 10 September, 1976.

10. Drew Middleton's essay in the *New York Times*, 24 June 1977. Also, Ch'ien Hsue-sen, a leading Chinese nuclear scientist complained about

the terrible backwardness of scientific technology in the P.R.C. in an article in *Hungch'i* (Red Flag), No. 7 1977. A PLA deserter stated in Taiwan that the plane in use by the Chinese which is identical to the Soviet MiG–19 is called the Chiencheng 6 and that he does not know the total number of Chiencheng 6 planes that China has, but that 2,000 to 3,000 would be a good estimate, in his opinion. (*Sankei Newspaper*, 29 July 1977).

11. *Wireless Bulletin*, Press Office, USIS, American Embassy, Tokyo.
12. Osamu Kaibara, *Watashi no Kokubō-hakusho* (My White Paper for the National Defence), Tokyo: Jiji Tsūshin-sha, 1975, p. 125.
13. In my opinion, the Australians, in contrast to the Japanese, have a good bargaining chip in negotiations with the United States, i.e. uranium. I suspect that Prime Minister Fraser, when he visited the U.S.A. in June, tried to use this issue in an effort to persuade President Carter not to withdraw ground troops from South Korea too rapidly.
14. No Japanese is allowed to export weapons to 1) Communist countries, 2) those countries to whom the weapon-trade-ban resolution of the U.N. applies, and 3) those who are engaged in active conflict.
15. e.g. Bunichiro Tabe, President of the Mitsubishi Corporation, advocated the export of weapons in a press conference on 7th July.
16. *Jen-min Ji-pao*, (People's Daily), 19 April 1975.
17. Hisashi Maeda, 'Hokutō-Ajia no Gunbi Kisei' (Arms Control in North-east Asia), World Economic Information Service (ed.) *Konnichi no Kokusai Taiseika ni okeru Shomondai* (Problems in the Present International System), Tokyo: 1977, p. 148ff.
18. Asagumo Shinbunsha (ed.), *Bōei Handobukku* (Defence Handbook), Asagumo Shinbunsha, Tokyo, 1977, p. 284.
19. H. Matsukane, 'The Soviet's Long Range Strategy in North Asia', mimeographed, submitted to the Symposium on North-east Asian Security, held at Stanford Research Institute on 20–22 June 1977, p.4.
20. Donald H. Rumsfeld, *Annual Defense Department Report, FY 1977*, Washington, D.C.; 1976, pp. 10–11.
21. To the best of my knowledge, the earliest warning voiced concerning the rapid development of Soviet sea power was made by Commodore W.B.M. Marks, R.A.N., in his letter to the editor of the *West Australian*, 19 March 1974.
22. Osamu Miyoshi, 'Semaru 1985–nen no Kiki' (The Coming Crisis of 1985), *Getsuyō Hyōron* (Monday Review), Tokyo; No. 338, 18 July 1977. In the light of domestic constraints, I personally doubt that the Japanese government will embark on a military buildup. Japan will continue to limit itself to the development of a defensive system and will not turn to the development of an offensive capacity. However, I do not think it likely that there would be any strong opposition to the development of a sophisticated surveillance system around Japan. Geographically, the Japanese archipelago is in a good position to establish an elaborate surveillance system to monitor the activities of the Soviet Pacific Fleet. Tokyo recently extended its territorial sea to

twelve nautical miles and the Tsugaru Strait has thus come under the control of Tokyo, although Japan has at least temporarily waived its rights in order to avoid a dispute with the Soviet Navy. The Korea Strait and the La Perouse Strait now have only a narrow belt of high seas remaining.

6
Weapons Proliferation and Security in South-east Asia
Khaw Guat Hoon

It is implicitly taken for granted that an armed force is vital for the protection of a country's national security. As such, states devote part of their resources, however limited, to military uses. Indeed, for the past several years, the military spending of most states has steadily increased. According to the U.S. Arms Control and Disarmament Agency (ACDA) world military spending totalled $US183.99 billion in 1966; nine years later, it surpassed $US371 billion.[1]*

Practically every region in the world, developed and developing, has contributed to the rise in global military spending. In Asia, for example, the level of military spending was higher in 1975 than it was in 1966. In 1966, the combined military expenditures of ten South-east Asian countries—Burma, Cambodia, Laos, North Vietnam, South Vietnam, Thailand, Malaysia, Indonesia, Singapore and the Philippines—came to a total of $US1,221 million. The figure reached $US3,703 million in 1975. Indeed, the expenditures of all the South-east Asian states were higher in 1975 than in 1966. As one measure which is commonly used to estimate levels of armaments is the quantity of resources devoted to military uses—or military expenditures—,[2] the increase in such expenditures therefore indicates that the levels of armaments of these countries were higher in 1975 than they were nine years ago. Table I gives figures of total military expenditures in the South-east Asian region in the period 1966–75. However, despite the overall increase within less than a decade, it should be noted that levels of military spending of several countries did not rise steadily throughout the years; in fact they waxed and waned.

It is the intention of this chapter to explore the interrelations of arms proliferation and security in the South-east Asian region. The regional countries have, at one time or another, emphasised the importance of possessing a strong and 'modern' armed force

Table 1³

Military Expenditures in South-east Asia, 1966–1975

(in millions of $US)

	1966	1967	1968	1969	1970	1971	1972	1973	1974	1975
Burma	120	102	104	117	135	155	157	189	139	171
Cambodia	32	36	38	42	100	98	141	84	64	68
Indonesia	96	219	301	356	410	479	545	535	709	1,050
Laos	17	18	18	19	19	20	18	19	18	19
Malaysia	133	132	131	131	163	190	304	308	397	515
Philippines	61	70	82	90	101	109	112	218	262	402
Singapore	25	33	54	136	154	197	200	226	252	305
Thailand	101	125	161	202	244	327	340	315	354	398
Vietnam,Nth	330	325	325	300	300	300	325	290	300	310
Vietnam,Sth	306	321	404	391	413	490	552	586	547	465
Total	1,221	1,381	1,618	1,784	2,039	2,365	2,694	2,770	3,042	3,703

for the protection of their national security and this partly explains the rise in their military spending. However, as noted, levels of military expenditure have fluctuated and at certain periods of time, there has been a greater demand for arms than at others. Levels of arms transfers to these countries under grant, credit or commercial sales terms will be taken into account in the discussion for they contribute to arms proliferation. The need to acquire arms and increase military spending is closely related to the country's perception of its security situation. Firstly then, the security problems faced by the South-east Asian countries will be briefly discussed as well as the conditions which lead to a greater demand for arms and a sharp rise in military expenditure. Secondly, the process of arms proliferation in the region will be examined. Attention is given to the arms trade and the role of extraregional powers in providing these countries with arms. Finally, the question of whether a policy of acquiring arms will lead to regional stability and a sense of greater security will be raised as will possible alternative policies for protecting national security.

Arms and National Security

Each country in the South-east Asian region is confronted with problems relating to its security. Within each state, internal problems of varying intensity exist, the more serious of which pose a challenge to the state as it is territorially and politically constituted. As is well-known, there are groups within most Southeast Asian countries which are disaffected with the established political and socio-economic systems for ideological, ethnic, religious or economic reasons. While some may not resort to armed violence to express their grievances, others do. In several countries, insurgency is a problem. Those disaffected have launched armed struggles or wars of national liberation which have as an objective either the overthrow of the incumbent government or secession and the setting up of an independent state. Besides being confronted with internal threats to their security, many states are also faced with problems arising out of their tensed relations with their neighbours. Ideological differences, unsolved problems of border demarcation, rival claims to disputed territories, suspicions of external interference in their internal affairs make these states acutely aware of the fact that their security needs protection. At the same time, their relations with some extraregional powers— particularly with the U.S.S.R., U.S.A. and C.P.R.—are fraught with difficulties. Many believe that the activities of one or the other of the great powers constitute a threat to their security. The non-communist countries of ASEAN—Malaysia, Indonesia, the Philippines, Singapore and Thailand—are especially wary of China. The Communist states of Indo-China harbour suspicions of American intentions. Indeed, it appears that the great powers' rivalry in the region, their tendency to support one or the other South-east Asian state in their conflicts in the past has made more acute the tense relations existing among them.

Of much concern to the South-east Asian countries is the fact that their internal problems may be exploited by unfriendly states situated in and outside the region to weaken their political and socio-economic structures. Countries confronted with internal threats are, as will be seen, worried about external interference in their internal affairs. Moreover, many are convinced that unfriendly states do in fact give support and even material assistance to rebels in their territories.

It appears that, as noted, levels of military expenditures of South-east Asian states are affected by the problems posed to their security. Many of the problems are chronic, having been in existence since they obtained their independence. Thailand, the only country in the region which escaped being colonised, also faces problems which are of long standing. However, these problems may constitute a greater threat at one time than at another. For example, the Communist problem faced by the non-communist countries has varied in intensity: it may erupt into an armed struggle the failure of which may usher in a lull in Communist activities; a few years later, insurgency may once again become a serious issue. Moreover, a dormant problem—such as the Muslims in the Southern Philippines—may develop into an armed struggle which requires urgent attention. Apart from chronic problems, a threat, hitherto nonexistent, may arise or the country may become involved in an armed conflict with another state. Such occurrences usually engender a greater demand for weapons and an increase in military expenditures. As the conflict or threat diminishes, there may be a decline in military spending.

Changes or political developments in the region may also contribute to a sense of insecurity in the South-east Asian states. For example, several decisions taken by extraregional states in the late 1960s and early 1970s were viewed by many non-communist countries as being directly relevant to their security. British withdrawal east of Suez, the American decision to disengage from Vietnam, the Nixon Doctrine and American-Chinese 'rapprochement' contributed to the increase in military expenditures in the early 1970s. The threats, internal and external, posed to the state, and the political developments in the region are among the factors which must be taken into account in discussing the interrelations of arms and security. The problems faced by the non-communist countries will be discussed first before looking into those confronting the Communist states.

Since 1975, the region of South-east Asia has been divided into two groups of states—one comprising the Communist countries of Indo-China and the other the non-communist states. With the exception of Burma, the latter are all members of ASEAN. Although tensions sometime arise between the Communist states and the ASEAN countries, these two groups should not be looked upon as 'blocs' confronting each other. The Indo-Chinese states do not by any means act in unison on all matters and the ASEAN members do not consider themselves a 'bloc' aimed at any country or group of countries. It is not inconceivable that the Communist states may experience problems in their relations. So may the non-communist ones. Nevertheless, the ASEAN countries have a common perception of certain threats to their security. The Communist countries, on their part, also share common views about the sources of possible external threats to theirs.

All the ASEAN countries have at one time or another expressed concern over the threat of Communist insurgency in the region. Their common outlook on this problem is understandable in view of the fact that all are confronted with an internal Communist threat. Some are cooperating bilaterally to deal with the Communist terrorists along their common borders. For example, both Thailand and Indonesia have agreements with Malaysia with regard to such cooperation. The ASEAN countries, moreover, are worried about an external Communist threat to their security. It is unlikely that such a threat would find expression in an armed attack against their territories although such a possibility is not discounted, especially by Thailand.[4] It is, however, more probable that it will take the form of subversion, assistance to the local insurgents and in other methods of interference in their domestic affairs. Most of these states have, at one time or another, accused China of interfering in their internal affairs. One—Thailand—has also alleged that Communist Vietnam has trained and provided material assistance to insurgents in its territory. It should be noted that some of the ASEAN countries are also confronted with non-communist threats.

Malaysia was faced with an armed revolt from the Malayan Communist Party (MCP) even prior to its independence. Begun in 1948, the revolt lasted until 1960; during these twelve years, the country was under a state of emergency which was declared over in 1960. However, the end of the Emergency did not mean the end of the Communist threat. From their bases in southern Thailand where they sought refuge in the 1950s elements of the MCP continued training and making preparations for another armed struggle. Indeed, since the 1960s they have launched attacks on Malaysian security forces within Malaysian territory itself.

Confronted as it was with a Communist threat, it is not surprising that on its independence in 1957, the country emphasised the need to build up its nascent armed forces. A navy and air force were thought essential to prevent assistance from reaching the insurgents from 'across the sea'. Indeed, as will be discussed, the problem of arms reaching the Communists from external sources has continued to cause concern. One objective in Malaysia's cooperation with Thailand is to prevent the smuggling of arms to the insurgents straddling their common border.

Malaysia was confronted with its first—and sole—external threat of armed aggression shortly after the formation of the Federation to include Sabah, Sarawak and Singapore. 'Konfrontasi' was launched by a non-communist country, Indonesia. However, from Kuala Lumpur's perspective, it was essentially a Communist threat inspired by the Partai Kommunis Indonesia (PKI) which was believed to have considerable influence over President Sukarno. Apart from the threat of armed aggression, Malaysia was also confronted with the problem of the Philippines' claim to part of its territory, Sabah. Faced for the first time with an armed attack as well as with a threat to its territorial integrity, Malaysia began to expand its armed forces and acquire more arms for its defence. Malaysian military expenditure was $US49.98 million in 1963. It rose to $US72.53 million in 1964 and further increased to $US96.04

million in 1965. Its armed forces increased from 14,000 in 1963 to 32,000 in 1964 and 37,000 in 1965. Moreover, its arms imports increased during 'Confrontation'. In the period 1963–74, 1964 and 1965 stand out as the years in which levels of arms imports reached the highest peaks:

Table 2[5]
Malaysian Arms Imports, 1963–1974
(millions of $US)

1963	3.0
1964	42.0
1965	45.0
1966	27.0
1967	8.0
1968	12.0
1969	22.0
1970	5.0
1971	26.0
1972	39.0
1973	34.0
1974	24.0

It was only in 1975 that a new peak in levels of arms imports was reached: the figure for that year was $US56 million. That Malaysia should have imported more arms in 1964–65 than in other years in this period is understandable. When a country is under armed attack, there is a greater demand for arms. Malaysia, like the other South-east Asian countries, depends on arms transfers from extraregional powers for its defence .With the end of Confrontation in 1966, arms imports fell to $US27 million and a year later to $US8 million. However, military expenditure did not fall with the end of Confrontation; it has been well above the $US100 million level annually since 1966 and has steadily increased since 1969 to reach a record $US515 million in 1975.

The steady rise in military spending can be explained in terms of the problems confronting the country in the late 1960s and early 1970s. Internally, it was faced with problems which threatened national unity. The Communist terrorists, moreover, were becoming increasingly bold in their attacks on security forces and in the selection of their targets. Externally, developments in the Indo-Chinese peninsular in particular and in South-east Asia in general aroused concern. The Vietnam war had spread to engulf both Laos and Cambodia, creating a situation of heightened instability in these two countries. It was feared that events in Indo-China would encourage the 'spread of subversion' in the region.[6] There was uneasiness about the impact the 1973 Paris Peace Agreement might have on Malaysia's security and regional stability. Moreover, in the late 1960s and early 1970s, some extraregional states made a series of decisions which would certainly have a bearing on its defence policy. Firstly, the British decided to withdraw from the Malaysia-Singapore region and to abrogate the Anglo-Malaysian Defence Agreement which had been the cornerstone of the country's defence policy since it achieved its independence. Under the Agreement, Britain was obligated to come to its assistance if it was under external attack and indeed Britain lived up to its commitment during Indonesian Confrontation. In 1971, the Agreement was abrogated and a loose Five-Power Defence Arrangement came into existence. Under this new arrangement, whose parties were Malaysia, Singapore, Britain, Australia and New Zealand, Britain made no firm commitment to come to the external defence of Malaysia. Neither did Australia nor New Zealand. Both, however, had not been parties to the Anglo-Malaysian Defence Agreement and had never been under any legal obligation to assist Malaysia should it be attacked. The abrogation of the Agreement meant that Malaysia could no longer depend on British assistance. Secondly, the Americans decided to disengage from Vietnam. Throughout the 1960s, Malaysia had expressed support for the American role in the Vietnam war, believing it to be important for the preservation of South Vietnam's 'political independence and territorial integrity' as well as political stability in the South-east Asian region. American disengagement, proceeding at a time when Britain was intent on reducing its military role in the region, aroused concern. Indeed, it was thought that a diminishment of the British military presence together with American disengagement might be a 'big boost to those who are trying to obtain power by violence and unconstitutional means'.[7] It also appeared that the country was worried about the impact of the Nixon Doctrine and Sino-American 'rapprochement' on political developments in the region.

In the 1970s Malaysia began to emphasise more and more the need to be self-reliant in defence matters. Unable to depend on its Commonwealth friends for assistance should a threat of armed aggression arise, having no defence agreement with any other country, it had few other options. As the late Tun Abdul Razak said, 'We cannot depend on others to defend our sovereignty and territorial integrity'.[8]

Under these conditions, Malaysia's military expenditure steadily rose in the 1970s. According to ACDA, expenditure was $US190 million in 1971, $US27 million more than the previous year. It jumped to $US304 million in 1972: one reason for the substantial increase was the termination of the Anglo-Malaysian Defence

Agreement in 1971. There was a slight increase of $US4 million in 1973 over the 1972 figure. In 1974, a year following the Paris Peace Agreement, expenditure rose to $US397 million. It was $US515 in 1975.

Thai military expenditures rose steadily in the latter half of the 1960s. (See Table 1.) There was a substantial increase in 1971 when expenditure climbed to $US327 million from the figure of $US244 million for 1970. By 1975, it had reached $US398 million. The increase in Thai military expenditure in this period was related to the security situation in the country.

First, like Malaysia, Thailand faces an internal threat of Communist insurgency which expanded in the late 1960s. Indeed, of the non-communist countries, Communist insurgency poses the greatest threat to Thailand. Because of Communist activities, 31 out of 71 provinces in the country were placed under a state of emergency by 1975.[9] Like Malaysia, Thailand too is worried about external assistance reaching the Communists.

China has apparently provided weapons and training to the insurgents.[10] Indeed, one obstacle in the normalisation of relations between the two countries was Thailand's belief that China was interfering in its domestic affairs by, among other things, supporting and assisting local insurgents. However, perhaps Thailand is currently more worried about Vietnamese interference in its internal affairs now that the two Vietnams are reunified. Even prior to 1975, it suspected Vietnam of abetting the Communist movement. Indeed, a Government White Paper in 1972 stated that North Vietnam had opened a school near Hanoi one of whose purposes was the training of Thai Communists in guerrilla warfare.[11]

Second, apart from the threat posed by the Communists, Thailand is also confronted with other internal problems from its ethnic minorities. The Lao in the north-east and the Thai Muslims in the south are examples. The Thai Muslims have set up a national liberation front whose objective appears to be secession. Thailand has always been concerned about external support given to the Thai Muslims and Pathet Lao intentions with regard to its Lao population. Since Laos turned Communist in 1975, Thailand has become more anxious than ever about Pathet Lao policies towards its north-east.

Third, Thailand was worried about the political developments in South-east Asia in the late 1960s and early 1970s. Given its close association with the U.S.A., American disengagement from Vietnam and the Nixon Doctrine, which served notice on the Asian states that they had to be more self-reliant in defence matters, naturally aroused Thai anxieties. Moreover, sharing as it does a common border with Laos and Cambodia, it could not but be disturbed about the political instability there and the inability of those governments to overcome the Communist threat.

The fall of Indo-China into Communist hands in 1975 intensified Thailand's concern over its security. The country now shares a 1,000–mile border with two Communist states, Laos and Cambodia, which in turn border Vietnam. It could not but suspect that, given its past role in their internal conflicts, the policies of the Indo-Chinese Communist states towards itself might not be friendly; it not only allowed American bases on its soil but permitted them to be used for carrying out bombing raids against North Vietnam and the liberated areas of Laos. It intervened militarily into Laos and Cambodia and despatched troops to South Vietnam. In doing so, it antagonised the Pathet Lao, Khmers Rouges and the Vietnamese Communists, all of whom turned out to be victors in 1975. What disturbed Thailand was the very distinct possibility that the Communist governments would pursue hostile policies in retaliation for its past activities in Indo-China.

The fact that there have been armed clashes between itself and the two Communist states of Laos and Cambodia only heightens its sense of insecurity. Moreover, Bangkok is worried about Vietnamese influence over Laos as well as the presence of about 50,000 Vietnamese in that country. Thai authorities suspect that Hanoi may be encouraging the Laotians in their acts of provocation against Thailand. Indeed, when one of the more serious incidents between the two countries occurred in November 1975, Thai Premier Kukrit Pramoj stated that 'another nation' was pushing Laos into confrontation with Thailand. It was believed that that nation was Vietnam.[12]

Sharing a long border with two Communist states with which it has had several skirmishes, having a common border with Burma, which too faces an internal Communist threat, and faced with Communist activities along the border areas with Malaysia, Thailand by mid-1975 had a police force of 80,000 patrolling its borders.[13] There have been suggestions that the force be strengthened and security forces in general be expanded.

The Communist insurgency in the Philippines is not as serious as the one in Thailand; nevertheless, it still constitutes a problem for the government. A revolt in the early years of independence was quickly quelled. However, in the 1960s Communist activities expanded and the Maoist New People's Army has posed a problem to internal security. In 1972, President Marcos estimated that there were 100,000 armed Communists and 100,000 sympathisers belonging to different organisations in the country.[14]

Like Thailand, the Philippines too is confronted with a problem from its Muslim population. Fighting between the Muslims and the governmental forces has been especially bitter following the declaration of martial law in 1972. An estimated 4,000–5,000 military personnel were killed in the period 1972–1976. Moreover, civilian casualties totalled about 10,000 while 500,000 people had been made homeless.[15] The rebels receive support, weapons and ammunition from abroad. One of the countries which have provided them with arms is Libya through the Malaysian state of Sabah. For example, two shipments of Soviet-made AK 47 rifles were landed near Malabang in 1969. The Muslims are apparently armed with American M16 rifles as well. Indeed, some observers have reported that they are often better supplied with arms than their governmental adversaries.

The government, concerned with the threat to internal stability, has attempted to reach a settlement with the Muslims. The Tripoli talks between the two parties took place in December 1976 with both agreeing to a ceasefire and the government giving a pledge to grant the Muslims a large measure of autonomy. However, President Marcos' announcement in early 1977 that a plebiscite would be conducted in the thirteen southern provinces to see if their inhabitants wanted them merged in an autonomous region was received with protests by the Muslims for, as only five of the thirteen provinces have Muslim majorities, it was unlikely that the results would be favourable to them. As matters stand, the problem of Muslim disaffection is by no means over. Internally, therefore, the country is confronted with two armed struggles—Communist and Muslim—both of which have apparently expanded since 1972.

Externally, the Philippines cannot be said to be faced with a threat. However, in the first half of 1970 it shared Thai and Malaysian concern over the developments in Indo-China in particular and South-east Asia in general. Although the Nixon Doctrine stated that the U.S.A. would stand by its commitments, the Philippines were nevertheless unsure about American readiness to provide assistance.

Philippine military expenditure steadily increased in the period 1966–1975. However, there were sharper increases in levels of expenditure in certain years. In 1972, the year martial law was declared, expenditure was $US112 million; it jumped to $US218 million in 1973, an increase of $US106 million. The sharpest increase occurred in 1975 when expenditure amounted to $US402 million, an increase of $US140 million from that of the previous year. Peak levels of arms imports occurred in 1972 and in 1975, the two years which saw sharp increases in military expenditure.

Indonesia, the largest country in South-east Asia, has one of the highest military expenditures in the region. If figures from ACDA

Table 3[16]
Philippine Arms Imports, 1966–1975
(millions of $US)

1966	20
1967	24
1968	22
1969	19
1970	14
1971	15
1972	31
1973	28
1974	29
1975	34

are used as a basis for analysis, Indonesian military expenditure in the period 1967–75 was surpassed only by that of South Vietnam for the years 1967–73 and by that of North Vietnam for 1967 and 1968. It should, of course, be borne in mind that the two Vietnams received considerable military assistance from the great powers which supported the one or the other. Of the ASEAN countries, Indonesian expenditure was the highest for every single year in this period. Military expenditure reached the figure of $US1,050 million in 1975. In that year, Indonesian military expenditure was the highest in South-east Asia.

The very size of the country necessitates a large armed force. As an archipelago, Indonesia needs a strong navy and air force to protect its territorial waters. However, the important role played by the army in domestic politics and in nation-building also calls for heavy military spending. Are there any specific threats to Indonesian security? There certainly exist remnants of the PKI and the problem of Communist terrorists along the Indonesian-Malaysian border. However, it cannot be said that the Communist threat is a serious one. What concerns military circles in Indonesia is the possibility that it may develop into a serious problem. Indeed, with an eye on the events in the Indo-Chinese peninsular in the early 1970s, the military have begun to talk about local guerrilla forces planning a long-term 'Vietcong style' war. President Suharto himself spoke of the possibility of a 'new and different' type of war following the Paris Peace Agreement.[17] Moreover, given the fact that there have been revolts against the central government in the past, the Indonesian leaders are also wary about possible threats to national unity.

In recent years, Indonesia has emphasised 'national resilience' which, among other things, means the ability of the nation to defend itself. This entails a strong armed force and indeed the country has embarked on a program of modernising its armed forces. Its military budget for 1976 was over $US1,100 million.

Although the island-republic of Singapore is not confronted with Communist insurgency, it is nevertheless worried about a Communist threat not only to its own security but to that of the region. Indeed, its Prime Minister, Lee Kuan Yew, has been among the most vocal of the ASEAN leaders in expressing anxiety over the Communist threat to South-east Asia. In a speech to the Commonwealth Summit in Ottawa in 1973, he noted that the collapse of Indo-China would advance the threat of Communist insurgency to Singapore's doorstep 'by way of Thailand and West Malaysia'.[18] From his perspective, the North Vietnamese had 'more guerrilla insurgency potential to export than China.'[19] Moreover, as a small island situated in a politically unstable region and one whose relations with its neighbours are often uneasy, Singapore is very conscious of the fact that a strong armed force is necessary for its security.

Like Malaysia, Singapore was affected by the British decision to withdraw from the Malaysia-Singapore region. It was clear that it could not depend on the British to come to its defence. Concerned with the Communist threat to the region, Singapore has been among the most outspoken of the non-communist countries in calling for an American military presence in South-east Asia. However, it is at the same time aware of American reluctance to become militarily involved in Asian conflicts. As the Singaporean Minister of State for Foreign Affairs, Rahim Ishak stated in 1972, Vietnam was the last war the U.S.A. would fight on the Asian mainland. Like the other ASEAN countries therefore, the island has begun to place more and more emphasis on self-reliance in defence. Not surprisingly, its military expenditures have steadily increased during the past several years. (See Table 1.) The peak level for its arms imports occurred in 1972 in the aftermath of the abrogation of the Anglo-Malaysian Defence Agreement:

It is interesting to note that in all the ASEAN countries, there was a sharp increase in military spending in the early years of the 1970s. Singapore's rose from $US154 million in 1970 to $US197 million in 1971. That of Thailand rose from $US244 million in 1970 to $US327 million in 1971; Indonesia's from $US410 million

Table 4[20]
Singaporean Arms Imports, 1969–1975
(millions of $US)

1969	9
1970	18
1971	19
1972	49
1973	26
1974	12
1975	14

in 1970 to $US479 million the following year; the Philippines' from $US112 million in 1972 to $US218 million in 1973. Malaysia's jumped from $US190 million in 1971 to $US304 million in 1972.

The increase can, as noted, be attributed mainly to the particular security problems faced by these countries individually. However, these countries also share a common concern over the political developments in the South-east Asian region which, directly or indirectly, affects their security. The British decision to withdraw from east of Suez had the greatest relevance for both Malaysia and Singapore; the implications of the Nixon Doctrine were especially important for Thailand and the Philippines. All the ASEAN countries were, however, worried about the political developments in the region in the aftermath of a diminished Western military presence. All five, as noted, thus began to lay stress increasingly on self-reliance and 'national resilience'.

The Communist victories in Vietnam, Cambodia and Laos in 1975 aroused a sense of unease throughout the ASEAN region. The outcome of the Indo-Chinese conflicts was unsettling for two reasons: first, the local insurgents, encouraged by the Communist successes, might intensify their struggle and launch people's wars of their own; second, some of the arms captured by the victorious Communists—estimated to be worth between $US2–5 billion— might be sent to help their revolutionary counterparts in the rest of South-east Asia.

Statements made by ASEAN leaders in the immediate aftermath of the fall of Vietnam illustrated the prevailing uneasiness. Lee Kuan Yew noted that the end of the Indo-Chinese fighting could trigger new outbreaks of trouble in South-east Asia. He especially noted that the arms which fell into Cummunist hands could be 'a source of incalculable mischief'.[21] Indonesian Foreign Minister, Adam Malik, said that the Communist victories in Vietnam and Cambodia might encourage the remaining Communist elements in Indonesia in their struggle.[22] The Thai Prime Minister expressed the view that an aggressive Communist thrust into the region was possible and that the threat posed by the Communist terrorists could reach 'unmanageable proportions'. The Yang-di-Pertuan Agong of Malaysia noted that the developments in Indo-China would to a certain extent encourage the terrorists in the country. Of the ASEAN countries, Thailand was the most concerned with the emergence of Communist Indo-China for obvious reasons: its past involvement in the internal conflicts of Vietnam, Laos and Cambodia.

While these five countries are uneasy about the policies of the three Communist states in the South-east Asian region, the latter on their part are suspicious of the functions and purposes of the Association to which the five belong. For example, although Hanoi is prepared to normalise relations with these countries, it has consistently expressed hostility towards ASEAN itself. Indeed, it has declared that the Association is a military organization functioning as a tool of 'US imperialists'. Moreover, it was critical of the presence of American troops in Thailand; they, however, were withdrawn in 1976. Thus, the three Communist states share common suspicions of ASEAN. However, it must be re-emphasised that they do not present a common front. Cambodia, for example, wants an independent policy and has little desire to be dominated by Vietnam, the strongest of the South-east Asian socialist states.

The Indo-Chinese countries too perceive the necessity of possessing a 'modern' armed force to protect their security. Vietnam has in no uncertain terms stated that it must prepare itself for the defence of its sovereignty and territorial integrity. This, among other things, means modernising the navy to protect its long coastline. It is, moreover, believed that the army which defeated the government of Nguyen Van Thieu is not suited for coping with an external threat and that the arms captured are outdated. However, Vietnam has not been specific about possible sources of external threats to its security apart from referring to 'aggressive powers' among which one might assume would be the U.S.A. That it should continue to harbour suspicions of that great power is understandable. American involvement in a war which it considered to be an internal one between itself and Saigon, American bombing and assistance given to right-wing factions in the other two Indo-Chinese states could not but leave a legacy of ill-feeling towards the U.S.A. Apart from the U.S.A., which countries, especially in the region of South-east Asia, could be considered 'hostile' to Vietnamese interests?

Difficulties have arisen in relations between Vietnam and China over rival claims on the Paracel and Spratly islands. Hanoi, as noted, is uncertain about the intentions of the ASEAN countries. Foreign Minister Nguyen Duy Trinh noted, for example, that these countries did not give support to the peoples of Indo-China during the war.[23] On the contrary, they supported the American role in the conflict. Two countries, Thailand and the Philippines sent troops to Vietnam; Malaysia provided Saigon with 'arms, war materials and equipment'[24] and trained South Vietnamese military personnel in jungle warfare. Singapore's stand on the war was less than neutral while Indonesia's attitudes towards Hanoi had cooled considerably since President Sukarno fell from power. Hanoi especially vented its ire on Thailand. Its criticism of Thai-Malaysian border operations against the Communists was in fact aimed mostly at Bangkok.

The other two Communist states also view Thailand with suspicion. Its past involvement in their internal affairs partly explains their current misgivings about Thai intentions. Moreover, some right-wing forces fled to Thailand when the Communists took over power in 1975. It is believed that they are plotting against the present governments. Bangkok is suspected of abetting these elements. While Thailand regards armed clashes with Laos and Cambodia as a threat to its security, the latter on their part look upon them as a threat to theirs. To the Thais, the clashes are started by their Communist neighbours; to the latter, it is Thai provocation which leads to armed skirmishes. Indeed, after an armed clash, Laos talked about Thai violation of its sovereignty and territorial integrity.

Despite attempts of the Indo-Chinese and the ASEAN states to improve their relations, it appears that they are still wary of one another. The former's ambiguous position on wars of national liberation is disquieting to the latter while the increased military cooperation of the latter is suspect to the Communist states.

The only non-communist state in the region which is not a member of ASEAN is Burma. The country has displayed a low political profile in South-east Asian politics and has attempted to maintain correct ties with states, Communist and non-communist.

Burma too has had its share of internal problems. The government has been engaged in various conflicts with ethnic minorities such as the Karens, Kachins, Mons and Arakanese as well as with Communist groups such as the White and Red Flags. Moreover, it is confronted with the problem of remnants of the Kuo Min Tang troops. Burmese military expenditures have fluctuated in the period 1966–75. Levels of arms imports have been low in comparison with those of the other South-east Asian states. This is due to two reasons: it does not have the resources to purchase large quantities of arms and until the mid–1960s, was generally reluctant to receive military aid. The peak in its levels of arms imports was in 1966 when it procured $US13 million worth. Internal difficulties as well as problems in its relations with China, which was then undergoing the Cultural Revolution, led to a greater demand for arms. Burma turned to the U.S.A. for support.

Given the fact that each South-east Asian country is faced with internal as well as external problems to its security, each stresses the necessity of possessing a 'modern' armed force to protect itself. Increases in military spending and demands for weapons have led to arms proliferation in the region. Two questions must be raised: How do these countries obtain the arms to equip their forces? Where do the arms come from?

The Process of Arms Proliferation in South-east Asia
In this section I intend to discuss the process of arms proliferation in South-east Asia. In doing so, three factors must be taken into account: the conditions which lead to arms proliferation, the ways in which the South-east Asian countries obtain arms for the protection of their security, and the role of extraregional powers in accelerating arms proliferation.

The conditions which lead to arms proliferation have been discussed above. As noted, it is concern with its security that propels each state to increase its military spending and stockpiles of weapons. The process of proliferation is accelerated when the states are involved in conflicts or when their security situation calls for further acquisition of arms.

The South-east Asian states—like any other state—are determined to exercise their sovereign right to possess an armed force to protect their security. The armed forces of several countries increased steadily in the 1966–75 period. (See Table 5.) At the same time, these states want their armed forces to be well-equipped with 'modern' weapons. They see the need to acquire 'sophisticated' arms to replace 'out-dated' ones. Indeed, several have sought to obtain progressively more sophisticated and lethal weaponry for their armed forces. The process of 'modernisation' is a continuous one: more and more sophisticated equipments are added to their military arsenals. 'Modernisation' in fact means the acquisition of, as far as possible, the latest weapons and military equipments which are available on the market and within the financial reach of these countries. The Royal Malaysian Air Force provides an example of the continuous process of modernisation.

Table 5[25]
Numerical Strengths of Armed Forces in South-east Asian Countries,
1965–1975
(in thousands)

	1966	1967	1968	1969	1970	1971	1972	1973	1974	1975
Burma	135	136	136	173	174	175	191	198	202	209
Cambodia	83	83	84	85	85	205	200	213	220	62
Indonesia	346	347	348	358	358	358	356	310	270	260
Laos	93	62	62	59	62	72	79	71	60	46
Malaysia	35	40	46	46	58	62	69	70	75	76
Philippines	45	45	51	55	59	58	62	63	90	120
Singapore	0	10	11	12	14	15	20	24	24	27
Thailand	151	151	167	175	175	195	205	233	221	227
Vietnam,Nth*	256	418	447	477	452	455	625	630	665	643
Vietnam,Sth	617	645	735	892	1,000	1,060	1,100	1,090	980	0

* The 1975 figure is that of the People's Army of Vietnam, including the South Vietnamese Liberation Army forces.

When the RMAF was formed in 1958, the main types of aircraft used were Twin Pioneers and later Chipmunks. In 1961, they were replaced by Provost aircraft. In 1963, Alouette helicopters were introduced, but in 1967 a very much bigger helicopter, the Sikorsky S61, was acquired. That same year, a strike capability was added to RMAF capability with the arrival of the Canadian CL 41G. In 1968, a base was formed in Butterworth which became the home for Sabres. Marconi S600 air defence radars were introduced in 1971 and in 1975 the RMAF acquired the American F 5E jet fighter.

In recent years, with the increased emphasis on self-reliance, modernisation has become more important than ever. Malaysia is studying ways in which to equip its armed force with the 'latest' technology and weapons. The Philippines are considering modernising their Navy and buying more advanced aircraft to replace the existing F54s. Singapore, Thailand and Indonesia are likewise in the process of adding new and more sophisticated equipment to their arsenals. Even Vietnam, which has emerged as the most powerful country in the region, has talked about the need to modernise its armed forces. The Communists took over an estimated $US2–5 billion worth of military equipment in 1975 which included jet fighters, tanks, armoured personnel carriers, 1.6 million rifles and 130,000 tons of ammunition.[26] However, it is believed that some of the equipment captured is out of commission.

Each state asserts that its armed forces are meant for self-defence and not for aggressive purposes. However, given the fact that many states view each other with suspicion, it is not surprising that plans by one state to modernise and expand its forces usually elicit uneasiness from the others. As weapons purportedly acquired for defence may be used for offence, the procurement of more arms by a country may be viewed by others with misgivings. They, on their part, may be propelled to strengthen their own military capability. The race to keep up with each other in the acquisition of sophisticated weapons is a vicious circle as increasingly sophisticated weapons are made available to the South-east Asian states.

Some military analysts of the South-east Asian region tend to compare the military capability of Vietnam with that of the ASEAN countries. For example, the defence columnist of *Sinar Harapan*, Madiri Sianipar, noted that the military forces of all the ASEAN countries totalled 627,300—about the same as North Vietnam's 600,000 before reunification with the South. North Vietnam had 198 combat aircraft, Thailand 179, Singapore 96, Malaysia 50, the Philippines 56 and Indonesia 30.[27] The ASEAN countries, it is argued, are militarily weaker than Vietnam. As such, these countries should increase and improve their armaments. Military circles in some countries—particularly Indonesia—have also argued that the ASEAN countries should have closer military cooperation, albeit outside the framework of the Association. There have also been suggestions that the weapons and equipments of the ASEAN armed forces be standardised. Indonesian Defence Minister, General Maraden Panggabean has for example argued that standardisation is desirable to facilitate ASEAN countries in helping each other should the need arise. It is, of course, pointed out that such cooperation is not aimed at any state. However, military cooperation may convince Hanoi that ASEAN is indeed an anti-Communist military organisation. It, too, may see the necessity of cooperating with, for example, Laos to counter a threat from 'aggressive' countries.

One reason for the ASEAN countries' current emphasis on military cooperation is an apparently genuine fear of an arms flow to the insurgents within their territories. Such a flow is another potential form of arms proliferation in South-east Asia, but in this instance proliferation is not among states but among insurgents.

The problem of the ability of subnational groups to obtain weapons is one of long standing in South-east Asia. Groups as diverse as the Khmer Serei, Khmers Rouges and the Muslims in the Philippines have, at one time or another, obtained military equipment for their struggles.

The ASEAN countries are worried about the fact that some insurgents—Communist and non-communists—appear to be well-equipped with arms. It has been noted, for example, that Communist terrorists along the Thai–Malaysian border use 'sophisticated' weapons against the security forces. The Muslim rebels in the Philippines are sometimes better equipped than the governmental forces. How do these insurgents acquire arms? And from what sources?

China is one country which is believed to have supplied weapons to some Communist insurgents. More recently, the ASEAN countries have become concerned about the possibility of Vietnam becoming another source of arms. These fears were especially widespread in the aftermath of Saigon's fall. Several countries expressed concern over the prospect of millions of dollars worth of arms falling into the hands of insurgents throughout non-communist South-east Asia. Thailand is especially worried about the problem. Thai military circles allege that arms supplies for the local insurgents have come mainly from Indo-China since 1965; the flow of weapons has apparently increased since the Communist takeovers.

However, although Vietnam is considered to be a source of weapons, several countries are quick to point out that Hanoi itself may not be channelling arms to the insurgents; it is more probable that such arms are smuggled into the countries by gun-runners who bought or obtained them in other ways in South Vietnam before its fall. They are then sold to the insurgents for profit.[28]

Arms, whether provided by governments or sold by gun-runners, enter the territory through smugglers. Indeed, arms smuggling is considered to be a serious problem. It is believed that an 'enormous' quantity of arms and munitions has been smuggled into the non-communist countries since 1975 although the actual value and quantity is difficult to estimate. It is apparently easy to smuggle arms into Thailand. The weapons are acquired along the Thai–Cambodian and Thai–Laotian borders and then shipped by trucks to high–demand areas.[29] It was reported that Communist supply lines lead from Thailand to Central Pahang in Malaysia and from there to Kuala Lumpur, Malacca and Johore Bahru.[30] Discovery of weapons such as M16 rifles and M79 grenade launchers in Thailand only serves to heighten anxiety concerning this problem. It is, moreover, estimated that an M16 rifle can be bought in Thailand for as cheaply as $M250 or less than $US100.

Whether large quantities of arms have or have not proliferated among insurgents is less important than the belief on the part of policy-makers that arms indeed have reached these groups. Those countries which take the issue of arms smuggling seriously are currently strengthening their land, sea and air patrols.

How do the South-east Asian states obtain arms? Are they produced locally? Or do they have to be imported?

Most developing countries do not have the resources to devote to a military research and development program. This is certainly true of the South-east Asian countries. Many are able to manufacture small arms and ammunitions for certain types of weapons. For example, the Indonesian armaments factory at Bandung is producing various kinds of light arms and heavy mortars. Some produce weapons under licence. Singapore's state-owned Chartered Industries produce the Colt AR–15 which is similar to the M16, Israeli-type explosives, grenades and mortars.[31] Licensed production of some major weapons such as military aircraft and armoured fighting vehicles is carried on in, for example, Indonesia, Thailand and the Philippines. However, it appears that the arms industry is at a nascent stage and as such the South-east Asian countries cannot produce sufficient weapons for their armed forces. Although some countries, such as Singapore, have exported arms, the value of their imports far surpasses that of their exports. Singapore exported $US6 million worth of arms in 1972 but imported $US49 million; it exported $US2 million in 1974 but imported $US12 million. All South-east Asian states in fact depend on arms imports. In the period 1966–75, the region imported more than $US1,000 million worth of arms annually. (See Table 6.)

Levels of South-east Asian arms imports have fluctuated. The peak was in 1972 when total regional imports amounted to $US2,428 million. Of course, levels of arms imports were affected by the progress of the Vietnam war. The two Vietnams imported more arms than any other country in South-east Asia.

Table 6[32]

Arms Imports of South-east Asian Countries, 1966–1975

(in millions of $US)

	1966	*1967*	*1968*	*1969*	*1970*	*1971*	*1972*	*1973*	*1974*	*1975*
Burma	13	9	4	5	1	1	0	0	5	1
Cambodia	7	2	7	5	60	54	82	79	302	128
Indonesia	6	1	3	13	16	24	35	20	35	17
Laos	43	87	72	55	69	111	109	96	68	22
Malaysia	27	8	12	22	5	26	39	34	24	56
Philippines	20	24	22	19	14	15	31	28	29	34
Singapore	0	0	0	9	18	19	49	26	12	14
Thailand	25	56	73	48	30	38	28	43	42	51
Vietnam,Nth	610	830	530	315	200	310	745	325	400	155
Vietnam,Sth	727	510	726	934	917	803	1,310	1,140	665	906
Total	1,478	1,527	1,449	1,425	1,330	1,401	2,428	1,791	1,582	1,384

Millions of dollars worth of arms were transferred to the region by extraregional powers. Indeed, it is not possible to ignore their role in the process of arms proliferation. First, if they were unwilling to supply arms, the process of arms proliferation would have been much slower. Second, it is from these countries that the South-east Asian states acquire increasingly sophisticated weapons. Some of these countries now possess long-range surface-to-air missiles and supersonic aircraft, all of which were imported. Third, by issuing licences, these countries help towards the development of local arms industries.

There is no dearth of suppliers of arms to South-east Asia. Extraregional powers are prepared to transfer military equipment under various terms—grant, credit or cash sales. Table 7 gives figures of arms transfers by major suppliers to the South-east Asian countries in the period 1965–74. While some regional states depend mainly on one supplier, others adopt a policy of diversifying their sources of procurement.

For various reasons, the extraregional powers are willing to provide arms to these states. For some, including the U.S.A., U.S.S.R. and C.P.R., political reasons are tantamount. Their arms supply policy must be seen within the overall context of their foreign policies. The U.S.A. in the past transferred large quantities of arms to countries which were in the front line of its containment policy. Lesser quantities were provided to the other non-communist countries. The U.S.S.R. and C.P.R. supplied arms to North Vietnam as well as to neutralist countries which were prepared to accept them. Each was willing to provide arms to countries which were aligned to it or with which it was on friendly terms; the arms supply policy of each was geared towards maintaining friendly governments in power and assisting them in pursuing their foreign objectives, provided they did not conflict with its own. Arms indeed were a tool used by the 'big three' in their rivalry with each other. To others, profit seems to be an important consideration. Whatever motives are behind their willingness to transfer arms to the South-east Asian countries, the fact remains that their arms supply policy has accelerated the process of proliferation in the region. The arms policy of three countries—the U.S.A., U.S.S.R. and C.P.R.—will be briefly discussed.

One prime objective of American policy was to contain Communism. Not surprisingly, the bulk of American arms transferred to the region in the period 1965–74 went to South Vietnam, Laos, Cambodia and Thailand.

Of all the countries in the region, South Vietnam was the biggest

Table 7[33]

Total Arms Transfer to South-east Asian Countries by Major Suppliers, 1965–1974
(millions of $US)

Recipient	Total	United States	Soviet Union	France	United Kingdom	Czecho-slovakia	People's Republic of China	Poland	Canada	Federal Republic of Germany	All Others
Burma	45	29	—	3	3	—	—	—	—	5	5
Cambodia	606	570	8	9	—	—	11	—	1	—	7
Indonesia	331	88	54	1	10	5	—	—	6	—	167
Laos	754	751	2	—	—	—	—	—	—	—	1
Malaysia	242	44	—	25	73	—	—	—	25	2	73
Philippines	221	210	—	—	—	—	—	—	—	2	9
Singapore	133	43	—	2	46	—	—	—	—	8	34
Thailand	397	378	—	—	13	—	—	—	—	6	—
Vietnam, North	4,630	—	3,245	—	—	—	1,355	10	—	—	20
Vietnam, South	7,969	7,969	—	—	—	—	—	—	—	—	—
Total	15,328	10,082	3,309	40	145	5	1,366	10	32	23	316

recipient of American arms. Between 1965 and 1974, the U.S.A. supplied $US10,082 million worth of arms to South-east Asia ; $US7,969 million went to that country. Indeed, Saigon depended exclusively on American arms. This figure, it should be noted, does not include the value of weapons sent to Vietnam for the use of American troops. Moreover, the costs of American intervention in the war, which were about 25 billion a year in 1968 and 1969, were in excess of the total value of arms supplies to all Third World countries put together.[34] Two other countries stood out as major recipients of American arms—Laos and Cambodia: transfers to Laos totalled $US751 million while those to Cambodia $US570 million. The fourth biggest recipient was Thailand which received $US378 million worth of arms. Bearing in mind that Laos imported a total of $US754 million worth of arms, Cambodia $US606 million and Thailand $US397 million, it is obvious that their prime supplier of weapons was the U.S.A.

American arms supplies to both Laos and Cambodia were dependent on who was in power at any one time. Where Laos was concerned, the U.S.A. was willing to provide arms to governments which were either right-wing or coalitions of right-wing and neutralist factions. (When right-wing forces were out of power, they were equipped with American arms and encouraged in their opposition to the government.) Cambodia provides yet another example of a country whose government must be acceptable to the U.S.A. before it could expect to be supplied with arms. In the first few years of its independence, it received substantial American aid. However, as Cambodian-American relations became strained due to various reasons, including Norodom Sihanouk's decision to recognise China, American aid stopped. The U.S.A. became increasingly critical of the Cambodian government's foreign policy. In the 1960s, Cambodian imports of arms were below $US10 million annually. In 1970, its imports rose to $US60 million, a $US55 million increase from the previous year's $US5 million. This jump can be explained by American readiness to supply arms to the new government which was established in the aftermath of the military coup which overthrew Sihanouk. Of course, the Lon Nol government was eager to accept American arms and, in fact, became almost totally dependent on the U.S.A. for its arms supplies.

American arms supplies to the three Indo-Chinese states did not prevent a Communist takeover in 1975. Ironically, the arms provided to fight the Communists fell into their hands. Inadvertently, American arms provision to non-communist Vietnam has made reunified Communist Vietnam the strongest state in South-east

Asia. Uncertain about Hanoi's intentions, the non-communist states are now, as noted, emphasising the need to build up their own armed forces. American arms supply policies regarding Indo-China have therefore contributed to a further proliferation of arms in the region.

Thailand, as noted, was the fourth largest recipient of American arms. With the expansion of insurgency in the 1960s, it was provided with large quantities of COIN (counter insurgency) weapons including helicopters and infantry weapons. Moreover, the U.S.A. financed, at a rate of $US26 million a year, Thai military intervention in Laos where Thai troop strength increased from 5,000 in the mid-1960s to 10,000 in 1971 and 20,000 in 1973.[35] Thailand's intervention in Cambodia and Vietnam was also financed or rewarded by the U.S.A. Despite the end of the Indo-China conflicts in 1975, the U.S.A. has remained an important supplier of arms to Thailand. In early 1977 American military planes resumed flights —which were suspended in July 1976 during the withdrawal of American forces—to bring supplies. For the fiscal year 1977, the U.S.A. decided to provide the Thais with $US16 million in military assistance and $US30 million in long-term credit for the purchase of military equipment.[36]

The other non-communist states in the region have received American arms in varying quantities. The Philippines depend largely on the U.S.A. for arms. Of the total $US211 million worth of arms imported in the period 1965-74, $US210 million came from the U.S.A. alone. Since Sukarno fell from power, the U.S.A. has become an important supplier of arms to Indonesia. Between 1971-75, the U.S.A. pumped about $US65.8 million into its military modernisation program. In 1975, the U.S. State Department recommended that Congress double military aid to Indonesia for the fiscal year 1976. It called for $US30 million in grants and $US12.5 million in credits amounting to a total of $US42.5 million. This sum was twice the aggregate figure for the fiscal year 1975. Of the $US45 million worth of arms imported by Burma, $US29 million came from the U.S.A. alone. Both Malaysia and Singapore are not predominantly dependent on the Americans for arms. Both import a significant proportion of arms from Britain but both, at the same time, have diversified their sources of procurement.

The U.S.S.R. ranks second to the U.S.A. in supplying arms to South-east Asian countries. As can be expected, it concentrated on supplying Vietnam, which until 1975 was the only Communist country in the region. In the period 1965-74, it exported $US3,309 million worth of arms to South-east Asia out of which $US3,245 million went to North Vietnam, $US54 million to Indonesia, and $US8 million and $US2 million to Cambodia and Laos respectively.

It appears that levels of arms supplies to Hanoi were influenced by American involvement in the war. Beginning in 1965, major weapons supplies rose rapidly and included highly sophisticated defensive weapons. The intensified American bombing of the North, the landing of American combat forces in South Vietnam and constant Chinese criticism of Soviet lack of support for wars of national liberation were among the factors which led to the increased levels of arms supply to Hanoi. Substantial numbers of radar-controlled anti-aircraft guns were provided during 1965 and these were followed in 1966 by the highly-sophisticated SA2 missiles and MiG21s. Soviet arms were provided to Laos and Cambodia when neutralist governments were in power.

The bulk of Chinese arms to South-east Asia went to North Vietnam. Of the $US1,366 million worth of arms supplied, $US1,355 million went to North Vietnam and the other $US11 million went to Cambodia. However, the C.P.R. could not provide Hanoi with sophisticated weapons while the U.S.S.R. could. Moreover, the total value of Soviet arms was almost twice that of the Chinese.

In the period 1965–74, the South-east Asian region imported $US15,328 million worth of arms. Of this total, $US14,757 million came from the three great powers. Chinese arms went to very few states: only two countries—North Vietnam and Cambodia—were recipients. Thus, compared to the U.S.S.R., its Communist rival, the C.P.R. had fewer clients. However, not only did the U.S.A. provide more arms to the region, it had more recipients than either the C.P.R. or the U.S.S.R. Nine South-east Asian countries at one time or another received American arms. It is of course not surprising that there were few importers of Soviet or Chinese arms. Given the predominantly pro-Western inclinations of several South-east Asian states, they would hardly turn to the Communist countries for arms.

The three great powers, moreover, supplied subnational groups with weapons. The Khmer Serei and right-wing factions out of power in Laos and Cambodia were among those which received American military equipment. The U.S.S.R provided the Pathet Lao and the National Liberation Front of South Vietnam (NLFSV) with arms via Hanoi. China sent arms to the Pathet Lao, the NLFSV, Khmers Rouges as well as Thai Communists.

It cannot be denied that the arms supply policies of these three countries contributed largely to the acceleration of arms proliferation in South-east Asia. Other suppliers also played a role. However, in the final analysis, it is the South-east Asian states themselves which must bear the responsibility for the proliferation of arms in the region. They are the ones which demand weapons; they are the ones which provide a market for foreign arms. The extraregional powers, although ready and willing to transfer armaments to the region, would not have been able to do so if there had not been a demand.

Conclusion: South-east Asian Countries in Search of Security

Has the acquisition of arms enhanced the security of the South-east Asian states? Does possession of increasingly sophisticated weapons contribute to their security?

To be secure, these countries must be able to overcome or at least cope with the threats, internal and external, to their security. Have they been able to do so with the arms acquired? From their point of view, the answer is yes. Their security forces, armed with locally-produced or imported weapons, have kept insurgencies under control. Their armed forces are regarded as a deterrent against armed attacks by unfriendly states and are seen to play a role in defending their political independence and territorial integrity. However, it appears that the root causes of insecurity have not been solved despite the procurement of COIN materiel and major weapons.

As noted, the causes of insecurity are two: disaffection on the part of subnational groups which may find expression in armed violence and insurgency, and uneasy relations not only with regional neighbours but also with extraregional powers. The security forces may keep the insurgents under control but insurgency remains a problem. It has its roots in the existing socio-economic and political grievances and for as long as these continue to exist, insurgency is always a possibility. The arms build-up has not made any less tense the relations among states; in fact, it may lead to increased suspicions among them. By expanding and modernising its armed forces, a South-east Asian state may acquire a greater sense of security; however, this inspires insecurity in those of its neighbours with which it is on unfriendly terms for, as noted, armed forces and weapons acquired purportedly for self-defence may be used for offensive purposes. It appears that arms proliferation has led to uneasiness among states in the region. Moreover, it seems that the South-east Asian states are aware of the fact that large quantities of arms and massive external military assistance are no guarantee for security. This was one of the lessons of Indonesia. However, they are not prepared to abandon reliance on arms. An arms control arrangement for the region, for example, has not received any serious consideration so far.

Arguments can be made for such an arrangement. To put it simplistically, if these countries do not have the arms which may be used to attack each other, the security of each would be enhanced. Each would have less reason to fear armed aggression from its neighbours. At the same time, the countries might be more inclined to resolve their differences in non-military means. The lessening of armed conflicts would perhaps make the region more stable. However, any suggestions for an arms control arrangement are at the moment premature, unacceptable and unworkable.

First, the South-east Asian countries are not interested in such an arrangement. All, on the contrary, are engaged in programs to strengthen and modernise their forces. As long as they are uncertain about the intentions of each other, as long as vital issues such as border demarcation and disputed claims to territories are not solved, it is unlikely that they will agree to any such arrangement.

Second, an arms control arrangement for South-east Asia *alone* would be totally unacceptable, especially if extraregional powers continue to take an interest in the region. Many of these powers, as is well-known, regard the region as important for political, economic and strategic reasons. For example, the U.S.S.R., U.S.A. and Japan believe the Straits of Malacca to be of strategic value. China has always expressed an interest in the region while its economic resources have attracted the attention of several extraregional states. Might not an arms control arrangement which applies only to the region encourage some extraregional powers to assert domination over it? Of course, it can be argued that if a powerful extraregional power attacks the region, the South-east Asian countries, without external assistance, may not be able to defend themselves successfully. However, the fact that they possess an armed force seems to give them a sense of security.

Third, any arms control arrangement would have to entail some sort of regulations on the arms trade for, as noted, it is through arms transfers that these countries obtain the bulk of their weapons. The suppliers would have to agree not to transfer or, at the minimum, limit the transfer of arms to the region. It is however doubtful if all suppliers and recipients would accept regulations on the arms trade.

Fourth, it is most unlikely that the South-east Asian countries would accept regulations on arms transfers if insurgents in their territories continue to obtain arms from external sources. From their point of view, armed struggles must be met with armed force and this calls for imports of weapons.

Yet, it appears that these countries all recognise the fact that arms alone cannot solve their security problems. Many of these problems are political and hence political methods for resolving them cannot be ignored. A major preoccupation of several states appears to be the improvement of the relations among themselves and with extraregional powers which have an interest in the region. This improvement is believed important not only for internal but also for external security.

As noted, the South-east Asian countries are faced with internal problems. All are concerned about external intervention in their internal affairs. Such interference and provision of assistance to insurgents are most likely to be undertaken by countries which are unfriendly. An important foreign policy objective of several states is to improve their relations with their regional neighbours as well as with extraregional states. If, somehow, they can come to an agreement whereby they undertake not to interfere in each other's internal affairs, they may feel more secure. At the same time, if they agree to base their relations on principles such as respect for each other's political independence and territorial integrity and resort to peaceful means in resolving their differences, they may feel more at ease.

It appears that some regional states—Communist and non-communist—are making efforts to lessen tensions which have arisen in their relations. The Treaty of Amity proposed by the ASEAN countries at the Bali Summit in 1976 includes provisions for peaceful methods of resolving disputes among its signatories. It is hoped that all the countries in the region will become parties to the Treaty. While the ASEAN countries have offered a hand of friendship to the Communist states, the latter, on their part, have given indications that they are prepared to develop friendly relations with individual non-communist countries.

At the same time, some of these South-east Asian states have attempted to deal with the problem of great power rivalry in the region which in the past has contributed to its political instability. The proposal of the ASEAN countries for a 'zone of peace, freedom and neutrality' aims at, among other things, putting an end to great power interference in regional affairs.

However, the fact remains that uneasiness exists. The relations between some regional states are still not free from tensions while their relations with one or another of the great powers are not without problems. Mere advocacy of principles such as respect for sovereignty and territorial integrity and non-interference in internal affairs is no guarantee that states would actually put these principles into practice. The 'zone of peace, freedom and neutrality' would be difficult to implement; it has not even been accepted by all states in the region, let alone the great powers. Thus, while making efforts to improve their relations and making proposals for enhancing regional political stability, the South-east Asian countries have by no means ignored the military aspect of security. They still place primary confidence in their armed forces for the protection of their national security.

Footnotes

* Figures on world, regional and national military expenditures as well as on arms transfers to South-east Asian countries are taken from ACDA unless otherwise specified.
 1. United States Arms Control and Disarmament Agency, *World Military Expenditures and Arms Transfers, 1966–1975*, Washington D.C. 1976 p.14.
 2. Stockholm International Peace Research Institute, *Arms Uncontrolled*, Harvard University Press, Cambridge, Mass., 1975, p.4.
 3. The figures are based on statistics in *World Military Expenditures and Arms Transfers, 1966–1975*.
 4. *New Straits Times*, 18 June 1977.
 5. *World Military Expenditures and Arms Trade, 1963–1973*, p.103 and *World Military Expenditures and Arms Transfers, 1966–1975*, p.68.
 6. *Malaysia, Foreign Affairs*, Vol.4, No.3, September 1971, p.17.
 7. *Ibid.*, p.17.
 8. *New Straits Times*, 4 April 1975.
 9. *Ibid.*, 29 June 1975.
10. SIPRI, *The Arms Trade with the Third World*, Penguin Books, Harmondsworth, 1975, p.142.
11. *New Straits Times*, 14 August 1972.
12. *Ibid.*, 20 November 1975.
13. *Ibid.*, 29 June 1975.
14. *Straits Times*, 24 October 1972.
15. *Far Eastern Economic Review*, Vol. 95, No.2, 14 January 1977, p.19.
16. *World Military Expenditures and Arms Transfers, 1966–1975*, p.70.
17. *Straits Times*, 17 November 1972.
18. *Ibid.*, 6 August 1973.
19. *Ibid.*, 9 August 1973.
20. *World Military Expenditures and Arms Transfers, 1966–1975*, p.72.
21. *New Nation*, 1 May 1975.
22. *Indonesian Observer*, 1 May 1975.
23. *Far Eastern Economic Review*, Vol. 92, No.22, 28 May 1976, p.13.
24. Tunku Abdul Rahman Putra, *Looking Back*, Pustaka Antara, Kuala Lumpur, 1977, p. 141.

25. From *World Military Expenditures and Arms Transfers, 1966–1975.*
26. *New Straits Times,* 2 May 1977.
27. *Ibid.,* 30 January 1977.
28. *Ibid.,* 9 May 1975.
29. *Ibid.,* 22 November 1975.
30. *The Economist,* 6 December 1975.
31. *Far Eastern Economic Review,* Vol. 94, No.52, 24 December 1976.
32. From *World Military Expenditures and Arms Transfers, 1966–1975.*
33. From *Ibid., 1965–74,* p.74.
34. SIPRI, *Arms Trade with the Third World,* p.15.
35. Usha Mahajani, 'U.S. Intervention in Laos and Its Impact on Laotian Relations with Thailand and Vietnam', in M. Zacher and R. Milne, ed. *Conflict and Stability in South-east Asia,* Anchor Press Doubleday, New York, 1974, p.265.
36. *New Straits Times,* 10 March 1977.

7
The Indian Ocean Littoral: Intra-Regional Conflicts and Weapons Proliferation
Mohammed Ayoob

Introduction

It is only since the mid or late sixties that it has become fashionable to speak of an 'Indian Ocean region'. The popularity of this term owes a great deal to the naval competition between the superpowers in the Indian Ocean proper which has influenced the perception of policy-makers in the major capitals of the world and prompted them into looking at problems, particularly security problems, in this entire area as parts of a single whole. Policy-analysts and academic strategists have also followed suit and the term the 'Indian Ocean region' has gained currency in scholarly and academic writings as a valid unit of analysis.

However, it is only with major qualifications that one can accept the validity of this term particularly if one is engaged in analysing the security problems of the littoral and hinterland countries of the Indian Ocean. The major security problems of the countries bordering on the Indian Ocean have very little to do directly with the Indian Ocean as such or with superpower naval presence in that Ocean. As Peter Lyon has pointed out, the Indian Ocean is either too big or too small to be considered a 'single strategic threatre'—too small for the superpowers because they are free to concentrate their navies in any ocean including the Indian, and too big for conflicts between the littoral powers.[1]

The major foreign policy and security considerations of the littoral and hinterland states are primarily sub-regional (i.e. if you concede the term 'region' to the entire Indian Ocean area) in character. They do not embrace the entire Indian Ocean littoral as a whole. Therefore, if one looks at the entire area from the stand-point of the regional countries one can divide the Indian Ocean area into at least five distinct regions: South-east Asia and Australia, South Asia, the Persian Gulf, the Horn of Africa and the Red Sea, and Southern Africa. It is within each of these regions that one finds 'interrelated problems that are discreet',[2] which is probably the best criterion to judge whether a geographic area is or is not a 'region' in the sense that the term is used in the literature of international relations. However, this does not mean that the policies pursued by regional powers towards the various regions can be divided into water-tight compartments. Given the particular geographical location of each country and the set of foreign policy problems it faces, policies towards and perceptions of each region are bound to be affected by policies towards and perceptions of other regions. But, while interacting with one another, these policies and postures towards particular regions are usually coherent enough to be viewed as distinctive categories or units of analysis.

As far as the non-regional actors, particularly the superpowers (because they are the only ones who have global reach), are concerned, once again it is highly questionable to state that they have a comprehensive policy equally applicable to all regions which make up the Indian Ocean littoral. For the strategists sitting in Washington and Moscow the Indian Ocean region is considered a valid unit of analysis and policy formulation only in the context of their naval strategies when such strategies are perceived as directly affecting the central balance). As for their overall policies towards the littoral states, the superpowers certainly differentiate between one region and another. As Kim Beazley, Jr. has pointed out:

> In developing their relations with the Indian Ocean littoral states, neither the Soviet Union nor the United States treated the Indian Ocean as a regional entity . . . Analyses of the policies of the superpowers have been bedevilled by the belief that British withdrawal produced a 'power vacuum' that nature demanded filled by powers with the global interests Britain once possessed. Quite minor initiatives by one or the other power were often seen as major incursions. Policies directed towards specific sections of the littoral have been portrayed as part of a 'grand design' for the region as a whole.[3]

If one looks closely at the superpowers' policies toward the Indian Ocean littoral, it would become clear, for example, that Soviet policy towards South and South-east Asia is intimately linked to its China policy, while its policy towards the Horn of Africa is an offshoot of its competition with the United States for influence in the Middle East. Similarly, the logic behind U.S. policy towards Southern Africa, if scrutinised closely, would appear to be quite different from calculations behind its policy towards South Asia.

Therefore, one has to be very careful in attributing unity of purpose to superpower policies in the region except in the highly generalised sense that both the United States and the Soviet Union, given the compulsions of superpower status, are engaged in a game of competition and collusion with each other for global domination and for the extension of their influence to all grey areas of the globe, viz., the third world. But in such a highly generalised sense the uniqueness of the term 'Indian Ocean region' is lost. At this level of generalisation, the term 'third world', despite all the vagueness surrounding it, appears to be a more valid category of analysis. For our purposes, however, it will be much more worthwhile to look at the security problems within each distinct region within the Indian Ocean area rather than at the Indian Ocean littoral as a whole. This becomes specially imperative since the major security problems around the Indian Ocean are primarily intra-regional in character (i.e. the major actors in the conflict-scenarios are confined to particular regions of the Indian Ocean littoral and it is only rarely that there is a case when the major participants in a dispute belong to two different regions of the littoral).

If one looks at the problems of regional security around the Indian Ocean, one would find that in South Asia the major security problem, traditionally, has been related to the Indo–Pakistan equation. All other security problems of the region are minor compared to this major contradiction in the region. In the Persian Gulf, the major security problem has so far been the relationship between Iran and Iraq. But the potential for a Saudi–Iranian conflict in the future should not be under-rated. In the Horn of Africa, the major security problems revolve around the Somalia–Ethiopia equation and the disintegration of the Ethiopian 'empire'. The Southern African region is unique in the sense that it is undergoing a complex process of decolonisation (defined not merely as a withdrawal of the metropolitan powers but also as an end to settler colonialism). The security problems of that region are primarily the outcome of this process and are definable in terms of racial conflict. But here also the major antagonists are regional actors, whether one defines the conflict in terms of a confrontation between the 'front-line' African States and Rhodesia or between the black majorities of Rhodesia and South Africa and their white-minority regimes.

As for external (primarily superpower) involvement in these and other intra-regional conflicts, the presence of naval fleets off the shores of the regional contestants has had only marginal effect on the regional contestants. The sailing of the *USS Enterprise* into the Bay of Bengal during the last few days of the Bangladesh war of December 1971 might have satisfied some egos in Washington but it made no contribution either way to the outcome of that conflict. Similarly, as Shahram Chubin points out:

> Superpower naval presence in the Indian Ocean has had no significant impact on events in the [Persian] Gulf. It did not deter Iran's assertion of her claim to half the Shatt-al-Arab or Abu Musa and the Tunb islands. There is no evidence that the Soviet naval presence in Iraq in April 1973 enhanced Baghdad's claim to two islands and a strip of coastline belonging to Kuwait, nor did the American presence in Bahrain deter an oil embargo.[4]

Such naval presence, however, does have some psychological effect on the littoral states, particularly because of the tradition of gunboat diplomacy which was a favourite pastime of European fleets in the area until not so long ago. However, the strategic balance between the two superpowers, coupled with the changed values of the international community, have prevented a repetition of such involvement during the recent past. This does not mean, of course, that a modern form of gunboat diplomacy will never be repeated. The debate in the United States in 1974–75 regarding the feasibility of Gulf oil fields as military objectives gives cause for serious concern.

This feeling of uneasiness and concern at superpower intentions plus the existence, actual or potential, of intra-regional conflicts susceptible to exploitation by external powers led most of the littoral countries to join together in the U.N. to propose that the Indian Ocean be declared a zone of peace where superpower naval presence would be drastically curtailed, if not completely eliminated. The rationale for the general agreement among the littoral and hinterland states that increased great power presence in the Indian Ocean was not in their long term interest was articulated remarkably well in the initial, unrevised report of the three experts appointed by the U.N. Secretary General to go into the matter. The report stated in part:

> The vast majority of the littoral and hinterland states of the Indian Ocean area are still developing socially, economically and politically. During this period of development there is, unfortunately, a considerable potential for local conflicts . . . Any attempt to derive advantage from this unstable situation by one great power will inevitably lead to a countermove by the other great power. Moreover, any attempt by one of the littoral or hinterland states to obtain undue support from one

of the great powers will probably in turn lead to some other littoral or hinterland state seeking countervailing support from the other great power. For these reasons, all the hinterland and littoral states perceive it to be in their common interest to eliminate great power rivalry from the area.[5]

Despite the recent preoccupation of the great powers as well as the littoral states with superpower naval competition in the Indian Ocean, this naval presence is not the major source of the regional security problems in the Indian Ocean area. It is important to the superpowers as part of their calculations relating to the central balance, in terms of the vulnerability or otherwise of certain targets that could be reached by SLBMs, or as a 'showing the flag' exercise in the Indian Ocean littoral. But in terms of most conflicts within the region the value of such presence offshore is extremely limited.

The influence that the superpowers wield within the countries of the littoral has very little, if any, correlation at all with the fleets they can muster in the Indian Ocean. Such influence is related to other factors which directly affect the capacity of the regional actors to hold their own in intra-regional conflicts and which help them to preserve a favourable regional balance of power or change one that is adverse. The most effective instrument which has been used to enhance or preserve such influence has been the supply of arms to the regional contestants or parties to the various intra-regional disputes. This instrument has also been the vehicle which has been most effective in exacerbating intra-regional conflicts. More often than not, it leads to an arms race which escalates at a frightening pace, adds to the psychological and physical insecurity of the regional actors, and is extremely detrimental to a rational allocation of scarce resources within the developing countries of the region. Therefore, any analysis of superpower contribution to the regional security problems of the various states of the Indian Ocean littoral must focus primarily on the issue of arms transfers, regional arms races and the consequent atmosphere of general insecurity in these regions, rather than the peripheral question of superpower naval deployment in the high seas of the Indian Ocean. Given the fact that the major security problems in the area are intra-regional in character and given the constraints of nuclear deterrence and superpower détente, one can reasonably conclude that calculations regarding ship-days, ship-ton-days and port calls relating to super-power naval deployment that have become the favourite pastime of Indian Ocean strategists are neither central nor, possibly, relevant to the real problems of regional security in the Indian Ocean area. Where the superpowers and other developed countries that are in a position to supply weapons to the regional contestants have left their indelible mark on the security problems of the area is in the sphere of arms transfers, whether on the basis of grants or sales—the latter being the more acceptable and popular form of arms transfer in recent years.

In Chapter 2,[6] Ron Huisken has gone into considerable detail to chart out the motivations behind and the mechanisms of arms transfer to the third world. I do not propose, therefore, to repeat the arguments in this paper, except to reiterate that the quantitative and qualitative explosion in the arms trade during the 1970s has added a frightful dimension to the problem.

As Huisken's chapter has demonstrated so well, since World War II the process of arms transfer has undergone four distinctive stages. The first was immediately after the war when obsolete weapons left over from World War II were provided either free or sold at nominal prices. Then, as the conventional arms race between the two power blocs intensified in the late 1940s and the 1950s, weapons which had become obsolescent in the European–North American theatres were transferred to clients in the third world. In the 1970s, particularly with the oil boom, one found the third process in operation when the most modern equipment found its way to selected countries of the third world sometimes right off the assembly line. This was attributable either to the greater buying capacity of the recipient states and the contribution they could make to the R and D account for the weapons (Iran) or to the greater political clout which the recipients have been able to muster in the domestic politics of a superpower (Israel). We are just entering the fourth phase where not merely weapon systems are available for sale but comprehensive package deals are arranged for the building up of total military capability, including base construction, etc., (Saudi Arabia).

Today, therefore, intra-regional conflicts, in certain areas of the third world, can be almost as destructive as major great power conflicts were not so long ago. This is a terrifying scenario, particularly because most of the countries involved are economically weak and politically unstable. Insecure regimes with narrow support bases can easily be tempted to transform issues of regime-security into those of state-security and thus get their countries and regions involved in catastrophic conflicts with the help of expensive toys sold or lent to them by the major industrialised countries, particularly the superpowers.

In the light of the foregoing remarks, this paper will attempt to identify major instances of intra-regional conflict, actual or potential, in the various regions of the Indian Ocean littoral and to evaluate how far superpower involvement, particularly in the field of arms transfer, has tended to exacerbate such conflict. For purposes of illustration this paper will limit itself to three regions of the Indian Ocean littoral, viz. South Asia, the Persian Gulf and the Horn of Africa. South-east Asia is the subject of a separate chapter (Chapter 6) and therefore does not require further treatment. Southern Africa is a region unique in itself, in the sense that it is still in the throes of de-colonisation and therefore requires to be treated differently from the treatment of intra-regional conflict proposed in this chapter. It will, therefore, not be included here but, it is hoped, will form part of a longer study which I am preparing.

South Asia

The major regional security problem in South Asia (or the Indian subcontinent as it was called until recently) has been the ongoing cold war between India and Pakistan occasionally punctuated by bouts of armed conflict as in 1947–48 and in 1965 over Kashmir and in 1971 over Bangladesh. The Indo-Pak relationship is a classic example of the 'security dilemma' where any accretion to one country's security has been perceived by the other as detracting from its own security. The historical and psychological reasons for this are too well known to need repetition in detail. Pakistan's search for identity, the dispute over Kashmir, and its almost insuperable problems of national integration had compelled Pakistan's rulers to adopt an aggressive anti-India stance to keep the fragile political unity of the geographically divided country intact. The Indian perception of Pakistan as a creation of British imperialism and as a case of both political and strategic secession from the subcontinent, plus the fact that Pakistan's religion-based nationalism threatened India's secular democratic experiment, created a degree of hostile reaction in India towards Pakistan unwarranted by the actual size of the threat that Pakistan posed to India's security.

Paradoxically, the war of 1971 and the emergence of Bangladesh seem to have had beneficial effects on the domestic environments in which Pakistani and Indian foreign policies are made, particularly towards each other. Prospects for a 'regional détente' between India and Pakistan are much brighter today than they have ever been during the last thirty years.[7] This does not mean, however, that the subcontinent has reached a significant stage of military de-escalation. Since both India and Pakistan also have other security threats to contend with—China in the case of India and

Afghanistan in the case of Pakistan—both New Delhi and Islamabad have plausible cases for resisting reduction of military
expenditure. Moreover, with the Pakistan army still a politically
significant factor in the domestic affairs of an unstable Pakistan,
no government in that country can afford to alienate the GHQ by
curtailing expenditure on the armed forces.

In the case of Pakistan there has been, in fact, a remarkable
increase in its defence preparedness, particularly as regard to
ground troops. The total number of armed force personnel has
grown by 33,000 in the past six years despite the fact that they
are now responsible for defending only one wing of what was
Pakistan until 1971. If you include the 90,000 POWs who were
held in India for almost two years after the 1971 war and were,
therefore, demobolised for all practical purposes during that period,
the accretion to Pakistan's armed forces strength between December
1971 and the middle of 1976 has been of the order of 123,000.[8]

This has meant the addition of four infantry divisions and one
armoured brigade during this period. The fire power of the army
has also been increased by the inclusion of M–4 tanks in the
Pakistan inventory. At the same time six Midget SX–404 submarines have been acquired for the Navy and three Daphne class
submarines (in addition to the three already in service) are on order
from France. During the same period Pakistan has acquired some
more MiG–19s from China and Mirage III and V aircraft from
France. Further Pakistani attempts to augment its air capability
have been thwarted by President Carter's recent refusal to sell 110
A–7 fighter bombers to that country, despite the Pentagon's
recommendation to that effect. With the break away of its eastern
wing in 1971, the Pakistani defence effort has been a heavy burden
on the economy. Islamabad's military expenditure as a percentage
of its GDP increased from 3.7 in 1970 to 7.2 in 1972 and fell slightly
to 6.2 in 1973, and remained around that figure until 1975.[9]

According to IISS estimates, India has added two infantry
divisions and two armoured brigades to its army since the war of
1971. At the same time it has more than doubled its number of
Soviet T–54 and T–55 tanks from 450 to 1,000. It has also more
than doubled its inventory of indigeneously produced Vijayanta
tanks from 300 to 700. India has also added to its naval strength
by acquiring four more Soviet F–class submarines thus reaching
a total of eight. It has also added some Petya–class frigates to its
naval strength. The IISS estimates also show a significant rise in
the Indian airforce capability by about 300 combat aircraft, but
this is not borne out by a detailed study of the Institute's figures

except in the case of three additional interceptor squadrons of MiG–21 aircraft produced indigenously under licence.[10] Indian military expenditure relative to its GDP has stayed stable through the early 1970s at a level of a little over three per cent. This in fact, compares favourably with the high of 3.8 per cent reached in 1963 immediately after the border conflict with China.[11]

Both India and Pakistan have been dependent to a large extent on external supplies for the development of their defence capabilities. This has been much more true of Pakistan which is almost totally dependent upon outside support. India has been able to build a respectable defence industry of its own which has been made possible by the existence of a highly developed industrial infra-structure in that country. MiG–21s, Gnat interceptors, HF–24 fighter bombers, and Vijayanta medium tanks are some examples of what India is capable of producing indigenously. Another major difference between Pakistani and Indian defence procurement policies has been that while India has paid for all items it has bought abroad, Pakistan was a major beneficiary of U.S. arms supplies on a grant basis under Washington's Military Assistance Program (MAP). U.S. military aid to Pakistan from 1954 to 1965 (when free military assistance was terminated) amounted to well over one billion dollars[12] although the official figure for military aid in the strict sense was put at $730 million.[13] The Pentagon, when it officially declassified information on 19 April 1972 about U.S. arms aid to Pakistan, through June 1965, put the figure at $671.6 million in grant aid and approximately $100 million in military sales.[14] The discrepancies between the SIPRI figure and those officially disclosed by U.S. agencies is related to the fact that, in addition to military hardware, Pakistan received between 1959 and 1963 about $565 million in defence supporting assistance, i.e. economic assistance designed for the maintenance of armed forces.[15] It would be realistic to assume that the actual value of arms transferred by the USA under the MAP to Pakistan was much greater than the book value because of various means by which such equipment could be drastically undervalued by the Pentagon if such under-valuation helped U.S. security needs as defined by the Pentagon. Under the MAP arms transfers, Pakistan received 120 F–86s, 26 B–57s and 12 F–104s as well as Sidewinder air-to-air missiles plus M–24, M–4 and M–41 tanks.

After 1965 when the U.S. imposed an embargo on the supply of arms to the subcontinent, Pakistan received the bulk of its equipment from China (most of it on a grant basis) and also shopped for arms in France (Mirage aircraft, Daphne class submarines, helicopters, etc.). Pakistan also made determined efforts to buy surplus U.S. equipment from Europe particularly through its CENTO allies. The most outstanding example of such a transaction was the purchase of 90 F–86s by Iran from West Germany in November 1966 at $87,000 each (10 per cent of the original price). These aircraft were then passed on to Pakistan by Iran. According to a reliable American estimate China supplied military hardware to Pakistan worth $133 million between 1965 and 1971.[16] According to another reliable American estimate $350 million worth of arms had been transferred by China to Pakistan between 1966 and 1975.[17]

As far as Indian acquisition of military hardware from abroad is concerned, throughout the 1950s it depended primarily on Great Britain, the traditional source of military supplies to the Indian armed forces, for military hardware. It was only in the 1960s— and particularly after the Sino-Indian conflict of 1962—that the Soviet Union became the major arms supplier to India. In the 1950s India avoided arms purchases from either of the superpowers, among other reasons because it perceived such a move to be detrimental to its larger policy of non-alignment. As one source has pointed out:

> When India was considering the purchase of Hunters and Canberras from Britain during the mid-fifties, an offer of bargain price MiG–17s and Il–28s from the Soviet Union was turned down. Indeed, apart from the gift of two transport planes from the Soviet Union in 1955, India did not purchase any Soviet equipment until 1960 . . . [and] until the summer of 1962, the arms deals between India and the Soviet Union were minor.[18]

It is interesting to note that even after Pakistan had started receiving U.S. military aid in 1954 under the Mutual Defence Assistance Pact, SEATO and the Baghdad Pact (later CENTO), India did not turn towards the Soviet Union to match U.S. supplies to Pakistan. What it did in the 1950s was to buy additional equipment from its traditional source of supply, Great Britain, to keep pace with major U.S. weapons transfers to Pakistan. During the 1950s Britain supplied two-thirds of India's needs. Thus, these two NATO allies shared the bulk of military supplies to the subcontinent, the British, in fact, supplying both armies. It is no wonder, therefore, that between 1955 and 1959, the U.S. and U.K. together were the source of approximately 80 per cent of the major weapons supplied to the subcontinent.[19]

India and Pakistan: comparison of the introduction of sophisticated weapons

	Aircraft and missiles[a]		Tanks and anti-tank missiles		Naval vessels	
	India	Pakistan	India	Pakistan	India	Pakistan
1950		Sea Fury (fighter)				
1951		Vicker's Attacker (bomber)			Destroyer, 'R' class	Destroyer, 'O' class
1952						
1953	Ouragan (fighter bomber) Vampire (fighter)		Sherman		Destroyer, 'Hunt' class	
1954				Chaffee Sherman Bulldog Patton		
1955						
1956		F-86 Sabre (fighter)	Centurion			Destroyer, 'Battle' class Cruiser, 'Dido' class
1957	Hunter (fighter)		AMX-13		Cruiser, 'Colony' class Frigate, 'Leopard' class Frigate, 'Backwood' class	Destroyer, 'CV' and 'Ch' class
1958	Canberra (bomber)[b] Mystère (fighter) Short Seacat (SA missile)	Canberra (bomber)[c]				
1959	Gnat (fighter)					
1960	Seahawk (fighter)					
1961					Frigate, 'Whitby' class Aircraft Carrier, 'Majestic' class	

	Aircraft and missiles[a]		Tanks and anti-tank missiles		Naval vessels	
	India	Pakistan	India	Pakistan	India	Pakistan
1962		F–104 Starfighter (fighter)				Submarine, 'Tench' class
1963	MiG–21 (fighter) Atoll (AA missile)					
1964	HF–24 (fighter) Guideline (SA missile)	Sidewinder (AA missile)	PT–76			
1965			Vickers 'Vijayanta'	T–59 Cobra (missile)		
1966		MiG–19 (fighter) 11–28 (bomber)				
1967						
1968	Su–7 (Fighter)	Mirage III (fighter)	T–54		Submarine, 'F' class Frigate, 'Petya' class	
1969			Entac (missile) SS–11 (missile)			
1970						Submarine, 'Daphne' class
1971	Styx (SS missile)	F–5 Freedom Fighter (fighter)			Missile boat 'Osa' class	
1972	Tigercat (SA missile)	Mirage 5 (fighter)			Frigate 'Leander' class	

[a] Excluding anti-tank missiles.
[b] India bought English Electric Canberra bombers from the U.K.
[c] Pakistan received Martin Canberra bombers from the U.S.A.
Source: SIPRI country registers.

Reproduced from SIPRI, *The Arms Trade with the Third World*, Penguin Edition, 1975, pp.184–185.

Pakistan's military alliance with the United States which was consummated in 1954 had a far-reaching impact on the politics of the subcontinent. It not only led to open Soviet political support for India in its disputes with Pakistan but also signalled a major Soviet involvement in economic assistance to and trade with India. However, this was not reflected in the value of military supplies until the 1960s, partially because of the Indian military élite's resistance to change from Western weapon systems, partially because of New Delhi's apprehension that such a move may compromise its non-aligned status, and partially because the Soviet Union had not entered the arms transfer game until 1955 and that only indirectly through Czechoslovakia.[20] Nonetheless, an arms race had been started in the subcontinent by the U.S. decision to supply sophisticated (in the subcontinental context) equipment to Pakistan and to equip five to five point five divisions of the Pakistan army as part of Washington's policy of 'containment' and 'roll-back'. The accompanying table makes it clear that in terms of introduction of sophisticated weaponry into the subcontinent, Pakistan led India on every count except in naval vessels. Even here, it was Pakistan which was the first country to acquire a submarine capability when the U.S.A. lent it a 'Tench' class submarine in 1964. Later renamed the PNS *Ghazi*, it was sunk off the coast of Visakhapatnam in the December 1971 conflict. The Pakistani acquisition of F–86 Sabre fighters in 1956 led to the Indian acquisition of Hunter and Mystère fighters. Canberra bombers (American in the case of Pakistan and British in the case of India) were acquired by both countries in 1958. The air race was escalated further with the Pakistani acquisition of F–104 supersonic fighters in 1962. This was directly responsible for the Indian decision made the same year to acquire MiG–21 interceptors from the U.S.S.R. In terms of armour, there was a major tank acquisition program launched by Pakistan in 1954 and Chaffee, Sherman, Bulldog and Patton tanks were introduced into the Pakistan army. India already had Centurion tanks on order from Britain and acquired additional AMX–13 tanks from France to match the M–41 Bulldogs in the Pakistani armoury.

After 1962 the Indian defence effort was geared to meeting a repetition of the Chinese incursion as well as to building up enough defensive capability to deter a two-front attack by Pakistan and China at the same time. The fear of a two-front war was heightened by strong criticism of the Pakistan government by certain elements in that country for its failure to take advantage of the Sino–Indian war to achieve Pakistani objectives in Kashmir by the use of force. The Indian build up, particularly in terms of air and naval power, can be explained to a large extent by this apprehension of a Pakistani attack in case of another round of Sino-Indian hostilities. As for the Chinese border, ten mountain divisions were raised by India to meet the Chinese threat from across the Himalayas.

Although the United States and Britain had responded to Indian appeals for support during and immediately after the Sino-Indian conflict, the Western powers were soon disillusioned with New Delhi for a number of reasons. First, India did not interpret the Chinese incursion as a sign of Communist aggression and continued to make a distinction between Peking and Moscow. As a corollary to this, it did not want to deviate from its policy of non-alignment and was willing to accept Soviet military supplies in addition to those from the West. It did not renege on the MiG deal although there were rumours that Moscow was not very enthusiastic about supplying the aircraft because of deterioration in Sino-Indian relations. India also refused to accept a U.S. and British commitment for air defence in case of attack. It preferred to purchase its own air defence system which the Western powers were unwilling to supply.

By 1963, the Soviet Union was ready to step in and fill the breach. Additional MiG–21 and Mi–4 helicopters were supplied and an agreement was reached for the assembly and manufacture of MiG–21s in India. Soviet credits, advanced for these items, were repayable in rupees at two per cent interest to be utilised by Moscow for the purchase of Indian goods.

The open split between China and the Soviet Union removed any qualms that the Soviets might have had in extending support to India's defence build up. The Sino-American rapprochement of mid-1971 and their joint 'tilt' towards Pakistan, led to the Indo-Soviet treaty of 1971 which was aimed primarily at neutralising Chinese moves in support of Pakistan during the impending conflict. After the victory in December 1971, Indian enthusiasm for the treaty has visibly waned (the treaty having served its purpose), but the U.S.S.R. continues to be India's major external source for arms supply. According to one American estimate, the Soviet Union had supplied India with arms worth $731 million between 1965 and 1971.[21] According to another American estimate this figure had reached $1.375 billion by 1975.[22] The Indian Navy is now primarily Soviet-oriented in terms of equipment although the shift from British to Soviet equipment had met with considerable opposition at Indian Naval Headquarters.[23]

However, this does not mean that India is totally dependent upon Soviet support for its defence needs. India has an expanding domestic defence industry, and recently there have also been interesting cases of diversification in acquisition of major equipment. Recent examples of Indian diversification include: (a) New Delhi's decision to opt for French *Magic* air combat missiles in preference to a Soviet offer, and (b) the debate in Indian Airforce circles over the production of the Anglo French *Jaguar* under licence instead of building an advanced version of the Soviet MiG.[24] France and Britain continue to be alternative sources of supply. As Ian Clark has pointed out, 'While there is no gainsaying that the U.S.S.R. is India's major supplier, neither should the degree of diversification be totally ignored.'[25]

The Indian nuclear explosion (PNE) of 18 May 1974 seems to have added a new dimension to the Indo-Pakistani security scenario. Islamabad has refused to accept at face value India's peaceful intentions and Prime Minister Bhutto made a pointed remark in his letter to Mrs Gandhi about the difference between 'intentions' and 'capabilities'.[26] The demonstration of Indian nuclear capability came in handy for Pakistan to justify (a) the development of its own nuclear capability and (b) to persuade arms suppliers, particularly the U.S.A., to liberalise their policy of conventional arms supply to Pakistan. This dual effort has, however, run into rough weather with the Pakistani purchase of a French nuclear reprocessing plant held up due to American pressure and President Carter's recent refusal to sell 110 A–7 fighter-bombers to Pakistan despite the Pentagon's recommendation to that effect. However, Pakistan was able to persuade Washington to lift the embargo on all arms sales to South Asia which had been imposed in 1971. This has allowed Pakistan to buy some arms and spare parts from the U.S.A. although not as much as it had hoped for.

It would be a mistake, however, to view the Indian PNE as being primarily related to the Indo-Pak power equation. India did not need to demonstrate its nuclear capability to prove its military superiority over Pakistan, particularly so soon after the 1971 war. The Indian explosion was aimed among other things at demonstrating to the nuclear monopoly powers that unless they did something concrete about halting vertical proliferation they would not be able to prevent horizontal proliferation of nuclear weapons or explosives. It was aimed also at adding to India's stature in the world community, particularly in the eyes of the superpowers, who, it was perceived in India, were not willing to grant India its due place despite its victory in the 1971 war. A sense of inferiority and, therefore, of insecurity vis-à-vis Chinese nuclear power also added to the desire to demonstrate India's nuclear weapons capability. One should not ignore the pressures from India's relatively large scientific establishment which must have wanted to demonstrate its technological-scientific competence through the PNE. The Pakistan factor if it figured at all in the debate within the Indian establishment must have been regarded as a restraining factor since there was a reasonable possibility (later demonstrated by Pakistan's actions) of Pakistan trying to develop nuclear capability following the Indian explosion. The recent categorical declaration by India's new Prime Minister, Morarji Desai, that India is not interested in manufacturing nuclear weapons (and not even undertaking nuclear explosions unless their utility is demonstrated) could allay, at least partially, Pakistani fears of a nuclear India if Indian statements are ever accepted at face-value in Pakistan.

To conclude, while there have been signs of a 'thaw' recently in the Indo-Pak cold war in the subcontinent, it still continues to dominate the security picture in South Asia. As has been demonstrated in the foregoing pages, great power, and particularly superpower, intervention especially through the medium of arms transfer has added to conflict-escalation in the region by providing regional actors with increasingly sophisticated weaponry, and thereby encouraging them to bring about change in the regional balance whenever they viewed it as being unfavourable to themselves. This has been more true of Pakistan than it has been of India because the former has been, traditionally, the anti-status quo power in the subcontinent. This has been the case partially because of Pakistan's dissatisfaction over Kashmir and partially because of India's inherent power-superiority in the region in terms of size, man-power, resources, weapons-production capability, etc. Pakistan's foreign policy, therefore, had been geared to a strategy of 'borrowing power' from abroad to counterpoise and neutralise Indian power-superiority in the subcontinent as well as help it attain its irredentist objective vis-à-vis Kashmir. More often than not, therefore, it has been Pakistan which has escalated the level of the arms race in the subcontinent. Indian military alignments have been usually in the nature of reactions to Pakistani moves in the political and military spheres. Pakistan's military alliance with the U.S.A. and the subsequent warmth witnessed in the Indo–Soviet relationship remains the most outstanding demonstration of the validity of this thesis.

In terms of great power, particularly superpower, competition in the fields of arms supply to the subcontinent, it is clear from the data presented above, that while Great Britain had been the traditional arms supplier for both India and Pakistan, the U.S.

decision in 1954 to extend military aid to Pakistan formed the major turning point in the history of arms acquisition by the regional antagonists. Even then it was not until 1962 that India turned to the U.S.S.R. for major weaponry and continued throughout the 1950s to rely upon British supplies and domestic production to maintain the balance with Pakistan. With the Sino–Indian war of 1962 and the perception of a 'two-front war' threat, the Indian defence build up was accelerated. The Pakistani decision to go to war in 1965 was to a large extent based upon its perception that if the projected Indian build up continued, the former would soon lose the edge that it seemed to possess in fire-power, weapons sophistication and combat-readiness over its larger neighbour. The Pakistani gamble failed in 1965 but it unleashed a chain of events inside Pakistan which reached its culmination with the separation of East from West Pakistan in 1971. A part of the blame for this tragic ending must lie with Pakistan's arms suppliers who encouraged its rulers to nurture ambitions far beyond anything its inherent military capability could achieve. Moreover, the infusion of military aid led to an inflated military establishment in a country with a weak political infrastructure. This, in turn, led to the West Pakistani dominated military playing a major role in the country's domestic politics thus adding to the alienation of an already resentful East Pakistani middle class and contributing immensely to the break up of Pakistan.[27]

Thus, the infusion of arms into the subcontinent, which began in large doses after 1954, not only led to the exacerbation of the major regional conflict, but it also contributed, however indirectly, to the disintegration of one of the regional contestants.

The Persian Gulf

The Persian Gulf region occupies a unique position among the littoral areas of the Indian Ocean because it is extremely rich in a very vital and relatively scarce energy resource, viz. oil. More than 55 per cent of the world's proven oil reserves are located in and around the Gulf and the Persian Gulf's oil production in 1974 was more than 70 per cent of the total produced by the 13-member Organization of Petroleum Exporting Countries, and more than 48 per cent of the non-Communist world total'. Since the countries of the area consume only 3 per cent of the world's total output of oil, the rest is available for export.[28] Western Europe and Japan are heavily dependent upon Gulf oil and U.S. dependence on the same source is increasing as its total oil imports increase. It is also reported that the Soviet Union, a net exporter of oil now, will become a net importer in the 1980s and its stakes in the oil fields of the Gulf may, therefore, increase correspondingly.

The strategic importance of the region was brought home to the West by the oil boycott imposed by the OPEC (all Gulf producers except Iran are Arab and members of the OPEC) against the U.S.A. and the Netherlands and a general reduction in oil production during and after the Arab–Israeli war of October 1973. It was in that context, that the then U.S. Secretary of State, Henry Kissinger, had made the remark in an interview to *Business Week* that the U.S.A. may contemplate the use of force against Arab oil producers 'if there is some actual strangulation of the industrialised world'.[29] Simultaneously, influential periodicals in the United States began printing a number of articles presenting arguments for and against such forcible seizure of oil fields in the Gulf, as well as presenting alternative scenarios if such action should take place.[30]

The whole debate seemed to take on such an urgent note that a special report entitled 'Oil Fields as Military Objectives: A Feasibility Study' was prepared by the Congressional Research Service at the behest of a special subcommittee of the U.S. House of Representatives. The Study, made public in August 1975, came to the eminently sensible conclusion that:

> Success would largely depend on two pre-requisites: Slight damage to key installations and Soviet abstinence from armed intervention. Since neither essential could be assured, military operations to rescue the United States (much less its key allies) from an air-tight OPEC embargo would combine high costs with high risks wherever we focused our efforts. This country would so deplete its strategic reserves that little would be left for contingencies elsewhere. Prospects would be poor, with plights of far-reaching political, economic, social, psychological and perhaps military consequence the penalty for failure.[31]

The strategic significance of Gulf oil has added a great deal to the importance of the region, particularly in an era of high oil prices (which has resulted in a bonanza for the oil producers) coupled with increasing demands and almost total control of the oil resources by the producer countries. The resources at the disposal of the major Gulf countries—Iran, Saudi Arabia and, to a lesser extent, Iraq—have increased considerably so that they can invest a sizable share of their petro-dollars in buying arms. While this has served various purposes as far as the superpowers are concerned (and to this we will return later), it has also set off an arms race in the region which can prove extremely de-stabilising for the Gulf in the long run. The arms build up in the Gulf (with Iran way ahead of all the others) is related primarily to Tehran's escalating ambitions, particularly since 1971, to dominate the region and, in fact, to extend Iran's security perimeters into the Indian Ocean. The major problems of intra-regional security in the Gulf revolve around these Iranian aspirations which led to increasing tensions with Iraq, a temporary breach with the Trucial Sheikhdoms (now the UAE) when Iran occupied three strategic islands near the Straits of Hormuz in 1971, and an involvement in Oman against the Dhofari revolutionaries. Given Iranian aspirations and Saudi Arabia's oil wealth (which potentially far exceeds that of Iran) the possibility of a future Iran–Saudi conflict cannot be ruled out. Iran's aspirations regarding the Gulf following the British withdrawal in 1971 and its desire to have a stable eastern flank also led Tehran to extend its protective umbrella over Pakistan thus bringing it, temporarily, into an antagonistic position vis-à-vis New Delhi.[32]

Behind much of the regional instability around the Gulf lies the traditional rivalry between Iran and the Arab world. In recent years this has been most visible in Iran's relations with Iraq. While until 1958 Iran and Iraq had both formed part of the Western-sponsored 'northern tier' alliance aimed against the Soviet Union, the Iraqi coup of that year put the two countries on different sides of the political divide in the Middle East. However, until the Arab-Israeli war of June 1967, Tehran had looked upon Cairo rather than Baghdad as the greatest threat to its security, particularly in ideological terms. With Egypt's defeat in 1967, Baghdad came to replace Cairo as the main source of Tehran's anxiety. Disputes soon arose between the two over navigational rights in the Shatt-al-Arab, over the Shia minority in Iraq and the Arab minority in Iran, over the Iraqi support to Baluchi dissidents in Iran and the latter's support to Kurdish rebels in Iraq and over the general orientation of their respective foreign policies with Iran firmly aligned to the West in general and the U.S.A. in particular and Iraq moving into a relationship of intimate friendship if not alliance with the Soviet Union.

The British withdrawal from the Gulf brought these Arab-Iranian rivalries to a head, particularly when Iran occupied the three islands of Abu Musa, and the Greater and Lesser Tunbs near the Straits of Hormuz. The tremendous increase in Iranian purchasing power, particularly its power to buy the most sophisticated equipment in the Western armoury, following the spectacular rise in oil prices in late 1973 and after, was further cause for Iraqi concern. Although Baghdad was able to persuade Moscow to supply it with some sophisticated equipment it could not hope to match Tehran in either quantitative or qualitative terms. This increase in Iranian capability was matched by Iranian initiatives in the region. These included a unilateral revision of the terms of navigation in the Shatt-al-Arab in favour of Iran and an escalation of support to Kurdish rebels in Iraq. Tensions heightened in the region until March 1975 when an agreement was reached between the two countries by which Iraq accepted the Iranian claims in the Shatt and Iran withdrew support to Kurdish rebels in Iraq thus reducing the internal security problems for Baghdad. Iran has also been interested in wooing Iraq away from the Soviet Union and the 1975 agreement formed the first step in that direction. It followed closely the success of American efforts at eliminating or reducing Soviet influence in Egypt and Syria and seemed to have Washington's blessings. As far as the Saudi-Iranian relationship is concerned, its conflict-potentialities lie dormant at the moment because of the pro-Western orientation of both countries and because they share an identical interests in propping up monarchical regimes around the Gulf. If, however, there is a change of regime in either country tensions between the two can be expected to rise and a Saudi–Iranian conflict may then overshadow the Iran–Iraq rivalry in the Gulf.

Given the Shah's interest in safeguarding the 'security' of the Gulf by preserving the anachronistic regimes in the region and the weak political base from which these regimes (particularly the smaller Sheikhdoms) operate, one cannot be too sanguine about the stability or the security of the region around the Gulf. The Shah has demonstrated his aversion to revolutionary ideologies by helping the Sultan of Oman with force of arms to bring the Dhofar uprising under control and this may be just a prelude to such other adventures.[33] However, this self-assumed role of the Gulf policeman may bring Iran, sooner or later, into confrontation with its Arab neighbours, since the Arabs are bound to resent at some stage (if they do not do so already) such Iranian intervention in intra-Arab affairs. There are, therefore, various issues with great degrees of conflict-potential within them in the Gulf region and the massive arms build up in the area may add immeasurably to the costs of future conflagration rather than preserve what goes under the name 'security' in the Persian Gulf littoral.

The strategic importance of the Gulf, in terms of its oil resources, to the superpowers has already been discussed above. In addition, the importance of the area in terms of the Arab-Israeli conflict and the conflict-potential within the area itself have made the Gulf region a fertile ground for superpower intervention. This has ranged from the reinstatement of friendly regimes (in Iran in 1953) to the supply of the most sophisticated military equipment that has been transferred to any part of the Third World. This arms transfer can be partially explained by the vastly increased capacity of these oil-rich states (particularly Saudi Arabia and Iran) to pay for costly weaponry and the natural desire on the part of the arms suppliers to benefit from the oil bonanza, particularly when their balances of payments have not been in terribly good shape. But arms sales are never undertaken exclusively or even primarily for financial gain —at least not by the superpowers. Therefore, the extent and quality of arms supplied to a strategically important region like the Gulf has very important political-security connotations from the point of view of the superpowers themselves.

The American desire to prevent repetition of the 1973 oil embargo as well as to enable Iran, and, to a lesser extent, Saudi Arabia to act as defenders of Western interests in the Gulf (after the departure of the British) seems to have played the major part in the U.S. decision to supply sophisticated equipment to these oil-rich countries. The very sophistication of such equipment has assured for the U.S.A. a continuing role in the security of these countries because without U.S. assistance in terms of know-how and spare parts neither Iran nor Saudi Arabia would be able to maintain an efficient fighting force. They are, therefore, securely plugged into the American security system and will be content to play their assigned roles (with only marginal variations) at least for the near future. The Soviet Union has tried to do the same thing with Iraq but has not been as successful as the U.S.A. Although the Soviet Union signed a 15-year Treaty of Friendship and Cooperation with Iraq in 1972 and has extended military supplies to Iraq, they have not been of an order to match U.S. arms supplies to Iran and the balance has continued to tilt further in Iran's favour. This can be explained partially in terms of Iraq's limited capacity (in comparison to Iran) to buy such hardware and partially because of the Soviet Union's unwillingness or inability to match American supplies to Iran and Saudi Arabia. Moscow has also been expanding its economic links with Iran and this might have inhibited it from going too far in its support to Iraq in the latter's confrontation with Iran. It was the increasingly un-favourable Iran-Iraq balance that persuaded the latter to enter into an agreement with Iran in March 1975 that conceded to Tehran what it had been demanding in the Shatt-al-Arab dispute. Accord-

ing to one American estimate the U.S.S.R. had by 1974 provided
Iraq with 'Modern arms (including MiG–21 interceptors) worth
approximately $1 billion', but 'it has not kept pace with U.S.-
sponsored arms build up in Iran'.[34] According to figures released
by the U.S. Arms Control and Disarmament Agency, the Soviet
Union had supplied Iraq with arms worth $1.343 billion between
1966 and 1975. Interestingly enough, during the same period
Moscow supplied Iran with $589 million worth of military hard-
ware, almost half of what it supplied Iraq.[35] According to the latest
IISS estimates, Iraq has also received 40 MiG–23s which provide
it with two of its fighter-bomber squadrons.[36] But with Iran receiving
quantities of F–14 fighters from the U.S.A., the overall superiority
of the Iranian airforce is assured. After careful consideration of
the type of equipment possessed by the armed forces of the three
major Gulf powers, Dale R. Tahtinen has come to the conclusion
that Iranian superiority over Iraq on the ground, in the air and
in the sea is not only assured but that the gap between the two
countries in power-terms is widening.[37] Moreover, Iraq's coastline
on the Gulf is very narrow and although the U.S.S.R. has access
to the Iraqi port of Umm Qasr and has, in fact, helped to build
naval facilities there, Soviet ships have to sail through the virtually
Iranian-controlled Straits of Hormuz to get there. Of late, Iraq has
also been showing signs of unease with its close Soviet connections
and has given indications that it would like to normalise relations
with the West, particularly with the U.S.A.

As far as U.S. supplies of arms to Iran are concerned, the latest
officially disclosed American figures put it at $10.4 billion for the
period FY 1972 to FY 1976. It is interesting to note that these
sales increased over seven–fold from $524 million in FY 1972 to
$3.9 billion in FY 1974 and then slackened off to $2.6 billion in
FY 1975 and $1.3 billion in FY 1976.[38] This transfer of arms to
Iran has included some of the most sophisticated equipment in the
American armoury including the F–14 fighter and the DD993
modified Spruance class destroyer. In fact, some of the equipment
being supplied to Iran is so modern that it has not even been
deployed in the American armed forces themselves. On the basis
of these facts and figures, a U.S. Senate Staff study came to the
conclusion that 'Upon delivery between now and 1981 of equipment
ordered to date, Iran, on paper, can be regarded as a regional
superpower.'[39] The staff study goes on to argue that because of
inadequate numbers of technically skilled personnel in Iran, U.S.
personnel will be increasingly involved with the Iranian arms build
up and, therefore, there is a danger of U.S. involvement in Iran

escalating to the point that American personnel may be involved in fighting an Iranian war. It quotes figures to prove that 'The number of official and private American citizens in Iran, a large percentage of whom are involved in military programs, has increased from approximately 15,000–16,000 in 1972 to 24,000 in 1976, it could easily reach 50,000–60,000 or higher by 1980.'[40]

Although the supply of U.S. arms to Saudi Arabia has not matched its sales to Iran—both in quantitative and qualitative terms—nonetheless it has been considerable. Among the sophisticated equipment that Saudi Arabia has acquired, F–5 aircraft from the United States and Mirage III from France stand out. According to estimates available, the U.S.A. had sold to Saudi Arabia $2.38 billion worth of arms up to the end of the third quarter of FY 1975.[41] In addition the United States is engaged in a major program for infra-structure construction for the Saudi armed forces and this may run into several billions of dollars in the next few years.[42] According to one estimate, that of Congressman Benjamin Rosenthal (a leading member of the Israeli lobby in the U.S. Congress), U.S. military sales to Saudi Arabia in 1976 were expected to total over $7.5 billion—of which over $5 billion were to be used for construction and training purposes.[43]

The quantitative explosion of arms in the Gulf region is matched only by the qualitative escalation. As has already been stated, some of the most modern equipments are being supplied to Iran right off the assembly line. American arms transfer policies towards Saudi Arabia, if recent reports are correct, envisage the setting up of vast infra-structure facilities needed to support modern equipments and a modernised army. This would mean the creation of total military capability and not merely the supply of weapon systems. While the Israeli lobby in Washington is worried about the effect such a build up of Saudi capability would have on the overall Arab-Israeli balance, what is more worrisome is the escalation of the arms race in the Persian Gulf itself. If Saudi capabilities came anywhere close to those possessed by Iran, the Shah is bound to aspire for more and the only sphere in which he can then outdo the Saudis would be that of nuclear weaponry. The United States may, therefore, be creating a situation in the Persian Gulf which might make nonsense of the entire Carter diplomacy relating to the control of nuclear proliferation.

Moreover, given the weak political infra-structure possessed by Iran and Saudi Arabia and the basically personal nature of the regimes in the two countries, the creation of inflated military establishments presiding over what are technologically the most advanced sectors of their societies is bound to create centres of power which may aspire to rival those of the throne thus adding to the possibilities of violent overthrow of the Gulf monarchies. The prospect of more Gaddafis appearing in the Gulf, with the help of American arms, can, therefore, not be completely ruled out.

The Horn of Africa
The Horn is one region of the Indian Ocean littoral where a conflict appears imminent. In fact, a major insurgency has been continuing in the Eritrean province of Ethiopia for a decade and a half and, unless external elements intervene in a big way, seems to be heading towards a successful conclusion for the insurgents. Moreover, Somalia and Ethiopia, relations between whom have remained tense since the former achieved independence in 1960, seem to be heading towards open conflict on the issue of Djibouti (the former French Territory of the Afar and the Issas) which has just attained freedom from French rule. Somali–Ethiopian relations have also been strained because of Somalia's claim to the Ogaden province of Ethiopia which is populated mostly by people of Somali origin. In recent months the insurgency in Ogaden has been intensified and the crumbling of the Ethiopian 'empire', as demonstrated by events in Eritrea, has encouraged the Somalis to look forward to the day when Ogaden can be re-incorporated into the Somali homeland. Similar Somali claims have also been made in neighbouring Somali-populated areas of Kenya. According to Thomas J. Farer, a leading authority on the region:

> Perhaps as many as one million Somalis occupy, more or less exclusively, nearly one-fifth of Ethiopia. Another quarter of a million inhabit the old Northern Frontier district of Kenya. And somewhere between sixty and one hundred thousand live in the French territory of the Afar and the Issa.[44]

The problem has been exacerbated by the harsh treatment meted out to the Somalis living in Ethiopia by Addis Ababa both under Emperor Haile Selassie and his successors. This attitude on the part of Ethiopia's Christian Amharic rulers formed a part of their general attitude towards the non-Christian and non-Amharic populations in the country and was particularly in evidence in Eritrea. The Djibouti issue has further complicated Somali–Ethiopian relations because the territory, with its sizable Somali population, has formed a natural target for Somali irrendentism. On the other hand, the Ethiopians have firmly opposed Djibouti's accession to Somalia since such an event would cut off their main access to the sea. The major Ethiopian ports, Assab and Massawa, are located in Eritrea and have been rendered increasingly unusable because of the uprising thus enhancing Djibouti's value in Ethiopian eyes.

The conflict-potential of the region is enhanced by its proximity to the major theatres of a future Arab-Israeli war and because of the 'strategic' importance, often overrated, of the Straits of Bab-el Mandeb to Israel. Therefore, the problems of this region have to a large extent come to be viewed, particularly in the West, as extensions of the Arab-Israeli issue. The accession to power of 'radical' regimes, particularly in Somalia and in South Yemen (PDRY), which have received political and military support from the Soviet Union, have further convinced policy-makers and strategists in the West that the area has become an important target for Soviet political expansion. On the other hand, Saudi Arabia, the major Red Sea power on the Asian side across from the Horn, seems to be firmly aligned to the United States and for the last 25 years (until a few months ago) the U.S.A. had been the major source of arms supply and political support to Addis Ababa.

The Arab support to the Somali Republic and to Eritrean nationalists adds another dimension to intra-regional security problems. This support is based on a number of factors, including sympathy for their Muslim co-religionists and as a retaliation for Ethiopia's traditionally pro-Israeli stance. Even though the Ethiopian stand underwent some change following the October war, Israeli military advisers still train the Dergue's counter-insurgency forces used primarily in Eritrea.[45] The Somali Republic, incidentally, has been accepted as a member of the Arab League, although it is ethnically non-Arab.

Superpower involvement in this region has been partially the result of the spill over of their involvement in the Arab-Israeli conflict into the Red Sea. Initial superpower investment in the area, in political and military terms, however, ante-dates the intensification of superpower rivalry in the Middle East and goes back to the early 1950s when the United States began its military and economic assistance program to Ethiopia. As J. Bowyer Bell has pointed out:

> To a degree the . . . American connection with Ethiopia resulted from an African initiative. . . . Despite the historic suspicion of the *ferenji*, the Ethiopians had sound reasons for seeking an American connection. America was an enemy of Communist revolution, and—to a degree—of European imperialism as well; a patron of Ethiopia's Israeli ally; and with the passage of the years, an advocate of conservative stability

in the Horn, and even a reluctant opponent of Arab ambitions.[46]

The United States looked upon its Ethiopian connection primarily in the cold war context. It not only gave Washington a foothold in a continent poised for de-colonisation, it brought with it certain concrete dividends, most important of all being the (formerly Italian) Kagnew communications base near Asmara in Eritrea. This base became an important link in the world-wide network of U.S. military communications stretching from the Philippines, through Ethiopia and Morocco to Arlington, Virginia. The U.S.A. acquired this base as a part of a deal with Ethiopia under which the U.S.A. extended support at the U.N. to the Ethiopian annexation of Eritrea and also promised military aid to Addis Ababa.[47] The Kagnew base, named after the Ethiopian contingent that fought in Korea,[48] was leased to the U.S.A. in 1953 for 25 years. While the lease has one more year to run, with the development of the Diego Garcia base in the Indian Ocean most of the functions of the Kagnew base have been transferred to the new facility.

John Spencer has pointed out that Ethiopia was able to persuade the U.S.A. to extend military assistance to Addis Ababa by exploiting the

'Northern Tier' concept being developed at that time by Secretary of State Dulles, culminating in the Baghdad Pact. The negotiators for Ethiopia presented the argument that it should form part of a 'Southern Tier' or secondary line of defense against Communism in the Middle East. That type of argument made it possible for the Secretaries of State and Defense to 'find' that the defense of Ethiopia was essential to the defense of the Free World. Again, as in the case of the base agreement, the arms assistance agreement was related not to Africa as such but to the Middle East and defense against Communism.[49]

On the basis of the abovementioned considerations, to which have been added new ones, particularly those of close Soviet-Somali relations from the mid 1960s onward, the United States supplied Ethiopia with $350 million in economic aid and $278.6 million in military assistance until 1976. An additional $6 million worth of military aid to Ethiopia had been programmed for FY 1977.[50] According to IISS estimates, this assistance has included 24 M–60 medium and 54 M–41 light tanks, about 90 M–113 APCs, four B–52 bombers, 11 F–86F fighter-bombers and 16 F–5 A/E fighter bombers.[51] According to SIPRI estimates, Ethiopia was the largest importer of major weapons in sub-Saharan Africa through the

1950s and 1960s,[52] accounting for over 12 per cent of the total throughout the period. It also became the first black African country to acquire supersonic aircraft when it received the F-5 Freedom Fighters from the U.S.A. in 1965. Moreover, up to 1962 nearly the entire U.S. military aid to sub-Saharan Africa went to Ethiopia and from 1962 to 1969 it averaged 70 per cent.[53]

Until 1960, when the Somali Republic gained independence, there was technically no 'arms race' in the Horn of Africa since Ethiopia was the only country receiving arms from abroad. With the emergence of the Somali Republic, however, conflict potentialities within the region increased. Somali aspirations for a 'Greater Somalia' consisting of Ogaden in Ethiopia, the Northern Frontier district of Kenya and Djibouti, in addition to the Somali Republic, was one major reason for increasing tensions in the region. Ethiopia's strong military establishment (strong in the African context and particularly vis-à-vis its neighbours) combined with the strategic interest of outside powers in the Horn were other major factors that led to the Somali arms build up.

During the initial years of Somali independence, Mogadishu received some arms supplies from the former colonial rulers of the two Somali lands—Italy and Great Britain—as well as from Egypt. However by 1963 Somali relations with the Western powers had deteriorated considerably, mainly because of British refusal to separate the Somali-populated northern district from Kenya before granting that country independence, and because of continued U.S. support to Ethiopia which kept the regional balance of power tilted very much against Somalia. In October 1963, Somalia accepted a Soviet offer of military assistance in the form of a long-term rouble credit worth $30 million. The main objective of this aid was to expand the Somali army from 4,000 to about 20,000 men and to build a respectable (by African standards) airforce. Somalia received its first supply of MiG aircraft (six MiG–15 UTI trainers) in November 1963 and additional MiG 15s and 17s in 1965–66. It also received T–34 tanks in 1965 from the U.S.S.R. The Somali-Soviet relationship has had its ups and downs, but since the accession of the military to power in 1969, they have remained close and, until recently, on an even keel. According to U.S. ACDA estimates, Somalia received $134 million worth of arms from the Soviet Union from 1966 to 1975.[54]

According to the latest IISS estimates, Somalia has an army of 22,000 (as compared to Ethiopia's 47,000) which has at its disposal 200 T–34 and 50 T–54/55 tanks. It has an airforce of 2,700 with 66 combat aircraft (as compared to Ethiopia's 2,300 and 36

respectively) which include 10 Il–28s, 44 MiG–15s and 17s and
12 MiG–21s. However, the latest *Military Balance* points out that
'spares are short and not all equipment is serviceable'.[55]

As a quid pro quo for Soviet military and economic assistance
to the Somali Republic, the latter extended certain base facilities
to Moscow at the port of Berbera. These included a military airport
and two Soviet communication facilities that opened in December
1972. Despite Soviet and Somali denials, the first report of the three
experts appointed by the U.N. Secretary General to report on great
power naval rivalry in the Indian Ocean identified Berbera as a
Soviet Base. There is enough evidence on record now—including
aerial photographic reconnaissance by the U.S.A. and the visits of
U.S. Congressional teams—to conclude that it is a naval facility
used by the Soviet Union and has storage and handling facilities
for naval missiles. However, as Geoffrey Jukes pointed out in
August 1976 in his testimony before the Australian Senate Standing
Committee on Foreign Affairs and Defence, 'Nothing has actually
been seen here that is bigger than the Styx [missile] which has
a range of about 20 miles . . . But the handling gear and the
buildings could obviously handle something much larger'.[56] In 1974
the Somali Republic and the Soviet Union signed a Treaty of
Friendship and Cooperation which makes provision for 'training of
the Somalian military personnel and in the mastering of weapons
and equipment delivered to the Somali Democratic Republic for
the purposes of enhancing its defence potential'.[57]

Until the overthrow of Emperor Haile Selassie in early 1974 by
an Ethiopian military junta called the Dergue, American and Soviet
positions in support of their respective allies in the area had
remained quite firm and rigid. The accession to power in Addis
Ababa of a regime apparently wedded to 'scientific socialism'
(though in a peculiarly Ethiopian fashion) seemed to queer the pitch
for U.S.–Ethiopian relations and a degree of unease was expressed
at this development in Washington, particularly in Congressional
circles. However, it was not until early 1977 that a major
transformation took place in the political and military alignments
in the Horn of Africa. A power struggle within the Dergue in
Ethiopia ended in February 1977 when Lieutenant Colonel
Mengistu Haile Mariam assumed supreme power after executing
the Head of State, Terefi Bante, and 16 of his supporters within
the Dergue.

In April Mengistu decided to cut off all ties with the United
States, thus abruptly ending Ethiopia's near-total dependence on
Washington for arms and other forms of military aid. He turned

instead to the Soviet Union to replace the U.S.A. as the major source of arms supply and military training. Among the reasons which seem to have prompted Mengistu, other than his Marxist predilections that had been coming under increasing attack in U.S. Congressional circles, was the way the war was going in Eritrea and the expectation of a showdown with Somalia over Djibouti when the French withdrew from that territory. Despite American military assistance, the war in Eritrea was moving slowly but surely towards a total Ethiopian rout. No government in Addis Ababa could have survived the fall of Eritrea. Mengistu must have reasoned that the Soviets would be a better bet to help him reverse the trend in Eritrea than the Americans, particularly because President Carter's new hobby-horse, 'human rights', prevented them from supporting Mengistu's genocidal plans for that region. Secondly, he had seen the Soviets in action in Angola where they did their best, including the introduction of Cuban troops, to help their allies win control of that country. The Soviets, therefore, appeared more reliable allies to him on the Eritrean front. Secondly, given the Soviet's leverage with Somalia, Mengistu must have reasoned that a Soviet Union friendly to Addis Ababa would be willing to restrain Somali intrusions into Djibouti which would have forced Ethiopia to open another front at a time when Eritrea itself was unmanageable.

The Soviet Union responded with surprising alacrity to Ethiopian overtures. Moscow's calculations seem to have been based, among other things, on the need to get a firmer foothold in the Horn than was provided by Somalia. Ethiopia with a population almost nine times that of Somalia and with two outlets to the Red Sea seemed a good horse to bet on. At the same time, it must have felt that with its influence in Egypt at an all time low and with Sudan following Cairo's example by expelling Soviet advisers and diplomats, a friendly Ethiopia might be a surrogate for losses in Egypt and Sudan. With these two countries and conservative Saudi Arabia the main supporters of the Eritrean nationalist movement, Moscow must have calculated that an Ethiopian victory in Eritrea, particularly with an avowedly Marxist government in Addis Ababa, might be in Soviet interest. Then again, Moscow might have been secretly worried that Saudi overtures to woo Somalia away from the Soviet orbit by dangling the carrot of massive economic and military aid, might prove too tempting for Mogadishu to decline and might, therefore, endanger Soviet influence in Somalia as a whole and its presence in Berbera in particular. On the other hand, Moscow may have been confident enough of its leverage—political, military and economic—with Somalia to take the risk of wooing its major rival and not alienating Mogadishu completely.

There is enough evidence to establish that Moscow has decided to assist Addis Ababa in the counter-insurgency and counter-secessionist campaigns by way of arms shipments and advisers. The inevitable speculation about the presence of Cuban advisers and/or ground troops in Ethiopia has followed. According to one fairly reliable report, Moscow's support of Ethiopia has so far

> been signalled by the shipment to Ethiopia of old Soviet weaponry, 34 tanks (exactly the strength of an armoured battalion), 20 personnel carriers plus small arms and a clutch of anti-aircraft guns. There are also Russian and Cuban military advisers attached to their respective missions in Addis Ababa but the reportedly pending arrival of Cuban troops appears doubtful.[58]

There have been subtle changes in Somali foreign policy also, although most of these have preceded rather than followed the Soviet decision to support Ethiopia. There have been reports all through last year of Saudi offers of assistance to Mogadishu— including funds for the purchase of arms in the West—if Somalia broke with the Soviet Union. According to one report,

> the figure of preferred Saudi aid mentioned most often in Arab circles here [in Mogadishu] is $300 million to $350 million, although Saudi diplomats in the region say that this is a vastly exaggerated estimate of Somali needs. Last year Saudi Arabia gave Somalia $28 million; so far this year it has furnished $16–18 million.[59]

At one stage last year, James E. Akins, former U.S. Ambassador to Saudi Arabia, charged the Ford Administration with having ignored a Saudi proposal to reduce Soviet influence in Somalia because the removal of the Soviet base at Berbera would have weakened the Administration's case for a base on Diego Garcia at a time when the U.S. Congress was considering the appropriations for it.[60] There have been reports that on his recent trip to Washington Saudi Arabia's strongman, Crown Prince Fahd, had tried to persuade Washington to supply arms to Somalia for which the Saudis were willing to pay, but apparently with no success. France, another potential supplier, seems to have told Fahd that it was willing to supply arms to Somalia but that backlogs of other orders would mean a long delay.[61] Paris, worried about the fate of Djibouti, is in no hurry to augment Somali capabilities.

On the other hand, Somalia also appears to be more than cautious in making a major break with the Soviet Union. While Mogadishu is 'concerned' about Soviet arms supplies to Ethiopia, it has not protested officially.[62] In a recent interview to Arnaud de Borchgrave of *Newsweek*, President Muhammad Siad Barre of Somalia stated:

> I can assure you there will be no conflict between Somalia and the Soviets . . . But it is no secret that we don't see eye to eye on Ethiopia . . . We are not thinking in terms of divorce and remarriage . . . But we would rather have good relations with all powers as this would reinforce our non-alignment policy.

In answer to the question about U.S. military aid to Somalia, he said: 'We have no proposals before us. It would depend on circumstances. What we now receive from the Soviet Union is sufficient.'[63]

The present Somali reticence in criticising or condemning the Soviet Union stems from the existence of strong pro-Soviet elements in the ruling Somali Politburo as well as because of Somalia's dependence on Soviet arms. The unreliability of alternative suppliers (particularly the U.S.A.) to deliver what Somalia may need and the time span required to switch from Soviet to Western arms are crucial factors which have deterred Somalia so far from overtly adopting an anti-Soviet posture. This does not rule out, however, that at some point in time Somalia may decide that Soviet support to Ethiopia has so drastically affected the regional power balance to its disadvantage that it would be better to do an 'Egypt' on the Soviet Union and opt for stronger links with Saudi Arabia and the West. But, as one Somali leader pointed out to a Western correspondent, 'Look at what happened to Sadat: Washington promised him the moon and left him defenceless against Israel.'[64] However a recent report has mentioned that Somalia has told the Soviet Union to begin phasing out an estimated 1,500 advisers from the Soviet base at Berbera. This has been seen by observers as the first definite sign of the growing schism between Moscow and Mogadishu.[65] Another report mentioned that Somalia had ordered all Soviet military advisers and technicians in that country, numbering nearly 6,000, to leave in what was termed 'the biggest set back for Moscow in Africa since Egypt expelled 18,000 Russians five years ago'.[66] While the report has been denied by Somali sources, it has been confirmed that an American decision has been made to sell major arms to Somalia. The arms will apparently be paid for by Saudi Arabia.[67]

Several conclusions appear from this analysis of events in the

Horn: (1) Intra-regional conflicts are more deep-seated than either ideological commitments or alignments with big powers. This was nowhere more apparent than in the effort made by Castro in March 1977 to get Mengistu and Barre together at Aden to work out a regional Marxist confederation among Ethiopia, Somalia and PDRY. It was a complete non-starter. (2) While the Soviet Union may at the moment appear to have 'succeeded' in its Red Sea/Horn strategy by having both Ethiopia and Somalia militarily dependent upon it, it may turn out to be a Pyrrhic victory. If disappointed with the extent of Soviet help or frustrated at the outcome, not only one but both the regional powers may decide to perform an 'Egypt' on the Soviet Union, thus leaving it high and dry and without Berbera. If, however, the Soviet presence in Ethiopia escalates to the extent where large numbers of Soviet military advisers become involved in that country, then Ethiopia may turn out to be Moscow's 'Vietnam'. (3) As for the induction of arms into the area from abroad, it has been very considerably less, both in terms of quantity and quality, than the arms provided to the Gulf region or to South Asia. This has resulted from the fact that there are no petro-dollars available here to buy arms, nor are there vital resources in the region (like oil in the Gulf) which may prompt one or both of the superpowers to invest heavily, in military and political terms, in the region. It should be noted, however, that while technically the 'arms race' in the Horn started after Somali independence—there could not be an arms race without two parties to the race—Ethiopia had started to acquire sophisticated weaponry (in the African context) from the United States for at least a decade before Soviet military supplies to Somalia began. (4) Despite the low level of arms supply in the Horn compared to South Asia or the Gulf, the area is much more unstable both in terms of intra-regional conflict and internal security problems than either of the other two regions studied in this paper, and therefore, prospects of an imminent explosion in the region are high.

Conclusion

The three case studies presented above plus the general trends noticeable in intra-regional conflicts in the Third World and in the supply of sophisticated weaponry to the regional contestants lead us to the following tentative conclusions:

1. As far as regional actors are concerned, their primary preoccupation has been with regional balances of power and their interest in superpower rivalry has been usually limited to assessing the effects, beneficial or otherwise (from their point

of view), of superpower involvement in these regional balances and the intra-regional tensions that flow out of them.

2. Regional actors have, however, often justified their political and military attachments to the rival superpowers in ideological terms. This has been the case particularly when they have had to 'sell' these alliance-relationships to strong pressure groups within the superpowers' decision-making machinery. This was particularly true during the hey-day of the cold war in the 1950s when highly 'moralistic' stances were adopted by the great power contestants. This has been especially true of the allies that the U.S.A. accummulated in those days. An ideological justification for a close political and military relationship with the U.S.S.R. would not have suited the élites of most of the countries which had such a relationship with Moscow.

3. The superpowers were, of course, primarily interested in utilising regional powers to further their own global ends. They found intra-regional tensions a convenient medium which they could utilise for their own infiltration into various parts of the Third World in the guise of political supporters and military suppliers of one or the other party.

4. The United States most often led in this game. The Soviet involvement in intra-regional problems, conflicts and tensions was, more often than not, a reaction to an earlier U.S. involvement. This was true in all the three cases we have studied —South Asia, the Gulf and the Horn of Africa.

5. A major factor which can help explain the earlier American involvement is related to the fact that in the initial years after World War II, i.e. through the late 1940s and up to the middle 1950s, the U.S.A. was the only superpower. The Soviet Union was merely a regionally dominant power with certain global aspirations. Because of its global reach, the U.S.A. found it easier to get into the game of influence-building in the Indian Ocean littoral, and, in fact, in the third world as a whole, than was the case with the U.S.S.R. It was easier to translate U.S. strategic superiority into political influence before the Soviet Union could catch up with the U.S.A. in strategic terms.

6. Moreover the new rulers of most Third World states were afraid of greater contact with the U.S.S.R. which was viewed primarily as an anti-status quo power in ideological terms. Such contact, they believed, would undermine their own support-base within their respective countries. This feeling was augmented by the fact that a large number of opposition movements or elements in the Third World countries swore by Marxism—

Leninism. Conversely, a political and military association with the U.S.A. was viewed as a major source of support for these regimes, most of whom had very narrow and highly élitist support-bases in their own countries.

7. Therefore in the initial years, non-alignment was considered a viable policy only by those ruling élite which had relatively broad support-bases and were confident of their internal position (e.g. India and Indonesia) or were forced into such a policy by U.S. support of regional rivals (e.g. Egypt). Since non-alignment was detrimental to the extension of U.S. influence in the Third World and prevented Washington from translating its strategic superiority into political influence commensurate with such superiority, it was condemned by the U.S.A. in the early and middle 1950s as 'immoral'. However, by the early 1950s the U.S.S.R. had realised that, given the nature of the Third World ruling élites, the best that it could hope for was that they would not ally themselves openly with the West and would not allow U.S. bases to be set up in their territories since base-building was a major aim of U.S. policy in areas around the Soviet periphery. Moscow, as the weaker of the two superpowers, therefore, welcomed the policy of non-alignment and even extended political (and later military) support to non-aligned countries in their conflicts with regional rivals supported by the U.S.A. This complex interplay of strategies was very much in evidence in the regions of the Indian Ocean littoral.

8. In terms of arms transfer, the U.S.A. started to supply major arms to regional actors from the early 1950s. (Before the U.S.A. got into the act the British and the French were the major arms suppliers in their respective spheres of influence.) The first arms transfer deal reached between a Soviet-bloc country and a Third World recipient was the supply of Czechoslovakian arms to Egypt in 1955 after the West had turned down repeated requests by Nasser to supply arms to Egypt which might help him match Israeli weaponry. As far as our three case studies are concerned, it was not until the early 1960s (Iraq 1958–1960, India 1962, Somalia 1963) that the Soviet Union started to supply major weapons to regional actors. Pakistan, Iran, Iraq and Ethiopia had all received American arms for almost a decade before the Soviets got into the act. Therefore, the initial responsibility for the destablisation of regional balances and the exacerbation of intra-regional conflicts rests upon the United States.[68] However, the Soviet

contribution to the exacerbation of such tensions has been particularly noticeable in the Horn of Africa where Moscow helped further Somali irredentism by building up its armed forces and has now become the leading patron and arms supplier of both the regional contestants, Ethiopia and Somalia.

9. The Persian Gulf region is unique—both in quantitative and qualitative terms—as far as transfer of arms is concerned. This is so not only among the regions of the Indian Ocean littoral but in the entire Third World. The oil boom, the consequent accumulation of petro-dollars in the hands of major regional actors and the strategic value of Gulf oil have combined to make the Gulf region the most important recipient of advanced weaponry anywhere in the Third World. The U.S.A., once again, bears the major responsibility for weapons proliferation that has taken place and is taking place in the Gulf. The Soviet supply of arms to Iraq, although considerable, does not match American supplies—current and projected—to Iran and Saudi Arabia. Iran is buying U.S. weapons right off the assembly line and Saudi Arabia is building 'total military capability' with U.S. help.

10. Given the weak political infra-structure of the regional actors, particularly in the Gulf and the Horn, accumulation of sophisticated weaponry and modernisation of their armed forces is likely not only to exacerbate intra-regional tensions but also to destabilise seriously societies and regimes. While the second outcome may not be without its good points, it is likely, in the short run, to add to the instability of the regions and promote external adventures by unstable regimes who may look upon such adventures as the easiest way of creating domestic support and meeting internal challenges.

11. While the competitive naval presence of the superpowers in the Indian Ocean has not proved to be the best means of influencing the course of events in the regions of the Indian Ocean littoral, nonetheless such presence has added to the general atmosphere of insecurity around the Indian Ocean. The apprehension that either one or both of the superpowers may revert to a late-20th century version of gunboat diplomacy was strengthened by the sailing of a U.S. task force led by the *USS Enterprise* into the Bay of Bengal during the height of the Bangladesh war and by remarks made by U.S. Secretary of State Kissinger and Defense Secretary Schlesinger regarding forcible takeover of oil fields in the Gulf following the Arab oil embargo in 1973–74.

12. The construction of a U.S. communications and naval base at

Diego Garcia provides Washington with a military facility much more secure than anything the Soviet Union has been able to acquire in the Indian Ocean area. Unlike its Soviet competitor, Berbera, Diego Garcia is an unpopulated island under direct American control, except for symbolic British involvement. With the Soviet position in Somalia undermined as a result of Moscow's recent support to Ethiopia, the latter could be in serious danger of losing its privileges in Berbera. The U.S. strategy of building a facility in an area not under the sovereignty of a littoral state, plus the better access routes it possesses to the Ocean and the presence of two strong and friendly powers—Australia and South Africa—at the two extremeties of the Ocean, make the American position in the Ocean much less vulnerable to changes in the littoral countries, and in the regional power-balances. The Soviet Union is much more at the mercy of the littoral countries both for access to the Ocean, from the Mediterranean and the Pacific, and for on-shore facilities. Its position is, therefore, much more vulnerable than that of its superpower rival. Moreover, French and British naval presences in the Indian Ocean should be added to the U.S. presence in order to make a realistic comparison with Soviet naval presence in the area. Once this is done, it becomes clear that Western presence in the Indian Ocean outweighs that of the Soviet Union quantitatively and qualitatively.[69]

Footnotes

1. Peter Lyon, 'The Indian Ocean as a Strategic Area', in *Collected Papers of the Study Conference on the Indian Ocean in International Politics*, Southampton (England), 1973, Mimeographed. Quoted in Ferenc A. Váli, *Politics of the Indian Ocean Region*, New York, 1976, p.39.
2. Wayne Wilcox quoted in Ferenc A. Váli, *Politics of the Indian Ocean Region*, p.31.
3. Kim Christian Beazley, *American and Soviet Involvement in the Indian Ocean Area, 1968-1975*, B. Phil. thesis, Oxford University, 1976, unpublished.
4. Shahram Chubin, 'Naval Competition and Security in South-west Asia', in *Power at Sea III: Competition and Conflict, Adelphi Papers*, No.124, p.23
5. U.N. Document A/AC.159/1, dated 3 May 1974.
6. See above, Chapter Two, 'The Development of the Conventional Arms Trade', by Ron Huisken.
7. For a detailed discussion of this issue, see Mohammed Ayoob, 'India and Pakistan: Prospects for Détente', *Pacific Community,* Tokyo, Vol. 8, No.1, October 1976, pp. 149–169.

8. These calculations are based on the figures provided by the IISS in *The Military Balance, 1972–73* and *1976–77*, London, 1973 and 1976.
9. *World Armaments and Disarmaments, SIPRI Yearbook, 1977*, Table 7A.16, p.231, and U.S. Arms Control and Disarmament Agency, *World Military Expenditures and Arms Transfers, 1966–1975*, Washington, 1976, p.43.
10. *The Military Balance, 1972–73* and *1976–77*.
11. *SIPRI Yearbook, 1977*, p. 231, and U.S. Arms Control and Disarmament Agency, *World Military Expenditures and Arms Transfers, 1966–1975*, Washington, 1976, p.33.
12. SIPRI, *The Arms Trade with the Third World*, Stockholm 1971, p.493.
13. Committee on Foreign Relations, U.S. Senate, *Hearings before the Subcommittee on Near Eastern and South Asian Affairs*, March–June 1967, Washington 1967.
14. Institute for Defence Studies and Analyses (New Delhi), *News Review on South Asia*, April 1972, pp. 16–17.
15. SIPRI, *Arms Trade with the Third World*, p.493.
16. President Richard M. Nixon, *U.S. Foreign Policy for the 1970s: The Emerging structure of Peace*, A Report to the U.S. Congress, 19 February 1972, Washington 1972, p.50.
17. U.S. ACDA, *World Military Expenditures and Arms Transfers, 1966–1975*, Washington 1976, p.78.
18. SIPRI, *The Arms Trade with the Third World*, p.481.
19. SIPRI, *The Arms Trade with the Third World*, Table 16.2, p.469.
20. The reference is to the Czech agreement to supply arms to Egypt.
21. President Nixon, *U.S. Foreign Policy for the 1970s*, 19 February 1972, p.50.
22. U.S. ACDA, *World Military Expenditures and Arms Transfers, 1966–1975*, p.78.
23. Raju C. Thomas, 'The Indian Navy in the Seventies', *Pacific Affairs* Winter 1975–76, p.502.
24. *Far Eastern Economic Review*, 15 July 1977 and 22 July 1977.
25. Ian Clark, 'Autonomy and Dependence in Recent Indo–Soviet Relations', *Australian Outlook*, Vol. 31, No.1, April 1977, p.155. This article also gives details of Soviet, British and French equipment supplied to India or produced under licence since 1971.
26. *Dawn*, Karachi, 10 June 1974.
27. For details see Mohammed Ayoob, 'The Military in Pakistan's Political Development', in S.P. Varma & Virendra Narain (ed.), *Pakistan Political System in Crisis*, Jaipur, 1972.
28. For details see Jahangir Amuzegar, 'Persian Gulf Oil and the World Economy', in Abbas Amirie, *The Persian Gulf and Indian Ocean in International Politics*, Tehran, 1975, pp. 321–345.
29. *Business Week*, 23 December 1974, reproduced in *Department of State Bulletin*, 27 January 1975, p.101.
30. The most notable examples of those which advocated such a step were,

Robert W. Tucker, 'Oil: The Issue of American Intervention', *Commentary*, January 1975, pp. 21–31 and Miles Ignotus (a pseudonym for a Washington-based professor), 'Seizing Arab Oil', *Harper's*, March 1975, pp. 45–62. Rebuttals included Earl C. Ravenal, 'The Oil Grab Scenario', *The New Republic*, 18 January 1975, pp. 14–16, and I.F. Stone, 'War for Oil?' *The New York Review*, 6 February 1975, pp. 7–8, 10.

31. Congressional Research Service, Library of Congress, *Oil Fields as Military Objectives: A Feasibility Study*, prepared for the Special Subcommittee on Investigations of the Committee on International Relations, U.S. House of Representatives, Washington, 21 August 1975, p.76.

32. For details see Mohammed Ayoob, 'Indo–Iranian Relations: Strategic, Political and Economic Dimensions', *India Quarterly*, New Delhi, Vol. 33, No.1, January–March 1977, pp.1–18.

33. For an interesting account of the Dhofar insurrection see John Duke Anthony, 'Insurrection and Intervention: The War in Dhofar', in Abbas Armirie (ed.), *The Persian Gulf and the Indian Ocean in International Politics*, pp. 287–318.

34. Michael T. Klare, 'The Political Economy of Arms Sales: The American Empire at Bay', in *Society*, September–October 1974, reproduced as Appendix 6 in Committee on Foreign Affairs, U.S. House of Representatives, *The Persian Gulf, 1974: Money, Politics, Arms and Power*, Hearings before the Subcommittee on the Near East and South Asia, July–August 1974, Washington, D.C. 1975, p.228.

35. U.S. ACDA, *World Military Expenditures and Arms Transfers, 1966–1975*, p.78. In November 1976 Iran signed another agreement under which Moscow will supply Tehran a further $414 million worth of arms. *SIPRI Yearbook 1977*, p.321.

36. IISS, *The Military Balance, 1976–77*, p.34.

37. Dale R. Tahtinen, *Arms in the Persian Gulf*, Washington, D.C. 1975.

38. Committee on Foreign Relations, U.S. Senate, *U.S. Military Sales to Iran*, a Staff Report to the Subcommittee on Foreign Assistance, July 1976, Washington, D.C., 1976, p.vii.

39. *Ibid.*, p.viii.

40. *Ibid*, p.vii.

41. *The Defence Monitor* (Washington, D.C.), May 1975, p.2.

42. For details see Committee on International Relations, U.S. House of Representatives, *Military Sales to Saudi–Arabia, 1975*, Hearings before the Subcommittee on International Political and Military Affairs, 4 November and 17 December, 1975, Washington, D.C. 1976.

43. *Congressional Record*, September 27, 1976, p.E5311.

44. Committee on Foreign Affairs, U.S. Senate, *Ethiopia and the Horn of Africa*, Hearings before the Subcommittee on African Affairs, 4–6 August 1976, p.75.

45. William Lee, 'Local Powers are drawn into the Ethiopian Vortex', *Middle East Economic Digest*, London, 6 May 1977, p.9.

46. J. Bowyer Bell, *The Horn of Africa: Strategic Magnet in the Seventies*, New York, 1973, p.39.

47. For details, see the testimony of John H. Spencer, former Chief Adviser to the Ethiopian Ministry of Foreign Affairs, in *Ethiopia and the Horn of Africa*, Hearings . . . , particularly pp. 26–28.

48. Ethiopia was the only African country apart from South Africa to have supplied a military contingent for U.N. operations in Korea.

49. *Ethiopia and the Horn of Africa*, Hearings . . . , p.27.

50. *Ibid.*, p.2.

51. IISS, *The Military Balance, 1976–77*, p.42.

52. Comparable estimates for the 1970s have not been made public by SIPRI.

53. SIPRI, *The Arms Trade with the Third World*, 1971, pp.650–651.

54. U.S. ACDA, *World Military Expenditures and Arms Transfers, 1966–1975*, p.79.

55. *The Military Balance, 1976–77*, p.44.

56. Commonwealth of Australia, Senate Standing Committee on Foreign Affairs and Defence, *Australia and the Indian Ocean Region, Official Hansard Report*, 10 August 1976, Canberra 1976, p.669.

57. Quoted in Australian Senate Standing Committee on Foreign Affairs and Defence, *Australia and the Indian Ocean Region*, Canberra 1976, p.21.

58. James MacManus, 'Russia's Red Sea Strategy', *The Guardian Weekly*, 5 June 1977.

59. *International Herald Tribune*, 4–5 June, 1977.

60. *New York Times*, 5 May 1976.

61. *Newsweek*, 13 June 1977, p.5.

62. *International Herald Tribune*, 18 May 1977.

63. *Newsweek*, 27 June 1977, p.12.

64. *Newsweek*, 27 June 1977, p.11.

65. *The Australian*, 14 July 1977.

66. *The Australian*, 18 July 1977, quoting *Sunday Telegraph*, London.

67. *The Australian*, 28 and 29 July 1977.

68. This is borne out by a recent U.S. National Security Council Report. According to CIA data published in that report, the U.S.A. accounted for more than half of the worldwide arms traffic to developing nations in recent years. With 56 per cent of the sales the U.S. share is more than twice that of the other non-Communist suppliers combined (26 per cent) and more than three times the sales of the Soviet Union and other Communist suppliers. *International Herald Tribune*, 13 July 1977.

69. A considerable amount of literature has been published in recent years on great power naval deployment in the Indian Ocean. See especially: T.B. Millar, *Soviet Policies in the Indian Ocean Area*, Canberra 1970; Geoffrey Jukes, 'The Indian Ocean in Soviet Naval Policy', IISS, *Adelphi Papers*, No.87, May 1972; Alvin J. Cottrell and R.M. Burrell,

Indian Ocean Littoral: Conflicts and Proliferation. 221
(ed.), *The Indian Ocean: Its Political, Economic and Military Importance,* New York 1972; Michael MccGwire, (ed). *Soviet Naval Developments: Capabilities and Context,* New York, 1973; and a Report from the Australian Senate Standing Committee on Foreign Affairs and Defence entitled *Australia and the Indian Ocean Region,* Canberra, 1976.

8
Weapons Proliferation and Security Problems in The South Pacific Region
T.B. Millar

In a world of ICBMs, cruise missiles, MIRVs, SSBNs etc., one area and only one area stands out as removed from the fray but still inhabitable, a haven from the storm, a sea of tranquility: the South Pacific. One does not have to make this a desert to call it peace: it is at peace in name and nature already. Wherever else the superpowers may confront, the local gladiators posture, the economic thrusters thrust, it is surely not the South Pacific. There is nothing here but some scattered islands, a few fish, and happy Polynesians strumming guitars beneath waving palm tress. What is such a paradise doing in a conference on arms proliferation?

It is there partly because of the irreversible fact of geography —one cannot talk about the Pacific and leave out the 30 million square miles of it in the south. It is there also because Australia and New Zealand occupy one corner of it. And it is there because there are some endemic instabilities, and because problems of superpower rivalry and resources competition are slowly moving into the region.

Leaving out the external powers for the moment, the states in the South Pacific (and this paper deals with the western two–thirds of the ocean) are small and scattered. Australia, with 14 million people, is by far the largest. New Zealand has an estimated population of 3.2 million, Papua New Guinea has 2.6 million, Fiji has 550,000, Western Samoa 160,000, French Polynesia 135,000, New Caledonia 135,000. The rest are smaller again. The distances are vast, and the number of islands runs to many thousands. There are thus considerable problems of communication and of population pressing on resources. The political tendency, as elsewhere, is not towards consolidation but towards fragmentation, and the creation of a plethora of vulnerable ministates.

If there are security problems among these island territories or states, they are almost wholly *within* the states rather than between them: there is no hegemonial or acquisitive power hungrily eyeing its neighbours. The Gilbert and Ellice Islands have already split. Fiji has its racial division between Polynesians and Indians which is threatening political stability. Several territories are barely viable, are facing real poverty for the first time in a century, and with such poverty could well come a breakdown in internal security. In a relative sense one could talk about an expansion of arms to meet such problems, but the largest local military force east of New Zealand is in Fiji, and this is only of the order of one regular rifle company plus a small reserve. The implication of this might appear to be that the assumption of power by an alternative elite would be relatively easy, and involve only a modest application of force, but this does not take into account established patterns of authority and behaviour in the region. Oceania is not Africa or Latin America. Threats to internal security could see a demand for some additional arms and perhaps patrol craft or air transport, but on a limited scale. For a new or old imperial power in Europe, America or Asia baldly to take over a Pacific island state would cause an outcry by world public opinion. No metropolitan state in recent years has shown any interest in such imperialism.

Yet there are situations which could give rise to security problems on a significant scale. For some time there have been separatist tendencies within Papua New Guinea, which the government with some skill has contained. It is still possible that the people on Bougainville may at some stage insist on separating themselves from the mainland, either to go their own way or to link up with the Solomons. Miss Abaijah's defeat of Sir Maori Kiki in the recent election is a blow on behalf of an independent Papua. If either of these movements succeeded, we would probably have a civil war in the state, and Australia would be involved at least in terms of providing logistical support for government forces. It is not inconceivable that if Australia refused to provide the arms, helicopters etc. that the PNG government considered necessary to enforce its authority, it might turn elsewhere for them.

But not only Australia would have an interest in the outcome of such a conflict. Indonesia, separated only by the thickness of the north/south line that divides the island of New Guinea, has a very direct interest in its neighbour. Some people in PNG fear Indonesian imperialism against them, suspecting it of wanting to take over at least the whole mainland area. The present Indonesian government has expressed no such intention, although the idea has been canvassed in Jakarta from time to time. If, with or without Indonesian assistance PNG were to split up into two, three or more units, there would be a strong incentive for Indonesia to establish a new and closer relationship with one or more of them. The Indonesia/PNG border is already porous, which Jakarta finds disturbing. It does not like West Irianese fleeing eastwards into PNG, as they have done periodically, no doubt for very cogent reasons. These refugees, or other more professional dissidents, are assumed to be sitting in Port Moresby or elsewhere plotting the disintegration of the fragile political archipelago which is Indonesia. In fact, the Port Moresby government heavily discourages such activity, and encourages refugees to return to Irian Jaya. The last thing PNG wants is an unpleasant border incident with Indonesia. But its writ does not run everywhere, certainly not everywhere at once. The border is unpoliceable without an army probably several times greater than the one PNG has. And the problem would be compounded if the separatist movements in PNG were successful —an aspect which does not appear to have occurred to the Papua Besena movement.

An Indonesian government contemplating what to do in the situation of a disintegrating PNG might conclude from recent events that, in the event of their intervening, Australian reaction would be limited to expostulation after the event.

Australian governments in the past ten years or so have been reluctant to indicate, in advance, support for the PNG government in the event of a separatism crisis, other breakdowns in internal security, or an incident with Indonesia. This may be understandable, but Australians need to remember that PNG is just as relevant, in principle, to the security of Australia as it has ever been, and that Australia's interests are best served by a united, strong and friendly PNG. Australia's dispute with PNG over the location of the boundary—or boundaries—between them is unlikely to create a security problem, although it cannot be ruled out altogether. The 'worst case' situation would be where a radical PNG government demanded a boundary unacceptable to Australia, and when refused sought foreign arms to bring it about. It could scarcely hope to win a conflict against Australia, but it might well hope to achieve its aim by the threat of force.

A second type of security problem that could lead to arms increases is the thrust by a local island state for independence from a metropolitan power. This does not apply any longer to Britain, which is delighted to afford independence to any colonial territory that wants it and even to some that don't. But France has two colonial situations where local populations are restive—in New Caledonia, and in French Polynesia. Both are important to France, for different reasons. New Caledonia, which is a French territory represented in the French National Assembly and Senate, is rich in minerals, especially nickel and iron, but also chrome, cobalt, manganese and others. There is a sizable white community (40 per cent of population), and a strong nationalist movement. While the evidence suggests that France would be most reluctant to relinquish sovereignty over the territory, it also suggests that any concessions made will be induced by political action rather than by violence involving substantial import of arms.

French Polynesia comprises some 130 main islands, totalling 1300 square miles, spread over nearly a million square miles of ocean, and with a total population of 135,000. It is a French overseas territory and since 1963–64 has been the site of the French nuclear testing operations (Centre d'Expérimentation du Pacifique, or CEP). The massive French investment in this program has overwhelmed the social life and the economy of the territory, and has made self-government both more desired and more difficult. Again, local nationalist activity is likely to be political rather than violent. The size of the French naval force in the area fluctuates depending on the nuclear testing program.[1] Although relatively small in size, this program seems likely to continue, at intervals, for the foreseeable future. Thus French control of this territory is likely to remain in much the state it now is, and any forcible dissent will be met by French colonial gendarmerie, reinforced by French troops if necessary.

More than anything else, the French nuclear testing program stimulated the move throughout the South Pacific for a nuclear-free zone, which was adopted by the South Pacific Forum on the urging of Fiji and the New Zealand Labour government. A change of government in both Wellington and Canberra in 1975 led to the Forum quietly dropping the nuclear free zone idea. It was never a viable proposition. The United States could not possibly give up the right to send its nuclear-powered or nuclear-armed vessels into the area. There would be no way of checking whether either superpower adhered to any undertaking it gave. There was no way of compelling the French to stop testing in the South Pacific, any more than the Russians could be compelled to stop testing missiles in the North Pacific, or the Chinese could be compelled to stop testing at Lop Nor. The Pacific island territories were understandably disturbed at the French tests, but New Zealand and (still more) Australia could be accused of hypocrisy, protesting rather too much over the French tests and rather too little over the Chinese. Australian trade union activity against France was counter-productive. The sending of a New Zealand frigate into a safe part of the French 'test zone' was an outrageous piece of protest fakery at which Australia connived. The nuclear free zone movement, designed to reduce nuclear deployments or tests, has had no such effect.

If there is going to be a major disturbance to the peace of the South Pacific region, therefore, it would seem that it will have to stem from the intervention of a large external power. If it is going to be a disturbance of a kind that would cause an arms build-up, the intervention will have to be from a significant maritime power. There are not many such powers.

For some years, Japan has been engaged in dynamic economic activity throughout the region, in trade, investment, and some aid. Nowhere has it been of a magnitude to arouse fear or antagonism of a political or military kind. The Japanese navy is not geared to remote operations involving 'power projection'. According to the 1976–77 edition of *Jane's Fighting Ships*, the Japanese navy (euphemistically called the Maritime Self-Defence Force) has no capital ships, 29 destroyers, 16 frigates, 20 corvettes, and 16 patrol submarines. Given the local security problems of the Japanese home islands, this is a modest force. In any case, domestic political opinion would be overwhelmingly opposed to the forced acquisition of territory in the South Pacific or anywhere else. The sanctions of world opinion, especially the United States, would also be severe. The Japanese government is sensitive to charges of economic imperialism. I think we must conclude that Japan is most unlikely for some years to cause any security problems in the South Pacific region. North of the equator, in the Marianas, constitutional changes whereby part of the U.S. Trust Territory has become a commonwealth territory of the United States would seem to have ruled out any attachment (or re-attachment) to Japan.

Throughout the Pacific, there are small Chinese minorities, and China has begun to seek diplomatic relations, perhaps as a counter to similar Soviet actions. It has an embassy in Western Samoa, a mission in Fiji, and diplomatic relations with PNG using the embassy in Wellington. It is not recognised by Tonga, which has a Nationalist Chinese (Taiwan) mission.

The Chinese navy, like the Japanese, is geared to the defence of its own environment. According to *Jane's*, it has eight guided missile destroyers, ten frigates, 35 corvettes, one fleet submarine, one missile firing submarine, 60 patrol submarines, and over 800 small attack craft. The Chinese navy is now twice as strong, in manpower, as the British navy. There are modernised shipyards, and an advanced nuclear and missile capacity. But for the past five years, all building programs except for light forces have been subject to delay. The Chinese navy is an important element in the strategic balance in the North-west Pacific, but at present it has neither the capacity nor the incentive to be active in the South Pacific.

The only other powers that might increase their own military capacity in the area, or force each other to expand, are the United States and the Soviet Union.

The United States has of course been a major Pacific power throughout this century. Since World War II, her Pacific interests have been predominantly in North-east and South-east Asia, with the central controlling base at Honolulu. According to the U.S. Department of Defence *Commander's Digest* of 13 May 1976, American military forces in the Pacific at that time amounted to 141,000 Navy, 48,000 Air Force, 57,000 Army and 68,000 Marines, located in Hawaii (43,000), Guam (9,000), Japan and Okinawa (47,000), the Philippines (14,000), Korea (40,000), the rest being afloat. U.S. forces have been withdrawn from Thailand, and are being run down in Taiwan and South Korea. The Seventh Fleet customarily consists of some 50–55 ships, including two carriers, 18 surface combatants, and numerous combat support units. Its personnel, including marines, number 55,000 and it is based on Honolulu, Japan and the Philippines. The Third Fleet, in the Eastern Pacific, includes four carriers and 59 surface combatants. (Details of U.S. and Soviet Pacific fleets are given in Appendix A).

The Pacific provides a series of maritime thoroughfares for American trade, especially to Japan and Australia. The Secretary of State, Mr Cyrus P. Vance, pointed out in his address to the Asia Society in New York on 29 June 1977 that the five ASEAN countries, with a population larger than all of South America, bought $US3.7 billion worth of American goods in 1976, and supplied the U.S.A. with a tenth of her crude oil imports and a much higher percentage of rubber, tin, cocoa, bauxite and other important raw materials. (In 1975–76, Australia bought $US2 million worth of American goods). The United States is the largest trading country in the Indian Ocean, and much of this trade passes through the Pacific and the straits' in the Malay-Indonesian archipelago. Both the U.S.A. and the Soviet Union have discussed with Indonesia the right of submerged submarines to pass through the straits. Unless both Malaysia and Indonesia were to come under the control of a superpower, which is unlikely, any attempt by either to restrict rights of passage by naval or mercantile shipping would be met (as it has been met in the past) by combined international protests, and perhaps action.

In March 1976, General George Brown, Chairman of the Joint Chiefs of Staff, told the Senate Budget Committee (as reported) that the United States lacked sufficient naval power in the Pacific to guarantee freedom of the seas west of Hawaii. This was partly because the number of carriers in the Western Pacific had been reduced from three to two. A layman might well question whether General Brown was not being, even so, optimistic. The Soviet submarine fleet in the Pacific (see below) could do immense damage to American shipping between Honolulu and California.

Bases on foreign territory must always be considered vulnerable, and U.S. bases in Japan and the Philippines cannot be assumed to be permanent. The ritual protests by the Philippines designed to squeeze more rent out of the rich uncle have some effect because the United States navy is so dependent on Subic Bay, the only major repair base under American control east of Suez. Should it come under threat from Filipino nationalism or cupidity, a replacement would have to be built. As the Department of Defense *Pacific Basin Study* of 31 January 1976 stated: 'Guam is the only location in the Western Pacific where we can support a forward defense and an early warning capability from U.S. territory.' That territory now extends to the northern Marianas, and this enhances the capacity of the Marianas to be used for a much wider variety of military functions than at present. As the Report indicated, the Guam-Tinian complex of support facilities and training areas would provide a better hedge than the U.S.A. has had against unforeseen changes or reductions in the American Western Pacific base structure. The United States will obviously delay such a transfer as long as possible because of the great costs involved. In the meantime, Guam is widely believed to be the base for U.S. SSBNs deployed in the Pacific and Indian Oceans. There would seem to be no present strategic reason for them to be deployed in the South Pacific, although the Trident might conceivably operate there.

Russia has also been a Pacific naval power throughout this century, largely preoccupied with the defence of its own Pacific coastline and the sea lanes around to its European ports. But the size of its Pacific fleet clearly involves a much greater interest than that. Like the United States, it can and does transfer vessels into or out of the Pacific as required. There are probably at present some 9 cruisers, 27 destroyers, 22 frigates, 17 to 19 ballistic missile submarines, and between 55 and 70 conventionally-armed submarines (for details see Appendix A). This gives the Soviet Union a considerable interdiction capacity. The fact that it has no bases in the Pacific outside its own territory could be considered an incentive for it either to acquire them or not to range too widely. As the Soviet Union expands its carrier fleet, presumably a proportion will be deployed into the Pacific, but this is several years away.

Over the past year or two, the Soviet Union has been showing a new interest in the South Pacific, beyond the monitoring of American naval activities and French nuclear testing, and general survey work. It has diplomatic relations with Western Samoa, although as yet no mission; it has relations with Fiji, the Ambassador to Australia being accredited. It has relations with Papua New Guinea, the Ambassador to Jakarta being accredited. It has diplomatic relations with Tonga, an Ambassador has presented credentials, but no mission has as yet been set up.

There are several reasons why the Soviet Union might wish to improve its relations with South Pacific states: (a) the simple workmanlike extension of diplomatic intercourse to new nations which have a vote at the United Nations; (b) as American submarine-detection techniques improve, the Soviet Navy may feel a little conspicuous in the North Pacific and deploy some of its SSBN fleet in the South Pacific, where its longer range missiles will still be able to reach U.S. targets; and (c) fish. The South Pacific is relatively un-fished; the Soviet Union has one of the world's largest and most technologically advanced fishing fleets, and a steadily increasing demand for protein which fish supply. To this requirement should be added consideration of the accompanying map of Oceania showing the very limited areas which would be open sea if every island is given a 200–nautical mile exclusive economic zone (EEZ). This situation may not eventuate, for various reasons.

The Soviet Union has been sending fishing fleets into the area, and would obviously appreciate access to refuelling facilities, perhaps minor repairs, an airfield or two for flying in and out exchange crews, and congenial townships for rest and recreation. Press reports say that it has already approached Tonga, Western Samoa and Fiji over the extension of Soviet fishing rights—perhaps the establishment of fishing bases; that it has offered extensive development aid to Tonga, has offered to upgrade the airport at Nukalova, Fiji, to international standards, and offered to help Tonga build an international airport. It even, according to Mr Muldoon,[2] approached the New Zealand Labour government with

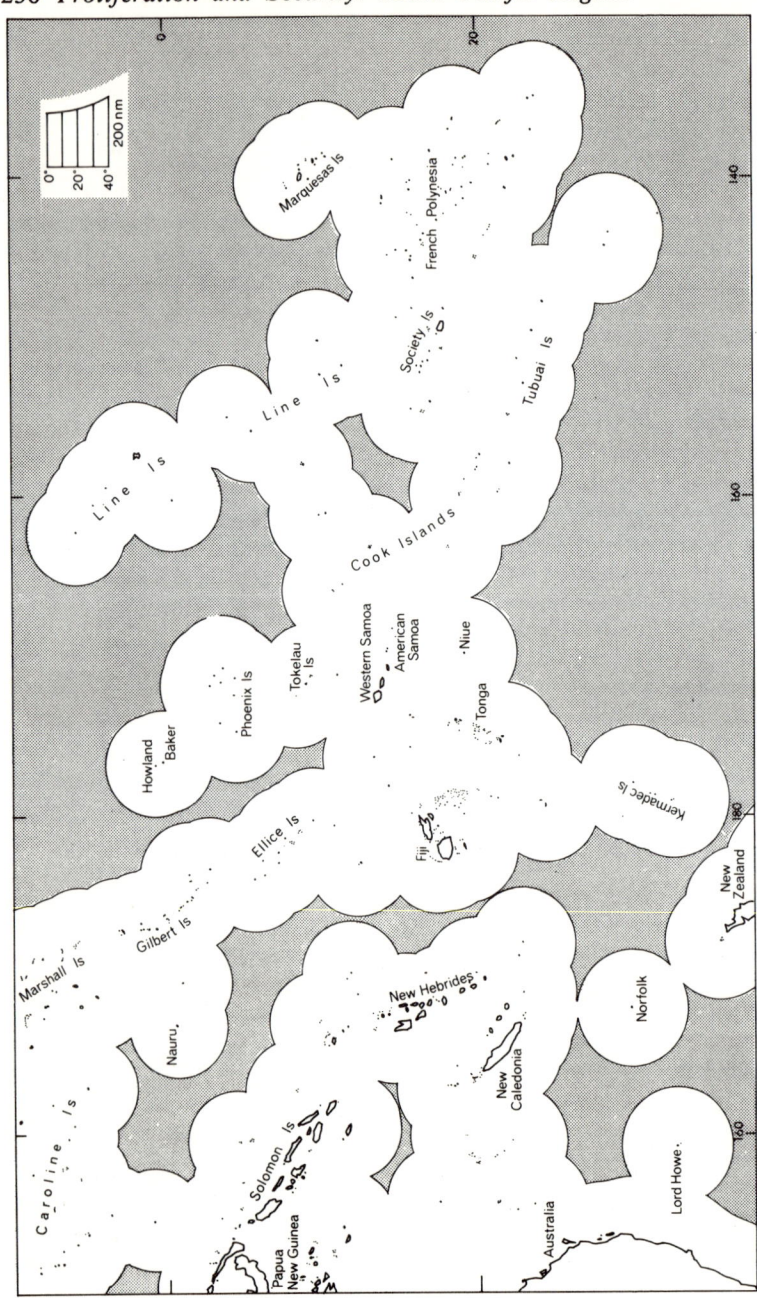

Extent of Possible 200 nm Economic Zones

a request for base and crew transfer facilities to service fishing fleets operating off New Zealand. The request was refused, but in a balancing gesture American nuclear warships were denied permission to use New Zealand ports.

Both the New Zealand and Australian governments have been disturbed by the Soviet activities in the Pacific. At the South Pacific Forum meeting in July last year, they offered to provide aid for fisheries development of the kind apparently promised by the Russians. The two governments have also discussed joint patrolling and policing of EEZs by the RAAF and the RNZAF. Both countries but especially Australia have a direct financial interest in the stability of many of the island states, through extensive investment and highly favourable trade. In Fiji, for example, the major banks, insurance companies and trading companies are owned by Australian firms and the pattern is repeated elsewhere. At the ANZUS Council meeting in Canberra in August 1976, the United States obviously took a more relaxed view of the Soviet presence than did her antipodean partners, and put the ball into their court. As the final communiqué, even more bland than usual, said: 'The Council reviewed recent developments in the South Pacific and noted the general increase in external awareness of the region. The Council noted the intention of Australia and New Zealand to give great priority to the South Pacific in their development programs.'

It is safe to say that Australia and New Zealand are not especially troubled by Soviet fishing activities, but rather by what those activities could lead to: in the worst case, an island 'people's republic' with a Soviet naval base and/or communications station; in less unpleasant but still regrettable circumstances, a Soviet political presence, civil or military aid program, and joint fishing ventures. The Soviet government has a poor record on economic aid, and has rarely done well with military aid. Where it has strings, it has the deplorable habit of pulling them, but not everyone is aware of this. Soviet aid may be seen as a useful supplement to that from Australia and New Zealand, or even a stick to beat them with. Sir Albert Henry, Prime Minister of the Cook Islands, said on 10 February 1977 (as reported by the *Australian*) that there was a limit to how long Pacific nations would 'wait and struggle under a charitable aid system' when Russia and China could help them survive and become self-sufficient. Some Soviet and perhaps Chinese aid projects are probably inevitable in the region, and Australia may just have to learn to live with them. But it is a big step beyond that to a Berbera, and one cannot easily discern any justification for such an investment on either strategic or economic grounds.[3]

Yet even if the Soviet Union built a Berbera-type base in the South Pacific, its main effect would be psychological. It would also no doubt affect foreign investment. It clearly would alter the strategic situation, but to a far lesser extent than might be imagined. In the event of a major war, such a base would be extremely vulnerable. Even in time of peace it would be subject to the local political leaders, and local political leaders sometimes change and they sometimes change their minds. Its naval or military value would be far less in an ocean so vast and relatively uncluttered as the Pacific. There are no bottlenecks between the east and western limits. No single port, airport, or route is vital to major maritime traffic: there are many alternatives. Outside the Euro-Asian continent, the Soviet Union has not shown itself to be an imperial power. It seeks targets of opportunity, but not controlled colonies. The Russians can cause problems for the West or for other states whenever they have even a temporary implantment: their intervention in Angola was made possible by their presence in Guinea, for example. Wherever they are, they are relevant, but we should not exaggerate the effect of their hitherto very limited interest in the territories of Oceania.

And what of Australia and New Zealand? Are there conceivable situations that could lead either or both to expand significantly arms production or procurement? Even ignoring the present economic constraints, it is not easy to foresee such a situation. Neither the present nor the last government in Australia has taken seriously the implications of Australia's being an island. Our oceanographic, hydrographic and sea-bed research—so far as a lay member of the public can tell—are geared to eternity. Our combat ship program is based on minimum and leisurely replacement. We cannot really control all our territorial waters, let alone the additional several hundred thousand square kilometres of ocean within the proposed EEZ. Without an enemy brandishing clubs on the horizon, Australian parliaments and people see little point in having much more than 'state of the art' armed forces. Several of the F-111Cs will be converted to a reconnaissance role. The Mirage fighter aircraft and the Attack class patrol boats will be replaced in due course, but any increase in arms capacity that could fit into the term 'proliferation', or in defence or resources research, seems highly unlikely. The only reason that we have the F-111s is that 14 years ago Indonesia confronted Malaysia in a tiny war, and sent an occasional Soviet supplied bomber cruising over our undefended and largely unaware north. In an excess of alarm at what this might mean at the 1963 election, the Menzies government ordered the F-111 off the drawing board.

Again, so far as we can tell, there seems little likelihood that the United States will expand its military or military-related facilities in Australia. The trend is the other way—to a reduction of facilities by technological advances. The only exception to this is the Omega navigation station, which the government and the Labor Party have agreed to and which will probably be built in Gippsland quite soon. Omega is a position-finding facility that will be available to merchant shipping of many nations. It will obviously be available to naval vessels also, and some writers claim that it will have a special value to the American fleet ballistic system,[4] and oppose it on those grounds.

There is one further area of the South Pacific—although it is not only in the Pacific—that may at some stage lead to arms proliferation: Antarctica. Under the 1959 Antarctic Treaty all territorial claims to Antarctica are frozen, military activities are prohibited, and anyone can go anywhere for research activites. As the resources of the other continents are depleted, it is inevitable that countries with the appropriate technology will seek at least to explore and eventually to exploit the resources of Antarctica. Some exploratory research may already have been carried out. The problems and costs of exploitation are so immense that it is hard to see this commencing for many years—perhaps a century or more. But well before then we could perhaps see the Treaty breaking down under the acquisitiveness of a technologically advanced power discovering what resources its bases are sitting on, putting up a military fence around them, and claiming 200 miles of the adjacent sea. Australia, with its extensive claims to Antarctic territory, would then have to consider its position very seriously.

But for the present and the foreseeable future, the South-west Pacific is not an area where the arms traders can do much business. It is comparatively stable. The scale of its problems is small. There is need for greater interest in the region by New Zealand and still more by Australia, not to see how much more they can get out of it but rather how much they can intelligently put into it without reducing the sovereignty and dignity of the small island states. Regional difficulties cannot be bought off with panicky injections of aid. Australia and New Zealand live in Oceania, and this has its problems as well as its responsibilities. If the islands of this paradise feel troubled by imperialism, it is less likely to be the imperialism of Moscow than of Canberra.

Footnotes

1. The French forces in the South Pacific number about 3000 men altogether. In French Polynesia, there are three destroyers and about 12 miscellaneous small craft, in New Caledonia three small craft and a hydrographic vessel. The two areas come under the Commandant Supérieur of the South Pacific zone, an admiral located in French Polynesia. The commander of the local forces in New Caledonia is a general.
2. *The Age*, 21 July 1976.
3. An interesting sidelight: the Soviet Union is now the largest operator of cruise ships in the South Pacific, and an important merchant carrier, offering cut-price freight rates.
4. See Desmond J. Ball, 'Some Military Uses of the Proposed Omega System', *Pacific Defence Reporter*, Vol. 3 No.12, June, 1977.
5. This estimate was made by Mr Geoffrey Jukes, Senior Fellow in the Department of International Relations, Australian National University, Canberra.
6. Mr Jukes notes that Golf is included by *The Military Balance 1975–76*, IISS, London 1976, among the SSBN submarines, but stated in fn. on p.8 to be recognised as *not* 'Strategic' under the SALT interim agreement. It is not clear whether 'Golf' is to be counted as part of the 'attack' force or not. He has counted it, because if it is not scrapped it will probably be converted to a torpedo submarine, as were the four Echo–I submarines built at about the same time as Golf.
7. Information provided by the Embassy of the United States of America, Canberra, July 1977.

APPENDIX
Soviet Pacific Fleet—Estimated Strength as at late 1976[5]

Cruisers		Destroyers	
Kresta–II	2	Krivak	3
Kresta–I	1	Kashin	5
Kynda	2	Kanin	2
Sverdlov	3	Krupny	0
	—	Kotlin SAM	2
	8	Kotlin	8
	—	Skory	7
			27

Frigates	
Mirka I & II	4
Petya I & II	10
Riga	8
Kola	0
	22

Submarines	
SSBN Yankee	8
SSBN Hotel II	3 or 2
SSB Golf[6]	8 or 7
Total, ballistic	19 to 17

SSGN Charlie	1
SSGN Echo–II	12 to 14
SSG Juliet	5
SSG Whisky Twin Cylinder/Long Bin	0
SSN Victor	2 to 4
SSN Echo–I	1 to 2
SSN November	4
SSN or SSGN, type unknown	0 to 5
SS or "padded target" Bravo	1
SS Foxtrot	12
SS Whisky	18 to 16
SS (Radar Picket) "Canvas Bag"	0 to 2
SS Zulu IV	0 to 2
SS, type unknown	0 to 2
Total, Attack and Cruise Missile	56 to 70

United States Military Presence in the Pacific[7]
(area between west coast of U.S.A. and east coast of Africa)

U.S. Army:	2 infantry divisions
	56,000 personnel
U.S. Navy:	2 numbered fleets (3rd and 7th)
	6 aircraft carriers and assigned wings
	76 surface combatants
	34 attack submarines
	10 fleet ballistic missile submarines
	32 amphibious assault ships
	12 air ASW-patrol squadrons
	157,000 personnel
U.S. Air Force:	2 numbered air forces
	9 tactical fighter squadrons
	1 B–52 squadron
	2 tanker squadrons
	39,000 personnel
U.S. Marine Corps:	2 amphibious force units
	(each MAF consists of 1 division, 1 air wing, any necessary support forces)
	71,000 personnel

9
Conflicts and Arms Races Between Littoral States of the Indian Ocean (A Background Paper)
Ferenc A. Váli*

The United Nations General Assembly at its 28th session in 1973 discussed the 'Zone of Peace in the Indian Ocean' plan and invited the Secretary General to prepare a report on Great power military presence in that region. The Secretary General appointed a Committee of three experts who submitted their Report on 3 May 1974. The main thesis of this Report was expressed as follows:

> The vast majority of the littoral and hinterland States of the Indian Ocean are still developing socially, economically and politically. During this period of development there is, unfortunately, a considerable potential for local conflicts. But the involvement of the Great Powers in a future local conflict would be neither in the real long-term interests of the Great Powers nor in those of the littoral and hinterland States. Any attempt to derive advantage from this unstable situation by one Great Power will inevitably lead to a countermove by the other Great Power. Moreover, any attempt by one of the littoral or hinterland States to obtain *undue support* from one of the Great Powers will probably in turn lead to some other littoral or hinterland State seeking countervailing support from the other Great Power.[1]

This original Report of the three experts was withdrawn because of the protests voiced by the United States, the Soviet Union, Britain, and China (a rather strange combination), as well as by some regional states. Henceforth, a shorter, revised version, dated 11 July 1974, was substituted. However, its main thesis remained unchanged. It reflected the thinking of K. Subrahmanyam, the Indian member of the Committee, who very much had the scenario of the eighteenth-century Anglo-French rivalry in mind. It was this rivalry which resulted in the subjugation of India to British rule and, eventually, in the control by Britain of almost the entire Indian Ocean littoral.

While the Report correctly pointed out the inherent instabilities of the region and the potential naval arms race between the superpowers, it is suggested that the causal link between these two situations is rather tenuous.

There is more than a parallelism; there is an interrelationship between what used to be the Cold War and the conflicts of regional Indian Ocean powers. Nevertheless, these conflicts did not originate from the Cold War. And they preceded the naval presence of the superpowers in the waters of this Ocean. These feuds exist independently of the Cold War, the subsequent East-West competition, and also of the Sino-Soviet conflict.

For instance, the Indian-Pakistani conflict originated from the partition of British-ruled India; Sukarno's 'konfrontasi' was due to Indonesian nationalism and the dreams of its hubristic leader; conflicts between Iran and Iraq are of a territorial character; the instability between Ethiopia and Somalia stems from the irredenta practised by the latter; and in Southern Africa it is the inherent racial antagonism which is the cause of instabilities and violent clashes.

None of these conflicts was foisted on these peoples by exogenous great powers. But they adjusted themselves or became adjusted into the frame of the East-West cleavage mainly because in such a way the interested actors were able to obtain support, and—what mattered most—arms from their respective protectors.

Without any doubt, there is thus an interconnection between the East-West and Sino-Soviet confrontations, on the one hand, and the regional conflicts, on the other. But it is not a causal nexus. The original causes of these regional conflicts are to be found in local circumstances and not in the Manichean division between East and West, or in the ideological-hegemonial competition between the Russians and the Chinese.

Furthermore, a linkage between the superpower naval presence in the Indian Ocean and the regional conflicts on land, including insurgencies against incumbent regimes, can hardly be substantiated. In times of crises, however, there may be a linkage when a local conflict is the cause and the effect is some action by the naval powers, and not vice versa.

Rivalries on Sea and Rivalries on Land

As mentioned before, most of the endemic feuds between the littoral countries of the Indian Ocean had been in existence for a long time prior to the appearance of Soviet naval units in that Ocean and are independent of any competition between the American and

Soviet Navies. These feuds probably would be unaffected by a potential arms race between these two navies. The first Report of the three experts was rather pessimistic in this respect when it predicted that a 'mutual balance between the Great Powers could not be maintained over a period of time,'[2] meaning the naval balance in the Indian Ocean.

However, this prediction has not been borne out by recent developments and findings of authoritative sources. Among them is the Australian Senate Standing Committee on Foreign Affairs and Defence. After a prolonged enquiry, this body came to the conclusions that a 'matching presence' existed between the navies of the superpowers in the Indian Ocean and that the likelihood of an arms race was limited.[3]

On the other hand, one cannot perceive any relaxation in the tensions between regional land powers in most of the corners of the Indian Ocean region. It is only in times of a local crisis that the superpowers may attempt to exercise pressures on the warring parties on land by the show of an increased naval strength. Otherwise, both the United States and the Soviet Union are careful not to expose themselves to accusations of practising 'gunboat diplomacy.'

Such instances of bringing naval pressures to bear in the Indian Ocean have been relatively few since the mutual presence of Soviet and American navies in those waters. And even so, it is doubtful whether the threatening presence of concentrated naval forces actually has had a restraining effect on belligerent or near-belligerent land powers. It cannot be substantiated that the entry of the nuclear aircraft carrier USS *Enterprise* and her escorting vessels into the Indian Ocean at the time of the 1971 Bangladesh War did restrain India in the pursuit of her war against Pakistan.[4] Side by side with the American squadron, British (for possible evacuation of British subjects) and also Soviet naval units (to counter the American presence) lined up in the Bay of Bengal. In 1973, during the Arab-Israeli War, we witnessed the simultaneous concentration of American and Soviet warships in the north-west corner of the Indian Ocean. And in 1975, after the Entebbe coup of the Israeli Air Force, an American frigate hastened to Mombasa, Kenya, to frighten away Uganda from attacking Kenya; it is rather improbable that this move had any effect on Idi Amin who actually used only empty threats against his African neighbour.

Developments on the land periphery of the Indian Ocean are thus largely independent of the developments or potential developments in the waters of this Ocean itself. Historic analogies are often misleading and are not always pertinent. Still they may place present-day situations into a better perspective and may contribute toward a better understanding of the present. A somewhat remote but still pertinent analogy with the present status in the Indian Ocean regions may be found in the historic developments of that part of the world during the sixteenth, seventeenth, and the earlier part of the eighteenth centuries.

In the sixteenth century Portugal maintained a less-than-watertight but still predominant control over the Indian Ocean and the trade with the countries of that Ocean. This monocracy collapsed in the seventeenth century when challenged by the Dutch and the British. By the end of the seventeenth century Dutch ambitions became territorially limited to what is now Indonesia, while the French and British rivalry for control of the Ocean and for trade flared up into several wars and lasted for over another century.

During this entire period the Mogul Empire was built up in India and firmly established on the subcontinent. It was the greatest concentration of land-power in the region.

These two projections of power—the Portuguese, Dutch, British, and French on the sea, and the Islamic penetration into India on land—took place without a major clash between them. Only in the middle of the eighteenth century (when the Mogul Empire had disintegrated) did the British and the French come into contact or collision with its successor states, which were by then seeking the protection of one or the other of these European powers. Wars by proxy were fought by the client states of Britain and France which eventually led to the victory of the British over the French.

This historic precedent demonstrates that competition and even struggle for mastery in the Indian Ocean may occur without basically affecting power struggles on land, and vice versa. However, to extrapolate these long-time past events into the present may be somewhat hazardous. Nowadays interactions between events on the sea and those on land in the Indian Ocean region may be much closer. Still, it is maintained that there exists no inevitable linkage, political or strategic, between what is happening along the littoral of the Indian Ocean and over the waters of the Ocean itself.

Since 1968 considerable concern has arisen over the presence of Soviet naval units in the Indian Ocean and the increased number of American warships entering those waters. Similarly, the establishment of Soviet base-facilities in the region and the construction of the United States naval-air communication facility on the island of Diego Garcia created resentment and fear in many parts of the world. Regional countries reacted with the proposal (which was initiated at the United Nations) of establishing a Zone of Peace in the Indian Ocean which would exclude the entry of non-regional navies and lead to the dismantling of all bases of non-regional powers in the area.

Both Washington and Moscow have been considering the possibility of mutual arms limitations of their respective navies and other forces in the Indian Ocean region. However, the Ford Administration was unwilling to consider these questions in isolation from other events. In an official statement it declined 'to consider seriously an arms limitation initiative focussed on the Indian Ocean without clear evidence of reciprocal Soviet willingness to exercise restraint in the region as a whole.'[5] The reference here was to the African continent in general, and specifically to the Soviet-supported involvement of Cuban forces in Angola.

On 9 March 1977, the American President Jimmy Carter offered to negotiate for a 'complete demilitarization' of the Indian Ocean. This offer was either deliberately vague or showed a complete disregard for accepted terminology used so far to describe the attempt to limit the presence of superpower naval forces in that region. When some days later, in his speech before the United Nations General Assembly, the President spoke of 'mutual restraint' by the United States and the Soviet Union in the deployment of their naval forces in the Indian Ocean, he (or his speechwriter) adopted the language which the State Department was using. But 'mutual restraint' by the superpowers does not embrace a restraint or arms control in regard to the arms proliferation among littoral powers of that Ocean.

In his above-mentioned first announcement, the American President listed the 'complete demilitarization' of the Indian Ocean together with some other topics to be taken up with Moscow. And he added that he would like to see any of these items quickly completed and then get down to the much more difficult negotiations on atomic weapons. It is believed to be rather unrealistic to expect that negotiations for the limitation of superpower naval presence in the Indian Ocean can be quickly completed.

Notwithstanding the halt in exchanges between Washington and Moscow in regard to arms limitation in the Indian Ocean, the U.S. Arms Control and Disarmament Agency has continued to study the options to be offered: how to formulate an agreement with the Soviet Union on this topic.[6] The advantage of such an agreement has been clearly perceived. No strategic requirement of the United States at present demands further increases in its naval strength in this Ocean; even a minimal presence would be satisfactory should

Moscow so reciprocate. And with an agreement to this effect concluded with the U.S.S.R., Moscow would no longer have a free hand to escalate its naval forces in those waters.

While entering into such a naval restraint agreement seems attractive, the American planners are in a quandary over how to translate the desiderata into quantitative and definitional elements. How should different types of warships be matched; what ships should be included (support vessels, or submarines which are hardly verifiable); should ship days be counted or the number of ships, or their respective tonnage; what constitutes a naval-air base or facility; should members of armed forces ashore also be limited (military instructors, repairmen, etc.); these are some of the questions which would demand an answer.[7]

Thus, there is the potential and even the possibility for an agreement mutually to limit naval forces and support installations between Washington and Moscow. But there is no planning or even idea on how to place restraints on a more imminent and perilous situation: the proliferation of highly sophisticated modern weaponry along the littoral and hinterland states of the Indian Ocean region. Apart from crisis situations, the superpowers' presence is likely to remain stable and constitute no imminent threat itself. In fact, their presence can be considered a natural projection of influence by great powers in time of peace. But the critical tensions between many if not most littoral powers, due to conventional arms deliveries, create a much more urgent problem.[8]

In the United Nations, the resolutions on the Zone of Peace in the Indian Ocean, adopted year by year, completely ignore the dangers created by the arms races between littoral powers of that Ocean. During these debates the question of potential or actual armed conflicts between regional states has been sidetracked by exclusively addressing the 'naval rivalry' between the superpowers and other great powers. But never did these resolutions deal with the 'undue support' by arms deliveries provided by exogenous sources for the use of local countries or revolutionary movements.

For the third time in recent years, during the Thirty-First (1976) session of the United Nations General Assembly, a number of Asian, European, and Latin American countries unsuccessfully tried to have the United Nations look into the trade of conventional weapons and to produce a study on the arms traffic. The issue was shelved again, mainly on the initiative of India, whereas it was strongly supported by the Philippines, Singapore, and Japan. Their representatives contended rightly that for the majority of the Third World countries the greatest peril came not from a nuclear menace or superpower rivalry but from conventional arms deliveries.[9] Two–thirds of the countries of the Third World are located around the periphery of the Indian Ocean.

Conflicts and Arms Supplies

Political leaders, journalists, and even scholars, immersed in details or day-to-day events, often disregard or forget the basic causes or motivations for international conflicts, especially when for ten, twenty, or fifty years no violent outbreak occurs between certain countries or in certain areas. But it is these 'fundamentals' or 'basics' which form the ultimate or primordial reason for armed clashes or wars between nations even if they remain apparently latent, subdued, or inoperative for a very long time.

The causes of these feuds, which are endemic or inherent to certain areas of the Indian Ocean region, may be either ethnic, religious, nationalist, social, or economic, or relate to the territorial status of these countries upon their establishment following World War II and their attainment of independence. National character or mentality also plays an important role in the circumstances or motives of potential or actual conflagrations.

These 'fundamentals' remain quiet or quiescent unless supplemented by further requisites likely to heat up violent outbreaks. Such a requisite is the capability to create instability, to threaten credibly or attack and invade another country, or revolt against the incumbent regime. Weapons are indispensable for acquiring such a capability. There are no substitutes for the equipment, training, possession and use of arms by a well-equipped foe.

Naturally, arms—whether simple or modern sophisticated ones —are unavailing or ineffectual without a determined, dedicated, and disciplined human element. The South Vietnamese, to provide just one example, were well equipped but after the American pull-out succumbed to the better-led, more-disciplined northern attackers.

Ideological fervour, messianic belief, or readiness to sacrifice one's life are also factors of great importance, especially against an opponent in disarray or one who is lacking determined leadership. In this respect, one is reminded of the famous conversation between Stalin and Churchill in Moscow in 1973. The British Prime Minister mentioned that the Vatican was sympathetic toward the Allies when Stalin facetiously interrupted him asking, 'How many divisions has the Pope?' According to perhaps apocryphal reports Churchill retorted, 'How many divisions had Lenin when he returned to Russia in 1917?'

We still have to assume that the acquisition of modern weaponry from outside sources is indispensable to nonindustrial, developing countries or revolutionary movements which seek to become a credible threat to their opponents and to be able to carry out an effective aggression. In the Indian Ocean region, with few exceptions, regional powers are being supplied by non-regional powers, or arms salesmen from these countries.

With respect to the support which regional countries of the Indian Ocean region are receiving from exogenous powers, the U.N. Report, it will be remembered, declared:

> . . . any attempt by one of the littoral or hinterland States to obtain undue support from one of the Great Powers will probably in turn lead to some other littoral or hinterland State seeking countervailing support from the other Great Power.

This statement is largely correct and constitutes a concise definition of the arms race, one of the principal additional reasons for the outbreak of conflicts. One should, however, ask oneself whether the 'undue support' mentioned in the text has necessarily been in every case a destabilising or stabilising influence.

In this context one is reminded of Talleyrand's rather cynical dictum: 'Intervention is the same thing as nonintervention.'

If you intervene in favour of one party in a conflict, you intervene. But if you don't intervene, you intervene indirectly in favour of the other party (so actually you also intervene).

Translated into the field of arms supplies, it would mean that, if you supply arms to a government or to an insurgent group, you support them in pursuit of their objective. But if you refrain from doing so, you indirectly support the opposing party, one perhaps already in possession of adequate weaponry, or able to produce it, or the recipient of arms from another source.

Briefly, Talleyrand's paradoxical proposition would imply that: no supply of arms is the same thing as a supply of arms.

However, the fact is that a country or revolutionary movement is generally incapable of being a threat or an aggressor unless provided with arms. If unable to produce them this international actor will have to rely on arms supplies from outside sources. And with these supplies of weaponry the supplier, will-nilly, acquires a stake in the outcome of a future armed conflict while the recipient, at the same time, becomes dependent on the supplier. Through this dependence the latter is able to extend its influence and increase its power and prestige in the area.

Factors Leading to Violent Outbreaks
The sale and delivery of arms constitutes a contributive factor to already existing basic antagonisms, a highly inflammatory factor indeed.

We have already mentioned the basic motivations as well as the requirements for a capability to exert pressure, to create a threat, or to initiate an aggression. These and the further factors required for the exacerbation of a conflict, possibly then leading to a violent outbreak, are listed as follows:

1. basic cause (motivation)
2. capability (arms)
3. leadership (determined)
4. opportunity or spark (trigger)

This listing, of course, envisages an oversimplified situation, namely one which is bilateral. It disregards alliances, involvement of third parties, nuclear capability, and others. It should serve only as a guide to this presentation. Further there are some brief points and caveats: it should be mentioned that the basic motivation is more constant than the remaining other factors.

Belief in capability may be erroneous. Leadership may be determined, but foolish. The opportunity to be exploited may rest on a miscalculation. Temporary relaxations may befog the latent but still virulent antagonisms.

Most of the peripheral zones of the Indian Ocean area studded with nations or would-be nations which are highly emotional and volatile. Their leaders embrace each other one day and are ready to stab each other in the back on the next.

Without wishing to be overly dramatic or alarmist, it seems no exaggeration to maintain that there are potentially, or in actuality, more critical, explosive situations around the Indian Ocean on land than at sea.

At the time of this writing the Cold War has admittedly come to an end. But American-Soviet rivalries (despite the détente) continue in many areas and the Sino-Soviet conflict shows no signs of abatement. Yet, a parallelism still exists between the various conflicts among regional powers and the great power rivalries. Parallelism means parallel action and reaction, but not necessarily a causality nor a coincidence. The Indian-Pakistani duel, Iran's and Saudi Arabia's massive armament purchases directed against revolutionary or Soviet encroachments in the Persian Gulf area, the feud between Somalia and Ethiopia, not to speak of the struggle in Southern Africa between African revolutionary forces and the white supremacist regimes of Rhodesia and South Africa—all these are not fights between proxies of great powers; but without the diplomatic, political, and especially military support of exogenous powers, the struggle would be carried out on a level of lesser violence or would remain a subdued antagonism.

Thus, it seems correct to assert that the violence of conflicts in the Indian Ocean region, or the probability and potentiality of such conflicts have largely been made possible or favoured by the military hardware made available to the regional actors.

This paper will attempt to illustrate and substantiate the guidelines listed above and apply them to the most important trouble spots of the region. Of course, these flashpoints of actual or potential violent conflict can only be highlighted here, a more detailed presentation would require a book-size analysis of each of the sub-regions discussed.

Since the end of the 'confrontation policy' of Sukarno, the south-east of the Indian Ocean has remained relatively calm though the invasion of the eastern half of the island of Timor by Indonesia and the border insurgencies in the Malay-Thai area occurred here. The continued relative tranquility of this sub-region depends largely on the attitude of the Indo-Chinese powers—Vietnam, Cambodia, and Laos. It is from this side that the stability and peace of South-east Asia could principally be disturbed.

Other corners of the region are more proximately threatened by major instabilities and conflicts. In some places violent struggles are taking place at the time of this writing.

This chapter considers one of the major trouble spots to be the Indian subcontinent. Here the main actors—India and Pakistan—while seemingly at peace and practising rapprochement moves, continued to implement an arms race which forecasts further violent outbreaks between them.

Another flashpoint of potential conflict which may escalate beyond the perimeter of their original explosion is the Persian Gulf area where the oil Croesuses—Iran, Iraq, Saudi Arabia, and, to a lesser extent, Kuwait and Abu Dhabi—are engaged in massive armament programs, an accumulation of modern weaponry that is replete with dangers.

The third area of tension to be discussed is the Horn of Africa and the adjacent parts of the Red Sea where the ancient and strategically located Ethiopian empire·is crumbling under internal and external pressures.

The fourth area of violent confrontations is Southern Africa where a battlefield has already been staged in Rhodesia between the black African forces and those of the white regime. Here the main target of possible revolutionary or conventional armed attacks is the Republic of South Africa and a major struggle for continued white supremacy in this country is likely to involve not only African but also maritime powers from other continents.

(1) The Indian Subcontinent
Basic Motivations

The perceptions which India and Pakistan hold of each other radically differ from the perceptions they have of themselves.

The partition of British-ruled India into the Indian Union and Pakistan was and is still considered by most of India's leaders as a temporary expedient to achieve the independence of their country.

India harbours the world outlook of a multinational empire; that is, an imperial and hegemonial world view. She not only considers herself to be the sole heir of the British raj but heir to the Hindu Maurya and Gupta kingdoms and to the Islamic Mogul empire. Even beyond these historical vestiges, these areas where the Hindu culture penetrated are considered culturally—and therefore also politically—subordinate.

Surrounding countries are regarded as temporarily broken-off pieces of the greater Indian body politic. Primarily, these include the 'secessionist' parts of the Indian subcontinent proper, such as Pakistan and Bangladesh, and also Nepal, Bhutan, Sikkim (recently incorporated into India) and even Sri Lanka (because of its former British rule). New Delhi conceives of Hindu culture as all-embracing and therefore not incompatible with the concept of being a 'secular' and not a special religion-oriented nation.

Because India wishes to embrace (if not formally incorporate) all the lands which formerly belonged to the British Indian Empire or to which Indian culture penetrated, she prefers to speak of a 'subcontinental unity' which is deeply disturbed, especially by the attitude of Pakistan. This 'subcontinental unity' is particularly infringed upon by the fact that Pakistan is 'bringing arms supplies by external powers into the subcontinent.'[10]

In 1975 the United States lifted the arms embargo imposed since the Bangladesh War of 1971 on both Pakistan and India; at that time, Indian Prime Minister Mrs Indira Gandhi declared:

> The decision of the United States to resume arming Pakistan shows that the policy-makers of that great country continue to subscribe to the fallacy of equating Pakistan and India.[11]

The Prime Minister wished to express the thought that—in the Indian view—it is inappropriate and incorrect to equate Mother

India with her ill-tempered child. The statement speaks for itself!

Pakistan, in turn, considers herself an 'Islamic Nation', *the* Islamic nation on the subcontinent. But since the loss of East Pakistan (Bangladesh) she feels more attracted toward the Islamic Middle East, thus sharing a cultural affinity with both geographic (but not Hindu) India and with her western Muslim neighbours.[12]

The frustration created by the secession of Bangladesh left Pakistan in a dichotomous mentality. The encirclement complex (which resulted from the lost war and ensuing feeling of insecurity) amounts almost to an obsession. Pakistan sees herself as surrounded by enemies—by India, the arch-enemy, and the Soviet Union, and Afghanistan—which wish to split her territory and destroy her independent existence as a nation by subversion or direct invasion. On the other hand, deep down and sometimes unconsciously, she has not given up her aspiration to free Kashmir from Indian rule and not even the dream to march on Delhi as did the great Muslim conquerors from Baber Khan to Nadir Shah.

Afghanistan is often thought of in Islamabad as a Soviet stooge. The separatist endeavours for Pushtunistan or in Baluchistan, supported by Afghanistan and also the Soviet Union, contribute to Pakistan's uneasiness. The lack of ethnic cohesion (only religious cohesion that proved to be too tenuous to keep East and West Pakistan together) is sorely felt in Pakistan as well as in India.

Capability

Since the 1971 war, India has systematically and gradually increased and modernised her armed forces. New Delhi now disposes of the advanced weaponry received from Moscow. More and more Indian divisions are being motorised and the number of tanks increased. The Indian Navy has also obtained many new units from the Soviet Union. Port Blair on the Andaman Islands is being developed into a naval base, and another such base is planned on the Laccadive Islands in the Arabian Sea, facing Pakistan.

The geostrategic status of India has greatly improved with the amputation of Pakistan which broke the uncomfortable embrace by the western and eastern portions of that country. The imbalance in every respect has been considerably tilted in favour of India.

Pakistan, with her more modest financial means, is trying to keep abreast with India's increased military power. An even larger slice of her budget than before the Bangladesh war is now allocated for military expenditures. An inflow of money from Islamic countries (Saudi Arabia, Iran, and the Arab Emirates) enables her to pay for arms on the international market. Islamabad receives arms from

China, the United States, and, possibly, also from Muslim countries.[13]

Beyond the objective truth, it is psychologically significant that both countries accuse each other of arming themselves 'to the teeth.' Such accusations, whether accurate or not, are likely to harden militaristic tendencies and create an atmosphere of tension. Both the Indian and the Pakistani press often include alarming reports of the massing of troops along their respective borders. Pakistani reports also include references to show that India is threatening Bangladesh.[14]

Leadership

India evidently has no desire at present to embark on adventures of a military nature. But under whatever government, New Delhi will remain determined to act as a gendarme of the subcontinent (including Sri Lanka), to prevent and oppose any aggression by non-subcontinental powers, and generally 'to preserve peace on the Subcontinent.' When acquiring an operational nuclear capability, it will want to employ such capability for such 'defensive' purposes.

Pakistan is headed now by a more rational leadership than during the sixties and early seventies. However, even a moderate and rational leader remains exposed to popular pressures which he may find himself unable to resist when a suitable opportunity for a forceful move offers itself.

Opportunity

While India is waiting for an opportunity to assert her hegemonial role in the subcontinent, Pakistan is waiting for an opportunity to take her revenge for the losses and humiliations suffered from India.

In Pakistan it is still believed and deplored that Islamabad 'missed the bus' in 1961 when China invaded India. At that time the Pakistanis were told by the United States and Britain to keep quiet. Both London and Washington then rushed arms for the rescue (as it was believed) of an India crumbling before the onslaught of the Chinese. Pakistani intervention would have been unthinkable at such a juncture.

To make up for the lost opportunity, Pakistan initiated hostilities in 1963. But its President, Ayub Khan, evidently miscalculated his country's strength and the strength of India's refurbished armed forces after the Chinese debacle.

In 1971 war between India and Pakistan became inevitable due to two incompatible aspirations. Pakistan could not be expected to acquiesce in the secession of its Eastern portion without resorting to massive suppression. However, India felt compelled, due to its hegemonial concept, to intervene as keeper of the peace. The ensuing war ended with the amputation of East Pakistan and the establishment of Bangladesh as an independent state.

Pakistan, aware of its inability to take on India once more, is still awaiting a favourable opportunity though she will observe more caution than on previous occasions. Such an opportunity, so it is hoped, might arise with possible internal troubles of India, or a possible disintegration of the Hindu superstate. China, Pakistan's ally, will grow in strength during the next two or three decades and may no longer be in fear of a Soviet invasion; in such a case, Peking might support Pakistan not only verbally as it did on the last two occasions when the Islamic State had to face India alone.

As India was always inclined to consider Pakistan nonviable (the combination of East and West Pakistan proved her to be so) so Pakistan disbelieves that the Union of India could *à la longue* survive as a unitary state. The mutual belief in the impermanency and eventual decrepitude of each other will stimulate in India or Pakistan, should such a real or imaginary occasion arise, the desire to administer the *coup de grâce* on her neighbour thus precipitating another armed confrontation.

The basic motivations, the increased capability to fight, a strong leadership on the one side opposing a possible weak leadership on the other, and an opportunity, real or imaginary, render another violent clash inevitable or most likely.

(2) The Persian Gulf
Basic Motivations
Antagonism between the countries of the Persian Gulf is kindled by old historic and inherent causes. There is the historic division between Semitic-Arab and Aryan-Persian ethnicity and culture, and the religious cleavage between Sunnites and Shiites. In the last two decades this division has been topped by political-ideological differences: Iran is an authoritarian monarchy; Iraq is devoted to Arab Baath-Socialism; and the other Arab states are Islamic fundamentalists.

The ambition of Iran has clearly been expressed by various pronouncements of her ruler. She wishes to play a hegemonial role in the Persian Gulf area; she wishes to grow by 1985 into one of the five great powers of the world (the five are the two superpowers, China, and either Britain or France); she wishes to protect the flow of oil out of the Persian Gulf and through the Arabian Sea and the Indian Ocean.

In return, Iraq is keen to develop her own brand of Arab

socialism, to increase her influence and power in the area which surrounds her. Saudi Arabia is anxious to be recognised as the bastion and lodestar of Islam. All the Arab states are suspicious and hostile vis-à-vis Iran's far-reaching hegemonial aspirations.

Capability

Iran, Saudi Arabia, Kuwait, and the United Arab Emirates have the financial capability to purchase any weapon which is on the market. Iraq also has the financial capability but is more restricted in its choice because of its close ties with the Soviet Union. Iran is supplied with arms, including the most sophisticated ones, by the United States, Britain, and France. Similarly Saudi Arabia can rely on purchases from any and all of the Western countries. Iraq's armament is mainly of Soviet origin.

The billions of dollars worth of armaments purchased by Iran (and also by Saudi Arabia) are well-known. To absorb these huge amounts of modern arms, Tehran needs the assistance of a great many (some 24,000 at present) arms experts and training personnel (mostly American) for the absorption by its armed forces of all this sophisticated weaponry. Saudi Arabia is even more dependent on foreign training personnel, and her development in the armament process is even slower than that of Iran.

The armament race is particularly sharp between Iran and Iraq. In 1975 the number of Iraqi tanks was still slightly higher than those of Iran. If current orders are implemented, Iran will have twice the number of tanks that she possesses at the time of this writing. Whether Iraq will maintain this tempo may depend largely on the speed of Soviet deliveries. In 1976 Iraq had 250 combat aircraft, including 30 MiG–23s, the latest Soviet attack plane; Iran had 240 combat aircraft, including 96F–4 Phantoms and 125 F–5 interceptors. Tehran has now placed orders for a further 300 aircraft with the United States (the F–16 and F–18, the latest models). Iran, additional to its three destroyers, placed orders for four highly sophisticated Spruance-class destroyers. She possesses further the largest hovercraft arsenal in the world as well as a helicopter fleet which is only surpassed by that of the United States.

The figures of the Saudi Arabian crash program for military expansion are equally impressive but, so far, behind that of Iran. Both, however, share the problem of assimilating the military equipment despite expensive help by the United States military and civilian personnel.[15]

Whether both Iran and Saudi Arabia will be able to implement their massive armament program seems somewhat doubtful. As to

Iran, even the financing of this program may run into difficulties; Tehran already has been forced to ask for credits because her current oil sales are insufficient to cover all the ambitious projects she has undertaken. And many if not all of the country's oil wells may run dry within the next twenty years or so. The operational capability of the Iranian armed forces to use all the sophisticated modern weapons is also questioned. On the other hand, the efficiency and reliability of her armed forces in operation against the Dhofari rebels was given praise.

The question also has been asked if Iran really needs this enormous arms input. Against whom is this military 'leap-forward' being directed? In response, Tehran points to its long border with the Soviet Union, to the necessity to protect the oil sources in the Gulf, and to secure the flow of oil into the Indian Ocean.

Leadership

Iran is certainly not lacking a determined leader. But her strength, in this respect, may someday be a source of weakness. Iran's gargantuan development and modernisation (including the armament) program appears to be dependent largely on the determination of one individual, the ruler. Should the need for a successor to the present monarch arise, the entire program may falter.

There is no lack of determined leaders in Saudi Arabia where the ruling family is strongly in power and rallies around the King. But in the other Gulf countries the position of the rulers appears to be less secure. Kuwait is threatened by the great number of disenfranchised non-Kuwaiti Arabs (Palestinians and others) who form half of its population; Bahrain is now vulnerable to democratic popular pressures; and Qatar and the United Arab Emirates are conspicuously unstable because of the feuds between themselves and between the members of each ruling family. There is also a threat from the side of nonindigenous Arabs and other ethnic groups who form a large percentage of the population. And Arab nationalists consider these rulers mere puppets in the hands of the oil companies and Western imperialists-colonialists. It is likely that sooner or later revolutionary groups will attempt to overthrow these governments in the name of Arab-Socialism. Under such circumstances it seems understandable that the Shah of Iran is anxious to provide for the defence of the Gulf.

Opportunity

Iran wishes to complete her armament and industrialisation program without being involved in international entanglements. For that reason, Tehran was ready to mend its fences with Iraq, her close neighbour and potential adversary, as well as with India, militarily the most powerful regional country. But even so, Iran will not hesitate to undertake steps (even of a military nature) to prevent attempts at endangering the Gulf area. For this reason, on the very day when the British protectorate over the future United Arab Emirates (the Trucial States) ended, that is, on 30 November 1971, Iranian forces occupied the strategic islands at the entrance of the Hormuz Strait (Abu Musa and the two Tunb Islands). Iran also supports Oman in its fight against the rebels in the Dhofar province and may intervene militarily if revolutionary forces would threaten or take over Oman or any of the Arab Emirates.

The Arab littoral states of the Persian Gulf (except for Oman) were reluctant to enter into any treaty for common defence with Iran, a treaty which was suggested by the Shah. They view the Iranian aspiration for a hegemonial role with utmost suspicion.

Iran has initiated an arms acquisition program of some length and duration. Orders and deliveries may be years apart and it will take years for inventories to be converted into operational systems. Nonetheless, if Tehran continues down the same path, she will turn out to become more powerful than all the other Gulf states put together.

It is not suggested that 'guns will fire by themselves', but an excessive amount of power may induce a government to become 'trigger-happy'. Sooner or later, Moscow will express some dissatisfaction with Tehran's imperial leap forward and may assume a threatening posture. Revolutionary forces, already active in the Gulf area and supported by the Soviet Union, may spark upheavals to which Iran will have to react and which may involve her and other Gulf States in a struggle whose consequences are difficult to foresee.

The worldwide importance of the Gulf, as a major source of oil, is bound to draw outside powers into any conflict that threatens to upset the existing balance of power in the area.

(3) The Horn of Africa
Basic Motivations

The historically dominant power in the Horn of Africa is Ethiopia with her distinct Amharic–Tigrean ethnic stock. The core of Ethiopia also is Christian and is surrounded by an Islamic sea. Hence, Ethiopians soon developed an isolation complex and a defensive urge to dominate their environment.

But for over three years Ethiopia has been the vortex of a revolutionary upheaval; much of the country is in revolt against the central government and the Eritrean revolt is even of a longer standing.

There also exists an acute external danger for Ethiopia: the Somali irrendentist claim to one-third of her territory, assumedly inhabited by a Somali ethnic population.

Somalia also lays claim to the former French Territory of the Afars and Issas, now the newly independent Djibouti and to northern sections of Kenya.

There thus exist in the Horn of Africa acute antagonisms of both ethnic and religious dimensions.

Capability

The Somali Socialist Democratic Republic has been excessively armed by the Soviet Union in proportion to its population (three million). The equipment includes tanks, aircraft, and missiles. Moscow has a special interest in Somalia: Berbera is the most important naval facility or base which the Soviet navy is using in the Indian Ocean. Somalia thus possesses a lever on Moscow (two other Somali harbours, Mogadishu and Kisimayu are also frequented by Soviet warships), and the Soviet government, under the Treaty of Friendship and Cooperation of 11 July 1974, is committed to support the Somali arms race. In return, by possibly withholding or stopping the arms supply, Moscow also has a lever over Somalia. This is referred to in Ethiopian circles as mutual blackmail.

The armed forces of the Somali Republic, reflecting her compact ethnic population and arms resources, are relatively so powerful that, according to a French analyst, she has become the fourth most powerful military force in Africa (evidently after South Africa, Egypt, and perhaps Nigeria).[16]

Compared to Somalia, Ethiopia is poorly equipped. Somali weaponry is modern whereas Ethiopia's is much outdated. In numbers of tanks (Somalia, 250; Ethiopia, 62) and combat aircraft (Somalia, 52, including 24 MiG 21s; Ethiopia, 37), Somalia already had outdistanced her prospective opponent by 1976. This disproportion is likely to increase in the coming years, also due to the losses Addis Ababa is suffering in the fighting in Eritrea. More than half of the Ethiopian army is engaged in this rebellious province. This disproportion may, however, disappear if Moscow will be ready to deliver massive amounts of arms to Ethiopia.

For a number of years Ethiopia has been seeking arms from everywhere. The United States was ready to supply only 'defensive' arms and even that delivery was stopped in early 1977. China had earlier delivered a few aircraft but by 1974 practically discontinued deliveries. While Emperor Haile Selassie was still on the throne, Ethiopia asked for financial aid from Saudi Arabia; King Faisal then offered to build an Islamic Institute in Addis Ababa. When Moscow was approached, the answer was, 'We only supply arms to friends.'

The present leader of Ethiopia, Colonel Mengistu Haile Maryam, a professed Marxist, again approached Moscow for arms in early 1977. Moscow then proceeded to deliver arms to Ethiopia and may, in the course of the coming years, provide considerable military hardware for the use of Ethiopian armed forces. If this should be the case, then an anomalous situation will arise in which Soviet-equipped Ethiopian soldiers will fight Soviet-equipped Eritrean guerrillas, and possibly also Somali armed forces provided with Soviet weaponry.

The Soviet diplomatic-military shift in favour of Ethiopia may convince the Somali leadership that the cause of their country is better served alongside Saudi Arabia, Sudan, and North Yemen (together with Somalia, strongly Islamic countries) than under the guardianship of Moscow. In such an eventuality, the Soviet naval-air bases in Berbera and elsewhere in Somalia might share the fate which similar bases suffered in Egypt when that country suddenly turned against Moscow and ousted Soviet military advisers and removed their installations from Egyptian territory.

Leadership

At the time of this writing, Ethiopia is governed by confusion and the mutual massacre of her leaders. The situation in this ancient empire is so chaotic that the central government is unable to exert control over most parts of the country. The ethnic-religious fragmentation in Ethiopia may also explain the low-quality performance of the Ethiopian military in Eritrea and, in a future emergency, elsewhere.

Somalia is controlled by a firm leadership and her ethnically compact population seems dedicated to achieve the unification of all the Somali nation now allegedly scattered among the former French Territory of the Afars and Issas, Ethiopia and Kenya.

Opportunity

In her present predicament, Ethiopia is unlikely to resort to any aggressive action, However, it is to be expected that Somalia will, in some way or other, avail herself of the opportunity to exploit her neighbour's confused and weakened condition. The spark which might trigger a violent conflict is the situation in what used to be the French Territory of the Afars and Issas before that country achieved independence on 27 June 1977, and then was to be known as the Republic of Djibouti.

Depending on whether this new Republic will be effectively defended by the French (a French military and naval presence might for some time survive in Djibouti), the Somalis may attempt to incorporate that area. So far the government of that territory has been controlled by the Afar ethnic group, but it may after independence fall into the exclusive hands of the Issas, a Somali ethnic group. Thus a unification with Somalia may become a close possibility.

In such an eventuality, Ethiopia, despite her enfeebled condition, would be committed to intervene. Although Addis Ababa has officially renounced any wish to succeed the French in the sovereignty of the Territory (a claim which was upheld until the early 1970s), she opposes the annexation of this area by Somalia in order to secure her principal outlet to the sea, the Addis Ababa–Djibouti railway, and her use of the facilities in Djibouti harbour.

Even a feeble attempt by Ethiopia to prevent the incorporation of Djibouti into Greater Somalia might lead to an all-out war along the long Somali-Ethiopian border. Somalia might then undertake to secure not only the formal annexation of Djibouti and the Ethiopian province of Ogaden, but also those areas beyond that province where Somali herdsmen wander with their cattle.

There is thus potential danger of a violent conflagration in and around the Horn of Africa. The union of the former French Territory and Somalia would also result in the control of the strategic Strait of Bab el Mandeb falling into the hands of Southern Yemen and Somalia. This event could have far-reaching significance for the shipping to and from the Suez Canal, especially for shipping bound for Israel. It seems certain that the Soviets have a great interest in tilting the balance of power in their favour in the Horn of Africa, as elsewhere in the Indian Ocean region.

(4) Southern Africa
Basic Motivation

The basic motivation for conflict in this part of the world is racial: the African-ruled countries and the black African population-at-large wish to eliminate what is known as the white supremacist regimes. On the other hand, the main bastion of European-descended populations, the Afrikaner element of the South African whites, has developed a conception of its own which motivates its struggle for survival.

According to the long-term strategic plan of the Organisation of African Unity, first the Portuguese colonies were to be liberated by their black majorities, next Rhodesia (which had been given the African name of Zimbabwe) is to be secured for black majority rule, then South West Africa (known as Namibia) is to be wrested from South African rule, and, lastly, the hardest nut to crack, the Republic of South Africa will be given to her majority African population to rule.

After the revolution in Lisbon in April 1974, Portugal gave up her colonial possessions, among them Mozambique on the shore of the Indian Ocean. At the time of this writing, Rhodesia is bearing the brunt of the battle for her existence under European rule. There now appears little chance that a realistic, peaceful transformation could take place in this country.

The motivation of the Africans is clearly racial: to free themselves from the domination of the whites. But the cause for which the South African regime is ready to stand up rests ultimately (in addition to the urge for self-preservation)on the particular ideological-political and religious *Weltanschauung* of the Afrikaner (Boer) people. This world view is embedded in the Afrikaner mind by historic experience and its importance is not to be underrated.

The Afrikaners are descendants of the Dutch settlers who came to the Cape province in the seventeenth century and were reinforced in numbers by Huguenot, German, and additional Dutch religious refugees in the eighteenth century. They escaped British rule (after the annexation by Britain of the Cape during the Napoleonic Wars) and in the late 1830s established the Boer republics of Transvaal (South African Republic) and the Orange Free State. While they moved north, Bantu tribes penetrated south into the area. The Boers thus can claim to have been the original settlers of the republics they founded. But surrounded from the Cape and Natal by the British, they fell victim to the British expansion in the second Boer War (1899–1902). After the foundation of the Union of South Africa (later to become the Republic of South Africa) the Afrikaner nation became the leading core of that state and converted it to the philosophy they wished to follow. Thus the policy of separate development (*apartheid*) was adopted, a policy which subsequently isolated South Africa from the rest of the world and denied her the ties of friendship which otherwise would bind her with the Western World.

The Afrikaner conception is Manichean: the world is divided between the forces of evil (Communists) and the Christian world. They identify the African revolutionary forces with Communism. With few exceptions their attitude is wholly defensive; they understand that they have to fight for survival as they did in the past. They feel beleaguered, encircled as they were when struggling against the Zulus and the English. Their symbol is the *Laager*, the ring of ox-driven wagons behind which they managed to defend themselves. Their missionary zeal and determination to fight or to die ('we have nowhere to go') makes any compromise solution less likely even if such a solution could be acceptable to the black Africans.

In such a way two completely inconsistent motivations and claims oppose each other: the claim for majority rule, and the South African insistence on maintaining their white regime with the 'separate development' for the non-whites (to be given autonomy in their respective 'homelands').

Capability

The principal actors in the power struggle in Southern Africa are the Republic of South Africa and her opponents: the African states, principally Tanzania, Zambia, and Mozambique, the various revolutionary movements for the liberation of Namibia and Anzania (the African name for South Africa), and their outside supporters, the Soviet Union, Cuba, China and other Communist countries. Rhodesia, from the South African point of view, is an advanced position or a glacis which can be written off without basically jeopardising her strategic position. Of course, it would be preferable to have a non-hostile black regime to succeed that of Ian Smith. Therefore, Prime Minister Vorster is eager to bring about a peaceful solution while, at the same time, Pretoria provides logistic and financial aid to Salisbury.

The African guerrillas who will attempt to subvert South African rule are armed by the Soviet Union, China, and some Soviet client states; arms are being delivered through the intermediaries of Tanzania, Zambia, or Mozambique.[17] There are also Cuban instructors operating in these countries, and the Cubans themselves, now mainly stationed in Angola, may join the struggle. So far, except for the Cubans, the guerrillas are provided with light arms, although missiles and heavy guns may also be made available to them in the future.

In return, South Africa is girding herself to defend her present political (and possibly physical) existence. Pretoria is engaged in a massive arms program The yearly defence budget has now reached almost U.S. $2 billion, approximately the same amount as Australia spends now on defence (the South African GNP is about half of the Australian). The period of compulsory military service has been extended to two years.

For a number of years an arms embargo has been imposed on weapons deliveries to South Africa by the United Nations Security Council. However, this embargo so far has had little effect on that country's military capability. To a very large extent, Pretoria is self-sufficient both in terms of raw materials and in the manufacture of arms. She is dependent on foreign supplies only in respect to some highly sophisticated weaponry and major naval craft. For such items, France and Israel were the official suppliers while through indirect channels arms of all kinds have reached South Africa. There is also some progress in the manufacture of more sophisticated weaponry: Mirage fighter aircraft, under a French licence, are manufactured in South Africa; also helicopters, missiles, and armoured vehicles. When on 10 August 1975, the French President Giscard d'Estaing announced that France would no longer sell South Africa arms 'likely to be used in air or land operations on the continent [of Africa]', he clearly meant that the embargo will not be extended to naval craft. South Africa possesses the financial means to purchase arms from anyone willing to sell them.

Pretoria also attempted to become more independent in the field of energy resources. It is believed that South Africa has oil reserves for two years so that an oil embargo would not have an immediate effect on her economy. She can also manufacture gasoline from coal which she has in abundance. It is also suspected that she has made fast progress in the manufacture of nuclear weapons.

Except for the narrow strip in the north-east, South Africa's terrain does not favour guerrilla operations. So far, if there have been attempts at infiltrations, they have proved to be highly unsuccessful.

Despite predictions to the contrary, [18] it appears that South Africa may prove to a 'nut too hard to crack'. But much depends on whether the leadership, the Afrikaner hard core of the population, will be able to maintain its present determination to resist meaningful changes.

Leadership

There seems to be no doubt that the African governments and the leaders of the various liberation movements will continue to insist that majority rule be established in South Africa, as they previously insisted in regard to the Portuguese colonies and to Rhodesia. They are also determined to pursue an armed struggle for the achievement of this goal. There is also little likelihood that the present suppliers of the anti-white regime's military forces—the Soviet

Union, China, and others—will abandon their arms deliveries.

The present South African leadership is equally determined to oppose any one-man-one-vote solution and to continue with the essentials of the apartheid policy. Pretoria wishes to gain time in order to implement its homeland projects—the setting up of officially independent Bantu States which would thus reduce the obvious statistical imbalance between the ruling white minority and the disfranchised blacks, coloureds, and Asians. The first such 'independent' state, Transkei, was established in 1976, but has not obtained recognition as an independent state by any government. However, no plausible solution has yet been envisaged for the millions of urban blacks and coloureds outside the future homelands.[19]

A partition of the country between Africans and whites (what would happen to the coloureds and Asians, rejected by both of the longer established racial elements, nobody has yet explained) has been proposed by academic commentators[20] but has received no endorsement by any official or unofficial sources in South Africa herself.

It is thus most likely that a solution will be sought on the battlefield.

Opportunity

It seems evident that the African liberation movements and their African as well as non-African state supporters will undertake no military operations before the Rhodesian question is settled according to their desire. In the timetable set by the Organisation of African Unity, the liberation of Namibia (South West Africa) is next on the list. However, it would be difficult to separate an onslaught on Namibia (which will be defended by South African forces) from that of South Africa herself. Even if the Pretoria government should be successful in establishing an autonomous regime in the former mandated territory (which is not recognised, however, by the United Nations or any government outside South Africa), the South African government is likely to continue giving military support for its defence. Thus, any action against Namibia will lead to an involvement of South African defence forces.

After the fall of Rhodesia, it seems certain that guerrilla activity is to be deployed on South African territory. Whether large numbers of the South African rural blacks will cooperate with such guerrilla forces is a highly important question which may determine the possibility of carrying out such harassing activity in the area controlled by the Republic of South Africa herself. Because the terrain in South Africa is much more favourable for defence against guerrilla incursions and the administrative and punitive capabilities of the South African police and military are relatively efficient, any such activity would be far less effective than similar activities deployed in the former Portuguese possessions or in Rhodesia. It will certainly be ineffective in overthrowing the present South African governmental structure without mass-scale black urban support by peaceful strikes or violence. And Pretoria, if determined to resist (and it appears likely that it will muster the determination to do so) will also be forced to cope with international diplomatic pressures and with economic embargoes or blockades. The sense of a life-and-death struggle will most probably lead the now critical English-speaking segment of the white population to rally finally to the Afrikaner governing element in a feeling of solidarity and commonality.

The intervention of Cuban forces which could result in a line-up and clash of conventional armies, operating from Angola or from Mozambique (or Rhodesia, if the latter is controlled by a hostile government), could easily be defeated by the military power of South Africa. The deployment of Soviet units against the well-equipped and well-led South African military defence forces is highly unlikely and could hardly be successful in view of the logistical difficulties and lack of experience and capability of the Soviet Union in implementing such a large-scale operation in a distant, overseas threatre. In Angola, only diplomatic reasons persuaded Pretoria to refrain from annihilating the Cuban forces and to withdraw their units from this former Portuguese territory.

An evident failure of a Cuban or Soviet intervention would cause the collapse of the entire action against South Africa and a loss of face which Moscow is most unlikely to risk.

Thus, a prolonged state of tension and attritional action by the African forces which would create instability and dangers of escalation is the most likely situation which could develop in and around the Republic of South Africa in the years to come.

'Mutual Restraint' and Regional Arms Races

The preceding survey of principal flashpoints along the littoral of the Indian Ocean inevitably leads to the conclusion that there are many critical, potentially explosive situations in its various sections. Violent struggles have already erupted in some parts of the region. Nor is it possible to avoid the conclusion that the Soviet Union —much more at present than Communist China—is intent upon exploiting these tensions in order to tilt the balances of power in favour of its protégés and to the detriment of pro-Western regimes. This tendency becomes even more evident when we realize that local conflicts tend to get polarised between East and West and, simultaneously, along the Sino-Soviet confrontation line.

These regional feuds, originally inherent or indigenous to the area in which they are carried, and independent of non-regional impulses, are likely to escalate due principally to two factors: one is the increased flow of arms supplied by non-regional sources, the second is the naval presence of the superpowers which provides a potential vehicle of support or menace.

Negotiations between Washington and Moscow to achieve 'mutual restraint' in the deployment of their naval forces in the Indian Ocean cannot be divorced from the present state of affairs and possible future developments in the coastal areas of that Ocean.

It should be recalled that the initial feelers between the two governments concerning the possibility of limiting their naval deployments in the Indian Ocean were discontinued in late 1975 because of developments on the African mainland—in Angola and also in the Horn. The Ford Administration considered that the question of arms limitation in the Indian Ocean cannot be envisaged 'in isolation from past and possible future events' in the areas bordering that Ocean. At the same time, the Administration pledged to encourage the Soviet Union to conduct itself with restraint and 'to avoid exploiting local crises for unilateral gain.'[21]

While the American pronouncements emphasise the existence of regional crises and their exploitation to its favour by Moscow, Soviet declarations on the question of ending the arms race between the superpowers in the Indian Ocean gloss over in silence the military threats and activities of littoral states. The Soviet 'Memorandum on Questions of Ending the Arms Race and Disarmament' submitted to the 31st Session (1976) of the United General Assembly exclusively discusses the military activities of non-littoral states which it proposes to reduce, and also to eliminate foreign military bases in that region (while asserting that there are no such Soviet establishments in the Indian Ocean area).

The developments on land and at sea originate from different motivations and impulses. A crisis or armed conflict on land creates a cause for superpower involvement. Not necessarily connected with the naval presence, there is yet another reason for interest and involvement by Moscow, Washington, or Peking (and possibly by London and Paris): arms supplies to littoral countries are likely to entangle the suppliers in the conflict. Arms deliveries by themselves are a surrogate form of intervention.

Superpower interventions, contingent on an outbreak of violent conflagration, may take place under certain circumstances in the four sub-regions listed previously:

(1) In the Indian subcontinent the polarisation between pro-Western (American) and pro-Eastern (Soviet) splits has been blunted by the ouster of Prime Minister Indira Gandhi. However, the arms race between the main antagonists, India and Pakistan, continues unabated. Internal troubles in both of these countries are likely to exclude, for the time being, an armed clash. However internal upheavals which threaten a dismemberment of the respective state or which result in a civil war, may be an invitation for aggression or to an action 'to restore peace'. India will now be even more prepared to oppose extremist governments in the area which she considers to be her hegemonial domain, not only in Pakistan but also in Bangladesh, Sri Lanka, and the Himalayan states. The Soviet Union, China, or both might then undertake to influence the outcome of a civil war by resorting to direct or indirect intervention, while the United States will feel obliged to make similar moves. A pattern which, in a limited form, evolved during the 1971 Bangladesh War, may be repeated but possibly with greater strength and vigour and with a more active involvement. American and Soviet warships may appear in force before the coast of the subcontinent and massive arms deliveries may be undertaken. Even if a direct military participation would be eschewed (which is likely in the case of the United States after the Vietnam experience, and impossible to perform by the Soviets because of logistic difficulties), the two navies might be brought close to a collision course.

(2) The dangers in the Persian Gulf area stem first from the geographic proximity of Soviet land power which could effectively provide protection to the Iraqi client state, should the latter be threatened by conservative forces; and then from the possibility that the vital flow of oil from that area might be interrupted by some local event or outside interference.

An unhindered delivery of the Persian Gulf oil is of vital interest to Western Europe and Japan, hence also to the United States. Forceful interruption of the oil supply by either regional or non-regional forces or a prolonged embargo or boycott by local powers (such as in the case of the 1973 Arab-Israeli War) might be countered by some American action ranging from a naval demonstration to the landing of marines. Soviet counter-measures cannot be excluded.

Iran, the dominating military power in the Gulf, may one day wish to demonstrate or safeguard her hegemonial position by resorting to military measures against either revolutionary forces in the Gulf area or against another regional state opposing Iran's control over the area. Or else Iran might be ready to cooperate with the United States in carrying out measures required to maintain the balance of power or status quo in the Gulf. Such measures may even reach out into the Indian subcontinent should Tehran feel obliged to prevent a dismemberment of Pakistan.[22] And another Arab-Israeli war might have a spillover effect, both in the Persian Gulf area and in the area around the Horn of Africa (Red Sea) with consequent American and Soviet interventions.[23]

(3) In the Horn of Africa and around the strategic Bab el Mandeb Strait, developments have already gained dramatic proportions. The relations between the two major antagonists, Ethiopia and the Somali Democratic Republic, have become more complex due to the fact that the Addis Ababa junta switched to the left, adopted Marxist–Leninist ideology, and moved away from Washington. The Soviet Union promised and began delivery of arms to Ethiopia. At the same time, Saudi Arabia undertook to lure away Somalia from her Soviet allegiance. The French withdrawal from the Territory of the Afars and Issas may expose that area to an invasion by Somali or pro-Somali forces. To quieten the Ethiopian leaders, France has been trying to come to an understanding with Somalia which would permit the stationing, after the attainment of independence by the Territory, of more than a token French force in Djibouti.

All these are delicate and perilous moves and countermoves. For Moscow to ride the Ethiopian and Somali horses simultaneously appears to be risky and may prove counterproductive. The Soviets may be deprived of the Berbera base without gaining the unreserved sympathies of Ethiopia. And Somalia can hardly be expected to avoid an exploitation of Ethiopia's confused situation, a country which is now divided by civil war and the protracted fighting in Eritrea.

Whichever directions the fortunes of these forthcoming struggles might take, it is unlikely that an involvement of the superpowers, and even France, can totally be avoided. Should the free transit through the Bab el Mandeb Strait be endangered, all the maritime powers might feel compelled to secure the freedom of movement through this waterway. Should the Strait fall under the prohibitive control of anti-Israeli forces (South Yemen and Somalia, or an anti-Israeli, independent Djibouti), during another Arab-Israeli military confrontation or otherwise, Washington might be compelled to intervene. Furthermore, should Ethiopia, in the place of Somalia, become the 'favourite daughter' of Moscow in that area (jeopardising the Soviet base at Berbera), the Soviet Union might possibly intervene to save an endangered and collapsing Ethiopia.

(4) In Southern Africa the disastrous situation described above suggests many possibilities for intervention by the superpowers.

The United States, together with Britain, is already involved in trying to bring about a peaceful transformation in Rhodesia from white supremacist to black majority rule. However, the Soviet Union, excluded so far from playing a part in the peaceful solution, is pressing for a military solution and for this reason is rushing arms to Mozambique and other centres of black guerrilla training. Eventually, Moscow may again resort to the use of Cuban forces in which case Washington, despite the Angolan fiasco, may come to use indirect methods to prevent a pro-Communist take-over in Rhodesia.

In one way or other, after the fate of Rhodesia is sealed, it will become South Africa's turn to defend her present politico-social structure. Then the reasons for superpower involvement could become even more pressing. As it is unlikely that a compromise formula (or any formula) can peacefully be reached which would allow for equality of the black, coloured, and Asian population with that of the whites, the probability of an armed clash is rather high. In any case, the alternatives at stake (control of the Cape of Good Hope area, or of the gold, diamond, and other mineral and industrial wealth of the country) will affect the outside powers more closely than in the case of Rhodesia. The armed clash which may threaten to erupt is bound to be more momentous and replete with dangers than that which is being waged for the future status of Rhodesia. The important, if not vital, interests of the superpowers and other great powers in the outcome of that struggle are bound to induce them to become involved, in one way or another, while the measure and method of future moves and countermoves cannot yet be conjectured at.

The eventualities described above will necessarily influence both Washington and Moscow in their negotiations for 'mutual restraint' in deployment of their naval forces in the Indian Ocean. They will be reluctant to be restricted in their naval movements in those waters because of the instabilities and potential clashes in that region, clashes in which they will be unavoidably involved. In case of any such involvement, the necessity of naval demonstrations or 'gunboat diplomacy', the need to secure shipments and military supplies to the affected areas will render the existence of a naval-military base highly useful if not essential. Under such circumstances the abandonment of Diego Garcia by the Americans, or of Berbera and other available facilities by the Soviets would amount to a sacrifice which either party would be reluctant to accept.

The case appears convincing that it is because of the conflicts among littoral powers or revolutionary movements operating in the areas adjacent to the Indian Ocean that the naval presence of the superpowers acquires an ominous meaning. These conflicts might even lead to the creation of such a state of affairs which would frustrate any attempt by the superpowers to limit their naval deployment in the Indian Ocean. All this leads to the conclusion that it would be more rational and more urgent to de-escalate these conflicts than to attempt to restrain the relatively modest deployment of naval forces of outside powers in the Indian Ocean.

As adumbrated above, an agreement of 'mutual restraint' by the superpowers would be difficult to reach. Still, such an objective would be infinitely easier to attain than a modest de-escalation of the conflict-potential among the littoral powers of that Ocean.

Arms Control among the Littoral Powers of the Indian Ocean
While a balanced arms control agreement between the superpowers for the limitation of naval deployment in the Indian Ocean (possibly including France and Britain)could pre-empt an arms race, there is no panacea for remedying the unfortunate state of tension and the potentiality for violent conflicts which exist between the littoral states of that region.

It would be futile to seek any one particular method which could be instrumental in lowering the intensity of antagonisms between most of these regional states and in removing the motivations for a violent outbreak between them. Nor would it be wise to attribute this tragic state of affairs entirely to arms supplied by non-regional countries. Even should the unthinkable happen, should the sales and supply of arms or military aid be miraculously discontinued, the more powerful regional countries would benefit from this restraint to the detriment of the weaker ones. Such a restraint on the part of the arms suppliers might have more of a destabilising than a stabilising effect.

Still, the military balance may in most cases become a catalytic factor for the outbreak of a war or armed revolt. But it is not the only factor and in some cases not the main factor.[24] However, history is the witness that states which have acquired excessive power, even if they commit no aggression, provoke fear and jealousies which, in turn, may induce their neighbours to take precautionary (and possibly even pre-emptive) measures of aggression.[25]

It would be a rather ungrateful, and even presumptuous endeavour to try to suggest methods of how to remedy the disastrous *bellum omnium contra omnes* which prevails in many parts of the periphery of the Indian Ocean. This author has always believed that his main task was to explain and analyse so that the international world could be better understood. In order to be improved, this world has to be understood first. But there are a great many who want to improve the world without even understanding it.

There may be a few suggestions of a general nature that can be made here. In order to establish among the littoral states of the Indian Ocean a modicum of arms control (in the broader sense), it may be advisable to consider proceeding in the reverse order of factors leading to a violent clash which was previously listed in this paper.

First, it would be necessary to avoid the 'opportunities' to spark a violent conflagration. Sometimes such opportunities are artificially created by persons, or groups of persons, who wish to promote the incidence of war. Sukarno launched his ' confrontation' because of the inclusion of the North Borneo states into the Malaysian Federation. The outbreak of the 1965 war between Pakistan and India may be another example for creating a pretext, or using an event as a justification for an aggression. But opportunities may also turn up spontaneously. It would be wise statesmanship to avoid the exploitation of such openings in order to preserve peace and to establish an atmosphere conducive to peaceful solutions.

In such a way the question of opportunities is closely linked with the character and composition of the leadership. Moderation by leaders, especially by leaders of a country more powerful than its neighbours is generally a rare phenomenon. Still, it is the key to ultimate (not immediate) success for hubris does lead eventually to failure and downfall.

Unfortunately, outside powers can mostly do very little to influence other countries in the choice of their leaders. It generally depends on the ruling or decision-making elements within each country to determine the choice of its leaders. Despite the technological and post- industrial developments of our age, the personal element remains to be an all-important if mercurial factor that shapes the world. In many if not most of the Third World countries, the devolution of leadership is combined with an internal crisis which makes it easier for irrational or irresponsible, however charismatic, figures to gain the upper hand.

The military balance is only one factor which may induce countries to resort to war. Still, it is an important factor.Because almost all of the countries around the periphery of the Indian Ocean have to rely on outside arms supplies, a limitation or reduction of arms deliveries (arms control in the narrower sense) will have a moderating influence and restrict capabilities to apply force. But due to the fact that the suppliers belong to different and opposing blocs of states, or because of the economic advantage of arms sales, the competitive character of this business prevents a concerted and agreed limitation. Thus, international understandings to limit arms sales are hard to arrive at. But the supplier countries may eventually come to the conclusion that it is in their long-range interest to reduce, limit, or balance such supplies, possibly by concentrating on certain trouble spots rather than on the region as a whole. This may be too much to expect in the present state of world affairs, but at least some cautious approach to this effect may not be impossible.

This purposeful reduction in arms deliveries may possibly be undertaken in conjunction with attempts to lower the intensity of basic motivations for conflicts. If such motivations are tempered or scaled down in their intensity so as not to offer a cause for armed conflict, the reason for arms races will also end.

As in the case of 'opportunity' and 'leadership', the elimination or scaling down of animosities can only be successfully handled on an individual, area to area or country to country, basis. Sweeping general pronouncements carry little weight. It might thus be possible to satisfy some reasonable demands and to compromise others. Of course, some of the conflicts will prove to be intractable. In this respect, one feels compelled to think of the black versus white situation in Southern Africa where mutual claims and vital interests are head-on incompatible. A particular solution which is attempted to be reached for Rhodesia may be totally unacceptable for South Africa. Somalia's irrendentist claims on Ethiopia and other neighbouring countries also are difficult to satisfy. In such cases at least attempts could be made to isolate the conflict, to prevent it from spreading into neighbouring areas, and from involving outside great powers.

In most cases of conflict the greatest obstacle which would prevent a peaceful solution rests not only with the local adversaries; it rests with the expansionist and ideologically motivated Soviet endeavours as well as rival Chinese attempts, to gain undue influence in the Third World, and in the Indian Ocean region in particular.

Moscow now seems to believe that its 'salami tactics' of placing Indian Ocean region countries one by one under its influence will be tolerated by the West and will not provoke a global confrontation replete with nuclear dangers. But certainly, should such gradual penetration be successful, there will come a point where the West will be bound to call a halt to further expansionism, as it did in the European arena of confrontation. Where the line is to be drawn, nobody can yet imagine but evidently there must be a line.

Should the Soviet advance continue, it will, in addition to the local conflicts, touch off an acute and most perilous confrontation between Washington and Moscow, joined by their respective allies. The conflicts and instabilities of the littoral countries of the Indian Ocean may thus become the source of a potential global and nuclear conflagration which is in the vital interest of all mankind to avoid.

Footnotes

* Professor Váli was a Visiting Fellow in the Strategic and Defence Studies Centre, January—May 1977 under the international security and arms control studies program. During this period he produced this chapter for use at the Conference as a background paper. Unfortunately he was unable to remain at the A.N.U. for the Conference.

1. United Nations Document A/AC. 159/1. Italics are the author's.
2. *Ibid.*
3. Australian Senate Standing Committee on Foreign Affairs and Defence, *Australia and the Indian Ocean Region*, Australian Government Publishing Service, Canberra, 1976, p.204.
4. See Ferenc A. Váli, *Politics of the Indian Ocean Region: The Balances of Power,* The Free Press, New York, 1976, pp.93, 175 and 187.
5. Report of the Department of State to the Congress of the United States made public on 21 April 1976.
6. Information obtained by this author.
7. Barry M. Blechman in his book on *The Control of Naval Armaments*, Brookings Institution, Washington, D.C. 1975, pp. 97–100, presents a 'Draft Indian Ocean Naval Disengagement Agreement'.
8. W.A.C. Adie in Patrick Wall, ed., *The Indian Ocean and the Threat to the West*, Stacey Int., London, 1975, p. 156, considers Soviet military involvement on land more important than its naval presence.
9. *New York Times*, 26 December 1976.
10. Evidently, only India is justified to 'bring arms supplies by external powers' into the subcontinent.
11. *New York Times*, 27 February 1975.
12. See in this respect Prime Minister Zulfikar Ali Bhutto's article in *Foreign Affairs*, April 1973, p.553.

13. The Indian Defence Ministry Report for 1975–76 expressed concern that advanced weapons supplied by the West to oil-producing countries of the Middle East might be transferred to Pakistan. According to the Report, Pakistan already had acquired missiles, tanks, anti-aircraft guns, artillery, gunboats, torpedo boats, submarines, helicopters, and different types of aircraft from various countries. *The Times*, (London) 4 April 1976.

14. See, for instance, *Pakistani Times*, 6 November 1975, *The Times of India*, 25 September 1975 and 2 March 1976; *Pakistani Times*, 2 April 1976.

15. The difficulties of absorbing all the modern weaponry purchased are well described in *New York Times*, 5 January 1977.

16. Yves Prats, 'L'Océan Indien, Zone Stratégique', in *Annuaire des Pays de l'Océan Indien* edited by the Centre d'Etude et de Recherches sur les Sociétés de l'Océan Indien, University of Aix-Marseilles, Vol. 1, 1974, p.124.

17. During his travel in Southern Africa in March 1977, the Soviet President Podgorny promised the delivery of abundant arms to the African countries he visited as well as to revolutionary liberation movements.

18. Andrew Young, the American Ambassador to the United Nations, has predicted that the South African regime will collapse in less than five years.

19. The fiction that these largely de-tribalised blacks would belong to these homelands and exercise their voting rights according to their tribal origin appears artificial and difficult to implement.

20. See, for instance, Jürgen Blenck and Klaus von der Ropp, 'Republic of South Africa: Partition a Solution?' in *Aussenpolitik* (English edition), Vol. 27, 3rd Quarter 1976, pp. 310–327.

21. See n.5 above.

22. See Sulzberger in the *International Herald Tribune*, 27 April 1977.

23. Blechman, *op. cit.*, p. 69.

24. See Laurence Martin, *Arms and Strategy*, Weidenfeld & Nicholson, London 1973, p.240.

25. Herbert Butterfield, 'Morality and International Order', in Brian Porter, (ed.), *International Politics, 1919–1969*, Oxford University Press, London 1972, p.355.

Conclusion
Robert O'Neill

I knew from the beginning of planning for the conference on which this volume is based that it would be no easy matter to prepare this conclusion. The nine preceding chapters have provided an excellent overview of current trends in weapons proliferation but they have not advanced many new suggestions for achieving effective control over these processes. Both the global and the regional chapters have set forth most convincingly the prospect that all kinds of proliferation, from vertical nuclear to horizontal conventional, appear likely to continue well into the future. We are all aware of the problems which this situation will cause but we find it extremely difficult to change the course of what seems, despite our best hopes, to be the inevitable march of human history.

It is not my purpose in this conclusion to recapitulate on the nine preceding papers. Rather I wish to raise some general questions and offer some comments on the feasibility of controlling the spread of weaponry in our area of concern.

The first of these questions is why should the nations of the Indian and Pacific Ocean region attempt special measures to control the growth of their own military inventories? I am not posing this question on the basis of any unstated assumption that a nation will see such action as being morally commendable i.e. it is not a question of the same kind as 'why should one obey the law?' There is no obvious consensus amongst national leaders that restriction of armaments is a good thing in the same way that there is about obedience to established laws. Indeed, it will be apparent from the preceding papers that states have different attitudes towards the first question according to whether it applies to their actual or potential enemies, to states which are neutral towards them, to states which are their allies, or finally, to themselves. Therefore, from this perspective, there is really nothing at all to be said of an objective nature about arms control.

However if a state should choose to free itself from the extremely subjective perspective of this crude, rivalry-based model, which tends to treat all nations as essentially similar except that some are friends and some are enemies, it may be frequently exhorted to consider another which takes into account an economic dimension. According to this model, the poorer states will tend to have a more positive attitude towards control of their own levels of armaments than the richer because the slender resource bases of the former are under much greater pressure than those of the latter. Indeed it is this model which underlies much of what has been written about arms control and developing countries in the past three decades.

This model is not much more useful than the first, as is evidenced by the lack of correlation between national income and national defence expenditure across a wide range of countries. Many of the wealthier countries, such as Canada, Australia and some Western European nations devote only some 2–3 per cent of their GNP to defence. Japan spends less than one per cent. Yet many poorer countries devote far higher proportions of their GNP to defence, e.g. Singapore 5 per cent, Pakistan 7 per cent, Nigeria 10 per cent, Turkey 9 per cent, Iran 17 per cent, etc. There are others which spend in the 3–5 per cent range and only a handful which spend less than 2 per cent.

Perhaps the most glaring lack of correlation between wealth and defence expenditure lies in the Soviet–U.S. duality. It is very difficult to know exactly what the Soviets spend on defence but there is wide consensus that with a smaller GNP than the U.S. they spend a much higher proportion, perhaps twice as much, on defence.

As an aside it might be noted from a Western point of view one should not be entirely discomforted about this level of Soviet defence expenditure. If, at some future point, they should reduce it to something like 5 per cent of GNP and use the money thereby saved for a major foreign aid program or to finance a major export drive of manufactured goods, some people may find themselves wishing for the good old days of the 1970's when the chief Soviet means of buying influence was the supply of tanks, missiles, guns and aircraft which did not compete seriously with either Western aid or Western commercial exports.

Furthermore, these disparities, which in the light of the economic model one would expect to be reversed, are not merely short-term phenomena. Their patterns are well established and indicate that there are much more powerful forces at work within nations than simple competition for economic resources.

Other factors therefore have to be brought into consideration, such as each state's own threat perceptions, the degree to which it depends upon allies for protection, the role of the military in each state's maintenance of internal law and order and the political power of each state's military establishment. It is of little use to criticise a poor state for heavy defence expenditure, if that state feels a substantial degree of external or internal threat, without offering some amelioration of that threat. It is similarly unproductive to criticise a state for the high expenditure associated with a more independent defence posture when that state does not believe participation in a major alliance to be in its best interests. It is probably expecting too much of human nature to imagine that military rulers, or militarily-based rulers, are going to be persuaded out of cultivating their own power bases so that they might be able to spend more money on those of their subjects who do not contribute to their tenure of power. Rather, to achieve significant results, arms controlling policies have to be concerned with the causes of weapons proliferation as much as, if not more than, the actual proliferation itself.

Thus, to return to the question why should states of the Indian and Pacific Ocean even seek to limit the growth of their armaments, one can state some fairly obvious answers such as to save money or to avoid provoking potential enemies into an arms race but one must admit that the motivation to achieve these ends is not strong. When placed alongside other motivations, such as the desire to have a substantial degree of direct security against attack by neighbours, or to cultivate a great power ally by agreeing to regard his potential enemies as one's own, or, in a domestic sense, to keep one's own political grouping in power, it is not surprising that arms control lobbies are scarcely to be detected in this region.

There are exceptions to this generalisation, most notably Japan, where historical experience has persuaded very many people that security is best achieved indirectly via allies and via economic strength. There are peace movements of various kinds which are active in most countries of the region but their views on the direction in which their own national policies should move tend to be regarded by those in power, and by electorates where these have a significant voice in foreign policy, as naive, as too far in advance of their time or as downright subversive. Politicians may give lip service to peace movement policies from time to time but it is hard to find a nation which puts such ideas into practice when it comes to the shaping of its own military forces.

If these pressures for arms limitations are weak in our region, what are the prospects for their development into effective political factors in the future? Unless the advocates of arms control can deploy arguments more telling than those of the economic costs of weapons, these prospects are slender indeed. Rather attention should be focused on the crucial areas of positive motivation towards defence expenditure—the security perceptions of the individual nations of the region and the internal, institutional factors which influence governments to build armed forces and equip them.

Neither of these fields will produce a heavy crop of results in return for a season's cultivation. However both offer some real prospects because they open a line of approach to the seats of decision-making power in the defence area. All states, like all individuals, have valid apprehensions about their own security. In the case of states, these apprehensions are a particularly serious matter for there is no supreme authority in the society of nations which can uphold rights by dealing with offenders against a recognised body of law. There is no safety net of a police force backed by a system of courts for the protection of individual nations. Each must be his own ultimate guarantor and each survives in the international system if his political, economic, diplomatic and military strengths suffice to meet the challenges of others. Therefore it is nonsense to preach disarmament to the society of sovereign states.

It is pointless to expect the U.S.A to restrict its nuclear arsenal while it fears the superiority of Soviet conventional forces over its own in Central Europe. It is just as baseless to suppose that the U.S.S.R. will be prepared to decrease this convential force while it feels threatened by NATO in the West, internal dissidence in Eastern Europe and China in the East. The Chinese Government, now visibly awake to the implications of the rapid advance of weapons technology in other countries, will not be impressed by those who argue against attempting to catch up.

Where then is there any opportunity for attempting to modify the growth of weaponry? I believe that one exists in questioning whether all of the contingencies for which armed forces are designed have not been outmoded by changes in strategic environment and weapons technology and whether armed forces are effectively and efficiently structured to meet these contingencies.

Armed forces, for very good reasons, tend to be slow to adapt their forces and structures to the changing natures of their possible future tasks and so can incite in other countries fears of contingencies which would now be counter-productive for an aggressor to realise. Military establishments do not surrender capabilities readily, particularly when they have been developed under the pressures of combat operations and at the cost of significant casualties. The Second World War has been a very powerful conditioning influence on the development of both contingency planning and force structure, leaving a legacy of large armed forces, trained and equipped to fight massive *Blitzkrieg* operations, which were then re-oriented and maintained to meet the needs of the Cold War. In recent years the levels of tension between the superpowers have subsided somewhat and their weapons systems are tending to make the use of massive numerical concentrations of ground forces extremely costly. The high pace of modern warfare is not likely to permit both the slow mobilisation of reserves and their transportation to the front over hundreds of miles in sufficient time to achieve or prevent the taking of a decision.

Hence the force structures of many states could be improved by surgery. In particular the members of both NATO and the Warsaw Pact would be well advised to reckon their opponents' strengths in terms other than numbers of divisions or of men, discounting particularly their lower categories of reserve formations. At least they may thereby individually come to question the utility of further numerical increases in their military establishments. They may even move towards modest reductions. While the pace of events in any clash between the Soviet Union and China may be slower than in a NATO–Warsaw Pact engagement, thereby conferring greater utility on reserve forces, both sides would be well advised to opt for qualitative rather than quantitative competition.

In the cases of regional conflicts, sharp questioning from appropriate places within the countries concerned may have more spectacular results than lecturing from outside in limiting the numerical expansion of existing forces. The high commands of some of the larger armies could be given a hard time in having to justify their existing establishments in terms of defence worth. What is the point of many of the obsolete destroyers of coastal navies which are inviting PGM attack by opposing small craft in time of hostilities? What is the value of the squadrons of MiG–15s and Sabres which fill out many of the smaller air forces of this region? Provided that these sorts of questions can continually be posed to and within defence establishments by officials, servicemen and politicians who are sufficiently well informed to be able to assess the replies given, I would be surprised not to see a move away from the predominance of numbers in most defence forces and towards better tactical defensive weaponry.

Similarly some of the contingencies for which states prepare might be shown to have lost their relevance to the external strategic environment which each state must face. In particular, scenarios of direct invasion to strategic depth by opposing ground forces look to be increasingly improbable, except in the cases of very confined battlefields such as in the Middle East, the Horn of Africa and the Korean peninsula. Indeed any major attack by a great power upon another nation as an intentional act, while still keeping peaceful relations with the remainder of the world, appears to be increasingly unlikely. The implications of such a move for the other great powers would be too serious for them to be prepared to tolerate any significant change in the existing balance of power by direct application of military force.

The growing accuracy and range of tactical weapons systems, both land- and sea-based, and the growing dependence of many nations upon their maritime environments, offer much higher prospects for effective application of pressure than massive force movements by those countries who wish to coerce their neighbours. The countering of such pressures can now be done much more effectively in most cases by long-range detection and warning systems, backed by small, sophisticated retaliatory strike forces, than by the numerically large, obsolescent establishments which frequently characterise regional powers.

Now, of course, it may be pointed out that what I am proposing is not arms control at all, simply a replacement of quantity by quality, and doing nothing to modify the existing animosities within the international system. And much of that charge is true. However I believe that, in many cases, change away from massive, World War II–type forces to more slender, new technology forces, can be a signficant step for arms control. There is an intrinsically threatening quality about numbers in the armed forces of a potential enemy which is not engendered by pieces of weaponry. Numbers of soldiers inevitably have a conditioning effect on their political environments, whether they run the country, whether they merely vote or whether through their collective opinions they simply act as a pressure group. They are people with initiative to be displayed, with morale to be sustained, with families to be appeased and with political causes to be supported. In particular they tend to look much more frightening to a potential enemy who naturally tends to give their effectiveness those benefits of the doubt which he usually denies to his assessment of the effectiveness of his own forces, quite apart from the benign nature of his own intentions compared with the obvious malevolence of everything his enemy does. The capabilities of technology-intensive weapons systems are more easily assessed with objectivity, which can be supported by the observations of other nations more reliably than can estimates of human capabilities. Also the intrinsic flexibility of weapons systems may be less than that of men in some cases, making the nature of the defence posture of a technologically- oriented nation less ambiguous than that of a manpower-intensive state.

This last factor is particularly important because if a state looks to have a reasonably effective defensive system it is not likely to invite attack. Although the absolute magnitudes of the forces of an attacker may be much greater than those of a defender, the former faces high marginal costs in subduing the latter if the latter is well prepared. Therefore the stability of a regional relationship is enhanced by the type of defensive strength which modern but modest tactical weapons systems can provide if possessed by both sides of a group of rivals. Hence I would agree with Michael MccGwire that the acquisition of weaponry by regional powers can be a very useful development in ensuring both a greater degree of independence of superpower involvement and an increased stability in that region.

The second area from which hopes for more effective control of arms proliferation emanate is that of the internal, institutional forces in any society which press its government for more defence expenditure. Even if these forces control the government, they still have to answer fundamental questions regarding the allocation of resources in such a way that their answers do not cause the state to collapse. In societies where the political power of the military is much less then so also is their capacity to evade such questions if their political masters know how to press them. Hence all kinds of societies have something to gain by encouraging the military by expert internal criticism and debate not to be wasteful and not to undertake activities which are unrelated to the defence function. This process of questioning can be pushed to the point of counter-productivity of course but in most countries, particularly in the developing world, it is quite difficult to assemble the expertise for even a modest dialogue, on equal terms, between government and military, between civilian and military members of defence establishments and within the professional military themselves.

I would be the last to claim that the total result of these various approaches to arms control is likely to be dramatic or spectacular. Armed forces and evolving weaponry are permanent features of our type of international society. States both rich and poor have demonstrated their power to raise and maintain their defence establishments and they are not going to be persuaded to reduce them substantially simply in order to save money, without modification of the external and internal factors which bear on the determination of those establishments.

However in order to achieve such modifications as may be possible, a deep understanding of threat assessments and response capacities is essential on the part of those who are concerned to question existing defence policies and postures. They must be able to comprehend why states fear each other and to conceive of responsible and effective counter-strategies. They must understand the strategic and tactical implications of new weaponry. They must be active within and not outside of the societies they seek to influence if they are to have any prospects of success. Preferably they should be within the governments and armed forces of the states they serve. Above all, they must understand the real nature of international behaviour and not just their concept of what should be its ideal nature. However, where are such people to come from, if not from universities which are equipped to train people in strategic analysis? Hence I hope I might be forgiven for believing that a volume such as this, in which the authors have addressed their subjects in a thoroughly professional manner and made us think deeply about them, is perhaps one of the most important single steps we can take towards the achievement of a greater degree of control over the development and application of military force, a more effective use of scarce resources and a safer international environment for us all.

Notes on Contributors

Dr. Mohammed Ayoob is an Associate Professor in the School of International Studies, Jawaharlal Nehru University, New Delhi, and a Visiting Fellow in the Department of International Relations, Research School of Pacific Studies, Australian National University. After taking his Ph.D and teaching at the University of Hawaii, 1966, he was a lecturer in the Indian School of International Studies, New Delhi, 1967–69, and a Research Associate in the Institute for Defence Studies and Analyses, New Delhi, 1969–70. He has published many articles and co-authored three books on foreign policy issues relating to South Asia.

Professor Shinkichi Eto is Professor of International Relations, University of Tokyo. He was born in Mukden, China. After studying law at Tokyo Imperial University 1943–48 his interests turned to East Asian international politics. He taught political science at Tokyo Institute of Technology, 1952–56 and since 1956 has taught at the University of Tokyo. His major publications have been in the field of modern East Asian political history, both national and international, and current foreign policy studies, focussing particulary on China and Japan.

Mr Ron Huisken is a Visiting Fellow in the Strategic and Defence Studies Centre, Research School of Pacific Studies, Australian National University. He received the degrees of Bachelor of Economics (Honours) from the University of Western Australia in 1968 and Master of Social Science from the University of Stockholm in 1970. He then joined the Stockholm International Peace Research Institute (SIPRI) and subsequently lectured in economics at the University of Malaya during 1970 and 1971. In 1972–1976 he again was at SIPRI before coming to the Australian National University. He has worked on both general and regional arms control issues and has been an adviser to the United Nations on the implications of weapons proliferation for developing countries.

Dr. Khaw Guat Hoon is a Lecturer in Political Science at Universiti Sains, Penang, Malaysia. After taking a B.A. at Ohio State University and an M.A. at the University of Wisconsin, she studied for a Ph.D in Geneva, Switzerland. She has taught at the University of Wisconsin and has held a Fellowship at the Institute of South-east Asian Studies, Singapore. Her major research interests are in the field of South-east Asian international politics.

Professor Michael MccGwire is a Professor of Maritime Strategy at Dalhousie University, Canada. After service in the Royal Navy 1942–67, which included specialisation in Soviet and strategic issues, he read for an Economics degree at the University of Aberystwyth. Since 1971 he has been at Dalhousie and has established an active centre for the study of Soviet maritime strategic matters. He has lectured and published widely and organised conferences on this theme. He served with the Royal Australian Navy on attachment, 1950–52.

Dr. T.B. Millar is Professorial Fellow in International Relations, Research School of Pacific Studies, Australian National University. A graduate of the Royal Military College of Australia and the Universities of Western Australia, Melbourne and London, he has been at the A.N.U. since 1961. He was the first Head of the Strategic and Defence Studies Centre, 1966–70, and was Director of the Australian Institute of International Affairs, 1969–76. He has been a Senior Research Associate of the International Institute for Strategic Studies, London 1968–69 and 1976–77. He has published widely on the United Nations, the British Commonwealth, the Indian Ocean, South-east Asia and Australia, specialising in both foreign policy and defence issues.

Professor Michael Nacht is Assistant Director of the Program for Science and International Affairs and Lecturer in Public Policy at Harvard University. He is also co-editor of *International Security*. He was trained in aeronautics and astronautics, received advanced degrees in statistics and operations research, and holds a Ph.D. in political science from Columbia University. He previously held positions in the National Aeronautics and Space Administration and in private industry. His research interests and publications relate to Soviet-American relations, the role of nuclear weapons in world politics, the implications of new weapons technologies and the broad security objectives of U.S. foreign policy.

Dr. Robert O'Neill is Head of the Strategic and Defence Studies Centre and Professorial Fellow in International Relations, Research School of Pacific Studies, Australian National University. A graduate of the Royal Military College of Australia and the

Universities of Melbourne and Oxford, he served in Vietnam as an infantry officer 1966–67. After lecturing in history at the Royal Military College, he joined the A.N.U. in 1969 and became Head of the S.D.S.C. in 1971. His work embraces both contemporary strategic analysis and the historical study of warfare. He is the Australian official historian for the Korean War, Armed Services Section Editor of the *Australian Dictionary of Biography* and member of the Editorial Advisory Board for the publication of *Documents on Australian Foreign Policy.*

Dr. Steven Rosen is a Senior Research Fellow in International Relations, Research School of Pacific Studies, Australian National University. He is a graduate of Hofstra University, the City College of New York and Syracuse University where he took his Ph.D. He was an Assistant Professor of Political Science at the University of Pittsburgh 1968–71 and at Brandeis University 1972–75. He has written extensively on the theory of international relations, strategic problems and the Middle East. He has studied these questions in many parts of the world, including Israel and Egypt.

Professor Ferenc Váli is an Emeritus Professor of Political Science at the University of Massachusetts. Born in Budapest he holds degrees from the Universities of Budapest and London, a diploma in International Law from The Hague and an honorary Doctorate of Laws from Wayne State University. He has taught law and political science at the University of Budapest 1935–43 and 1946–49. He was a political prisoner in Hungary 1951–56 when he escaped to Austria. Since 1957 he has been in the U.S.A. at Harvard University 1958–61 and at the University of Massachusetts since then. He was a Visiting Fellow at the A.N.U. in 1977. He has published extensively in the fields of international law and international security problems, recently completing a book on the Indian Ocean area.

Professor Wang Gungwu is Professor of Far Eastern History, Director of the Research School of Pacific Studies, Australian National University and Chairman of the Advisory Committee of the Strategic and Defence Studies Centre. Born in Surabaya, Indonesia, he was educated in Malaya and at the Universities of Nanking, Malaya and London. He lectured in history at the University of Malaya 1957–68 before coming to the A.N.U. He has published extensively on Chinese and South-east Asian history and on current policy problems facing East and South-east Asia. In 1964–65 he was a member of the Commission of Inquiry on the Singapore riots of 1964.